High-Performance Managed Futures

Founded in 1807, John Wiley & Sons is the oldest independent publishing company in the United States. With offices in North America, Europe, Australia and Asia, Wiley is globally committed to developing and marketing print and electronic products and services for our customers' professional and personal knowledge and understanding.

The Wiley Finance series contains books written specifically for finance and investment professionals as well as sophisticated individual investors and their financial advisors. Book topics range from portfolio management to e-commerce, risk management, financial engineering, valuation and financial instrument analysis, as well as much more.

For a list of available titles, visit our web site at www.WileyFinance.com.

High-Performance Managed Futures

The New Way to Diversify Your Portfolio

MARK H. MELIN

John Wiley & Sons, Inc.

Published by John Wiley & Sons, Inc., Hoboken, New Jersey.
Published simultaneously in Canada.

For general information on our other products and services or for technical support, please contact our Customer Care Department within the United States at (800) 762-2974, outside the United States at (317) 572-3993 or fax (317) 572-4002.

Wiley also publishes its books in a variety of electronic formats. Some content that appears in print may not be available in electronic books. For more information about Wiley products, visit our web site at www.wiley.com.

Library of Congress Cataloging-in-Publication Data:

Melin, Mark H.
High-performance managed futures : the new way to diversify your portfolio / Mark H. Melin.
p. cm. – (Wiley finance series ; 598)
Includes index.
ISBN 978-0-470-63793-7 (cloth); ISBN 978-0-470-88667-0 (ebk); ISBN 978-0-470-88684-7 (ebk); ISBN 978-0-470-88685-4 (ebk)
1. Portfolio management. 2. Investments. 3. Risk. I. Title.
HG4529.5.M45 2010
332.64′52–dc22

2010012326

Printed in the United States of America

10 9 8 7 6 5 4 3 2 1

Contents

Preface

This book reveals a unique method of investing independent of stocks and the economy—a method that studies have shown has outperformed the stock market for the past 27 years, judging success by the major indexes, their drawdown statistics, recovery time, and total returns.

The investment method is derived from a Nobel Prize–winning theory that was later revised by a legendary Harvard University professor. But what is most amazing is that many investors and even financial professionals are not aware of the asset class, or they misunderstand the investing method.

WELCOME TO HIGH-PERFORMANCE MANAGED FUTURES

This book is divided into two sections: The fundamental section from Chapters 1–5 contains information that might surprise even the most experienced investor. Here performance is discussed—and performance can be both positive and negative. The book then reveals managed futures portfolio-building fundamentals, showing how risk targets are established and basic portfolios built. After these headlines have been discussed, the book dives into the structure of the asset class and industry regulation, including performance auditing. Upon completing Chapter 5 readers should posses a basic understanding of the managed futures asset class, at which point sophisticated investors are encouraged to move to the second section of the book, Chapters 6–12, where unique portfolios are built, traditional academic thought is challenged, and most importantly, risk and risk management are discussed in frank detail, a topic for all investors.

IT'S NOT FOR EVERYONE

Some investors might consider the book's ideas exciting and cutting edge with significant potential; call this group the optimists. Others, the traditionalists, might be less receptive to changing their fundamental belief system and will complain and nitpick. Still others, call them the intelligent risk managers, might say "there is no free lunch," as my father always told me. Everything is a matter of understanding true risk and reward. While realistic optimists are welcome, this book is written for sophisticated, intelligent risk managers.

This book is appropriate for intelligent, qualified investors who desire higher performance and consider acceptable risk an intelligent concession to appropriate reward, and recognize some risks simply deserve a polite "no thank you." It is written for investors who use only risk capital to diversify investments with the goal of not becoming entirely dependent on the stock market or the economy at large; for those who understand performance measures are tools that measure past performance and do not indicate future results. For that matter, they recognize no one has a magical crystal ball or can predict the future; future projections are based on logical thought process and making intelligent connections, but any projection into the future is nothing more than opinion—pure conjecture. If this describes you, then read on and discover a truly interesting investing method.

This book provides insight into what for many is a very different concept: a new world; indeed, the world of *High-Performance Managed Futures*. It will be new for those who live their lives in the confines of a stock-centric world. The reason for this starts in the educational system that all but ignores futures and options, with a few exceptions, and mirrors societal values and dictates the source of investing power is centered on the stock market and a little island in New York. This book indeed leads a stock-centric world on a journey of discovery.

A HIGHLY REGULATED INDUSTRY

Managed futures is a highly regulated investment. The tight industry regulation can be a major benefit to investors, particularly when it comes to audited returns performance and specific intelligent regulations regarding transparency and how client investment capital cannot be directly manipulated by the investment manager under the limited protection of account segregation. These investor protections should be used as an international template when considering prevention of hedge fund fraud.

Communication with potential investors is highly regulated. While this book is considered free speech, anyone regulated in this industry is required to provide a reasonably balanced view of risk and reward. Facts must be supported by reality and anything deceptive is considered fraud, plain and simple. While it may be annoying, in this regulated environment participants are also required to consistently point out that past performance is not indicative of future results. Readers must also understand opinions can be right or wrong; no guarantees available. This book is significantly based on the author's opinions and in many cases those opinions may be evident to some but not stated.

DISCOVERY FOR THE RIGHT REASONS

The trend in managed futures has started, as evidenced by what has been one of the fastest growing major asset classes over the past decade. In part, the goal of this book is to educate investors and nudge a powerfully emerging investing trend over its tipping point. While this is exciting, it is not a reason to invest in anything. Investing involves intelligent risk–reward decisions that all investors must individually make; all will not travel this path, as it should be. The hope is those that venture down what can be an exciting and rewarding path first focus on intelligently understanding and managing risk and avoid being dazzled by powerful returns alone. It is when risk is properly managed that sweet reward comes into most appealing focus.

In addition, to the valuable information and concepts provided in this book, I have also developed a web site—www.wiley.com/go/managedfutures—that expands upon the information provided in each chapter. It also links you to valuable white papers, videos, interactive calculators, and recommendation tools; grants you access to CTA performance data and portfolio building tools; and provides you with discounts on books, white papers, and software products. Although most of this material will be available to the general public, some information will only be available to registered book users. (Since you bought this book, you will receive a free six month standard membership. Your membership code and password instructions will be provided on the web site.) So, at the end of each chapter, be sure to look for the "On the Book's Web site" icon and continue learning of new ways to diversity your portfolio. I hope you enjoy reading this book as much as I enjoyed writing it.

MARK H. MELIN

Acknowledgments

This book has been written in a number of different environments, with thanks to friends and family at each location. It started with the fresh ocean breeze of L.A.'s South Bay, constantly annoying a friend by the reciting of book passages and analogies while he was trying to watch his Saturday morning EPL soccer; to the edgy, invigorating force contained in Chicago's Wicker Park, where the laptop often shared a park bench with those who called the street home; to the gritty power of the West Loop where friends would congregate to watch Sunday football and I tackled my laptop; to the more trendy River North and then out to the leafy suburbs where much time was spent on a long, wide back porch overlooking the ever-changing beauty of a tranquil lake, with a supportive father and family when it mattered.

The futures and options industry is really a community. A cultural foundation in a Midwestern city of strong shoulders, it is dominated by an innovative futures exchange that fosters growth in what could be one of the fastest growing investment opportunities in history.

This community has several anchors, including the brokerage community, which was once dominated by strong families. I had the good fortune of entering this world first as a managed futures program manager, a consultant to many of the exchanges, and then by working for a trading family that found its origins in the hog pits of Chicago. The family patriarch was one of the legendary figures during the heyday of pit trading, a bygone era to be sure. His sons and daughter, forging their own identity, first started an introducing brokerage (IB) business out of a college dorm room that stepped up and later became one of the top 50 futures commission merchant (FCM) brokerages in the world. They later sold this company to another legendary Chicago family who traces its roots to Iowa and Hollywood. This company was founded by a former movie producer who had a vision of a commodity future while shooting a film in Japan, just as the Nixon administration issued a soybean embargo on the island nation. The family business was essentially passed from father to son, who shares the father's vision but runs the firm with his own professionalism, flair, and mission to create sustainable futures investing—the perfect home for a managed futures focus.

These are stories from a powerful industry that has a small-town feel, where people know the players, centered in one of the country's largest cities that at times doesn't feel large at all. A place where futures trading is integrated into the strong cultural identity, an industry that is an icon surrounded by urban legends, with stories upon stories of interesting personalities and situations—of which I consider myself fortunate to be a part.

This book doesn't mention many names, but now is an exception. Dr. Carl Peters is one of the industry's original commodity trading advisors (CTAs), along with the likes of Boston Red Sox owner John Henry. Carl is the noted author of the book *Managed Futures,* which was an industry standard when published in 1992. Carl visited Chicago in 2006 as the managed futures industry was in liftoff mode. Greeted by an exchange official, our group lunched at the Union League Club and visited with an algorithmic electronic option market maker, a hot topic at the time. As the September sun dimmed to orange, Carl ended the day by walking down Monroe Street and turned south onto LaSalle, when he was struck by majesty.

The canyon-like view looking south on LaSalle ended at the Chicago Board of Trade (CBOT), topped by the statue of Ceres, the mythological Greek goddess of the harvest that stood as a citadel over the CBOT building since 1930. Now with an iridescent glow, the moment took Carl's studied breath away, if for just a second. The educated man who spent more time on either coast than in "fly-over territory" made an interesting observation:

"This is an interesting place . . . at an interesting time."

There is no predicting the future; at that point Carl didn't know for certain the industry he helped build was about to embark on an industry growth spurt. But more exciting, he didn't know the one-time second-class asset class would emerge to take an important place in investment history as new paradigms for diversification are developed. Innovative solutions for uncorrelated portfolios are required for a new age, driven by forces of economic uncertainty as well as massive governmental and societal debt. The need for true uncorrelated performance from the stock market and the economy at large is knocking and an asset class will answer. This thought might not have crossed Carl's mind at that exact moment in time. But the realization that a point in history is upon an industry is more poignant than ever; a light will shine on a solution designed to work regardless of the stock market fluctuation, spotlighting how true uncorrelated asset diversification could matter most . . . right here, right now.

This book is dedicated to my kids: Life has practical limits that everyone must recognize and respect. Live life by giving 100 percent. Know in your heart that when the horn ending the third period sounds, you left everything inside you on the ice. All anyone can expect is you do your best.

Disclaimer

Everything expressed in this book is the sole opinion of the author, and is based on his investing perspective, experience, and research. Nothing in this book is to be construed as individual recommendations or advice but rather broad conjecture, and is not represented as a complete look at any topic. The author's opinions are not right for all investors. Much of the author's opinions are based on past performance, and past performance is not indicative of future results. The opinions and content in this book have not been endorsed or approved by any exchange, brokerage firm, regulatory body, or managed futures program. While the opinions are clearly biased in favor of managed futures, the facts speak volumes and are outlined in what the author believes is a balanced and fair approach.

The names of many firms have been masked throughout this book for several reasons. First, performance is a relative concept and with book production delay, the most recent performance information, both positive and negative, is available online. Second, in itself this book is about an entire industry and does not seek to promote any single managed futures program, brokerage firm, or exchange. Third, the goal of this book is not to provide individual recommendations or advice but rather expose broad concepts. The goal is to shine a light on an entire industry and achieve academic enlightenment; readers can conduct individual research online.

Managed futures risk is outlined in a frank and transparent format, but no attempt is made to diminish the risk in managed futures investing. When stock market risk is compared to managed futures risk, it is a comment on true stock market risk and not a comment on the lack of risk in managed futures investing. Managed futures investing involves significant risk, it is not right for everyone, and only risk capital should be used. Risk and risk management are topics for sophisticated individuals and if a reader does not understand the risk issues or is generally uncomfortable with the investment they should not invest in managed futures.

CHAPTER 1

Understand It

The Truth about Risk and Misunderstood Investments

There is an asset class that has been generally ignored by Wall Street—despite outperforming the stock market over 27 years, according to one of the most recent studies on the topic from the Chicago Mercantile Exchange (CME). (See Figure 1.1.)

While many Wall Street institutions benefit through their portfolio investments in this asset class, the investment has been misunderstood by many financial advisors, as well as generally and perhaps deliberately obscured from qualified investors.[1] This is despite the asset class performing positively in nine of the last ten stock market declines with such low drawdown numbers it would even make the most talented hedge fund manager blush.[2]

The asset class is managed futures, a relatively unknown and misunderstood investment. Managed futures has provided investors several benefits, including diversification, tax benefits, the potential for high returns, lowered portfolio volatility, and lack of correlation to the stock market.

In fact it could be argued that managed futures is the most uncorrelated major asset class in history, the most diversified from stocks.[3] Here is why:

Success in managed futures investing is not necessarily dependent on the positive or negative price movement of any market. This is relatively unique in the history of investing.

To illustrate this point, some market-neutral managed futures investments are designed to be profitable regardless of core price movements in the underlying markets in which they invest. Further, it is common in popular trend trading, and discretionary programs, for strategies to be designed

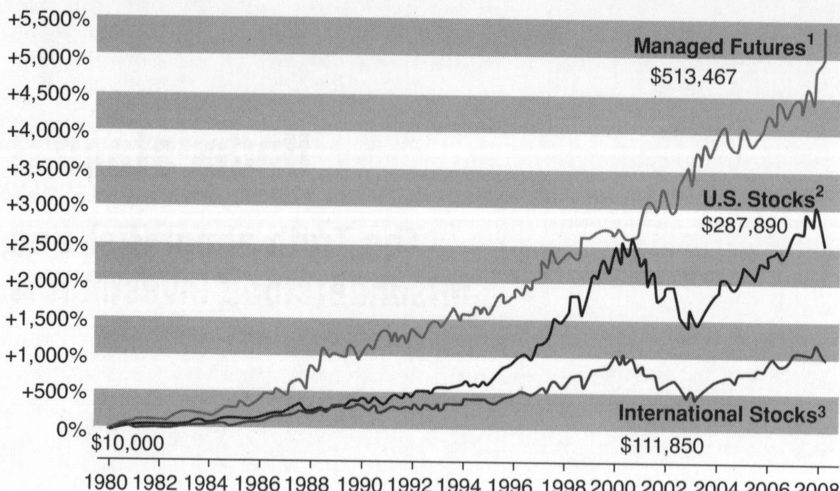

FIGURE 1.1 Comparison of Performance, 1/1980–2/2008
Source: Courtesy CMEGroup.

so as not to be tied to the positive price movement in any market in which they trade.

This bold statement is based on empirical correlation statistics outlined in this chapter and throughout the book. But it also comes from a conceptual knowledge of the unique and very different option and spread strategies that are based on futures and option contract structures: different delivery time frames for spread trading, option premium collection strategies, and other opportunities only available in the *regulated* derivatives markets. This book isn't about technical details of futures and option contracts, but it is about how to use these unique structures to create truly powerful investments using what is an interesting asset class.

WHAT IS THIS "MANAGED FUTURES" I'VE NEVER HEARD ABOUT?

Managed futures is similar in some ways to a mutual fund for the commodities industry in that talented money managers with audited past track records invest client assets in worldwide futures and options markets.[4] The core structure of the futures contract allows for very unique investment strategies; sometimes long, sometimes short, and at times market neutral, indifferent to the up or down price movement of any market or economic factor at large. Managed futures is defined further over the next three chapters, and throughout the book, as is the idea that managed futures could be the world's most uncorrelated asset class.

Stock investors should understand managed futures and consider it as a component in their portfolio. However, this investment method is not for everyone. It involves risk and managing risk, as does all investing, to varying degrees. The key is to understand true risk and then appropriately manage it. The word *true* is used because investing risk is at times unclear, obscured behind a veil of mistaken perception. This is true in the stock market when one considers real drawdown and volatility as it is in hedge funds and managed futures when different hidden risks are exposed. In this book the investor will discover the truth—for better or worse.

And it's about time.

This chapter lays the foundation for the book, calling into question commonly held investing beliefs—societal norms, really. This book in part echoes the voices of Lintner and countless ignored academic studies since that have compared stock market risk to more diversified risk that includes managed futures, and the book does so in what the author believes to be a balanced and fair approach. Chapter 1 highlights risk statistics that those beholden to stocks might not want you to see:

- Stocks are not as "conservative" as you might think—just ask several Nobel Prize winners.[5]
- The truth about risk: The new "conservative" is asset diversified with risk.
  - Conservative should be defined by the level of diversification, not based only on the risky assets inside a portfolio.
- Intelligent investing, and this book, are about using diversification and reducing correlation to stocks and the economy; performing under a variety of economic circumstances—the good, the bad, and the ugly of economic times.

STOCK MARKET "SAFETY" AND OTHER MYTHS

Prior to September 2008, investors might have considered stock portfolios reasonably diversified, conservative, and maybe even the unthinkable: "safe," to a degree. Investors might have believed that buy and hold was the best long-term strategy and that stocks were the only traditional investment that met their needs. These images, call them core societal beliefs, were generally marketed by the same firms that were kind enough to give birth to the credit-default swap and mortgage-backed securities that were so beneficial to the economy. Yes, these societal beliefs are wrong. Dead wrong.

For some, the consequences of these incorrect beliefs have been dramatic—a nightmare of life-altering proportions. For others, stock market stagnation represents just a number change on paper, nothing altering daily life. But in either case, the impact, the scare, the failure, and the realization of investor vulnerability can lead to emotions that foster bad dreams. The problem is that nightmares don't end until you wake up.

It is time to wake up.

Waking up is a process, and investors may have problems, particularly if they support the societal value that says the source of investing power—its heart, its liver, all its vital organs—is only centered on the stock market and a little island of thought. It is time to challenge tired traditions and usher in new choice, the option for real asset diversification.

As stock investors look upon a decade without financial reward, commonly called the "lost decade," they shake their heads with a disgust that comes from a man hoodwinked by a trusted friend. Ten years without capital gain or any appreciation in their stock investments; not even a thank you. How could the "safe" stock market fall off a cliff . . . again?

But here's the unwanted punch line: The coming 10 years could bring more uncertainty, kind of like raising a child. Stock investing could exhibit patterns of moody, unpredictable behavior with volatile price swings driven by economic forces beyond the control of mere politicians and governments, not to mention investors. At times everything might smell like roses; the stock market will experience bull runs to profitable ground; a new day will appear to be born. The market will rise in price along with investor hopes and dreams. Investors' emotions will drive them to think happy days are here again, the stock market is "normal," back on track. However, normal in most contexts is relative. Investors entirely dependent on their equity savior will also realize that hope is a four-letter word, because the stock market will likely have difficulty navigating what can only be described as a unique and uncertain economic environment. It is said that a stock market crash is an anomaly, like a 100-year flood. If so, investors will do well to prepare a sturdy boat, because stock market 100-year floods might occur on a more regular basis.

And this leads to one point of this book:

Wouldn't it be nice if investing wasn't entirely dependent on the stock market or the economy at large?

INVEST WITH STOCK MARKET NEUTRAL PROGRAMS

To be clear, this book does not seek to replace stock investments. Stocks are too engrained as a cultural norm. The goal is to create a balanced portfolio that includes stocks, but uses uncorrelated assets so that the portfolio is balanced and more neutral to wild stock fluctuations.

True asset diversification and uncorrelated returns performance is something to which all investors should aspire. In fact, those who regulate the investing industry advocate diversification. In *Ten Tips for 2010* the Financial Industry Regulatory Authority (FINRA), one of two regulators of U.S. securities investments, advocates spreading investments among different asset classes and within each asset class, a sentiment echoed by the National Futures Association (NFA), which is one of two organizations that regulates the managed futures industry and audits its performance.[6] "Although the concept may sound simple, the National Survey found that one-quarter of those who rated their financial knowledge as 'very high' could not correctly answer a question about risk and diversification," the FINRA report noted. Separate studies have found that only a small but growing number of financial professionals understand how to properly diversify a portfolio from stocks and the economy using managed futures.

FINRA is not just a singular pillar in the stock-centric world that recognizes the value of diversification.

"In 2008 investors discovered what financial advisors touted as a 'diversified portfolio' was not," noted Nadia Papagiannis, the Alternative Investment Strategist at Morningstar, a highly respected equity research firm. "Investors didn't realize the true volatility in the stock market—nor understand their individual risk tolerance—until in 2008 when they experienced firsthand the true risk and volatility in the stock market."

Papagiannis views managed futures from a unique vantage point as one who provides alternative investing insight for Morningstar, but more pointedly her previous experience as a commodity trading advisor (CTA) auditor at the NFA has allowed a firsthand knowledge of the strong performance reporting requirements demanded of the managed futures industry.

"Most investors had no idea managed futures and their uncorrelated strategies existed and that they are not as volatile as people think," she observed. "What's more, investors didn't really understand they can manage volatility (dialing it up and dialing it down)."

There is indeed valuable information on managed futures and related diversification opportunities of which both professional and individual investors should be aware. The way to achieve enlightenment on the world of true asset diversification using managed futures involves an interesting formula of Nobel Prize–winning lineage, a graphical risk measurement technique developed over 60 years ago. This concept was later advanced by a legendary Harvard University professor: a man who showed the world how to create portfolios diversified from stock market risk and volatility. It is a formula that in fact uses a volatile and risky investment, managed futures, with the goal to reduce overall portfolio volatility. In short, uncorrelated volatility will be used to reduce overall portfolio volatility, an interpolation of the work of Harvard's Dr. John Lintner.

To understand this formula and recognizing the reality in risk and reward is important, particularly when an opinion is drawn about stock market safety.

THE STOCK MARKET IS NOT "SAFE" OR "CONSERVATIVE" AND DOES NOT OFFER TRUE DIVERSIFICATION

Considering potential outside activities, driving to the local store for a gallon of milk in the morning is generally considered a safe activity; alternatively, flying as a plane passenger could be considered risky. But did you know, on a statistical basis, flying as a plane passenger is much safer than driving down the street? It is all a matter of perception.

Managed futures and hedge funds are risky investments. So is the stock market, when considered on a cold, statistical basis. It is all about understanding the degree of risk versus the degree of reward. Author Emanuel Balarie points out in his book *Commodities for Every Portfolio* that "concluding commodities are more volatile than stocks is purely a myth." Balarie cites several studies, including a 2004 Yale University study, a tilting academic opinion that showed over a 45-year period of time a portfolio would have been more volatile invested in stocks than commodities.[7]

This isn't something investors are being told. But that's not all.

Always Understand, Then Balance Risk and Reward

When considering managed futures risk and reward it is difficult to avoid the work of two legendary minds: Harvard's Dr. John Lintner and Nobel Prize winner Harry Markowitz. For those unfamiliar, details are revealed in Appendix F of the amazing work of these bright minds, work that has been generally overlooked by those blinded by a stock-centered world. Here is the point of their work for this chapter:

> *Understand, then balance, risk along with reward and only take risks for which the investor is compensated.*

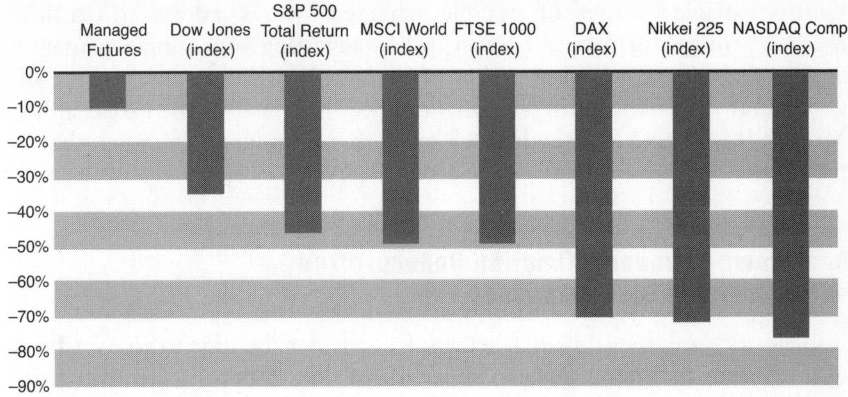

FIGURE 1.2 Comparison of Worst Drawdowns, 11/1990–2/2008
Source: Courtesy CMEGroup.

That sounds so simple and logical. But if it is so logical, why have investors not been largely exposed to the following information?

One measure of past risk is an index's inevitable drawdown, or negative return. Consider Figure 1.2. This is interesting because drawdown is such a blatant measure of risk in any investment: bottom line risk in many respects. It shows the worst sustained losses of the major stock indexes and a managed futures index. For most investors, Figure 1.2 may come as a surprise. The NASDAQ had a worst drawdown of 70 percent, an amazing dilution of investor wealth. Based on index drawdown alone, any investment that loses close to three-quarters of its value in the blink of an eye can only be described as a very risky investment, indeed. By contrast, the managed futures index in the CME study had a worst drawdown of 9.3 percent. This is not to claim that managed futures is not risky; managed futures is risky. The point is to take an honest look at stock market risk. If managed futures is even a twinkle of a thought on investors' investment horizon, they might consider the asset class as risky. It is risky, but in some very different ways than that of the stock market. Judging the asset class through the lens of the index's worst drawdown, risk becomes a relative concept, and 70 percent is a massive drawdown number in any investment—the sign of a very risky investment, indeed.

To provide balance, this interesting managed futures index drawdown might not tell the whole story. There is currently no single investment that allows access to invest in the CASAM CISDM managed futures index, unlike stocks. While the CASAM CISDM index was used by the CME for their study and *Barron's* magazine utilizes data from the index for publication, there are a wide variety of credible managed futures indexes to consider that vary in performance. Further, when investing in a single manager, as opposed to a diversified basket of managed futures programs, the investor may experience different performance from that of the broad index. Much like investing in a single stock, performance might differ from that of the index.

Drawdown Recovery Time: An Underutilized but Significant Risk Measure

If investors think the stock market is safe, consider the time to recover from negative returns performance. The length of time it takes to recover from sustained investment loss is a very interesting statistical measure of risk, particularly as it relates to managed futures. In Chapter 10, readers will discover a unique managed futures portfolio building method that features drawdown recovery time, volatility management and true diversification across five key points of correlation as a key risk management features. As the different drawdown recovery times are considered, understand that drawdown recovery is an underutilized yet potentially powerful risk statistic.

Figure 1.3 from the CME is illuminating. Managed futures in the CME study are represented by the CASAM CISDM managed futures index, and stocks by the S&P 500 Total Return index. The study shows the worst stock market meltdown took two years to recover, essentially working in the red from September 2000 to September 2002 with a 44.7 percent loss at its worst point, as measured by the S&P 500 Total Return index. By comparison, the managed futures index in the study had a relatively quick drawdown recovery period, lasting just two months. Its worst period of

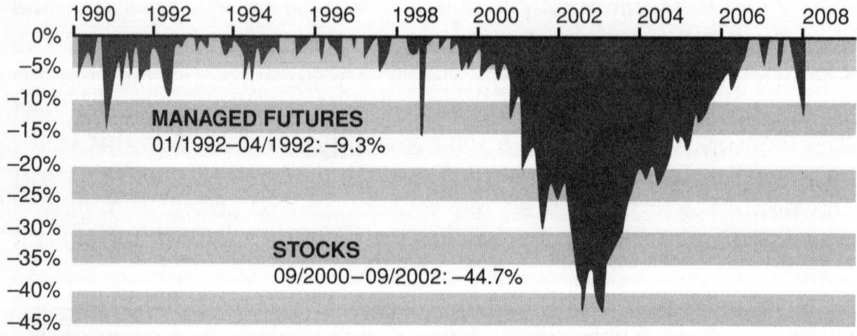

FIGURE 1.3 Comparison of Drawdown Duration, 1990–2008
Source: Courtesy CMEGroup.

back-to-back negative monthly performance lasted just three months, from January 1992 to April 1992, with only a 9.3 percent negative performance.[8]

Not only did stocks have the worst drawdown, they also exhibited the longest recovery time from this prolonged negative loss. That is the worst of all possibilities. Not only did stock hangovers hurt with a harshness not often experienced, but they took an excruciatingly long time to recover.

While these "headline performance numbers" are interesting, the book is about digging beyond the headlines, looking past strong returns alone and considering risk. In fact, this book advocates an approach that considers risk before return. In large part this risk is managed through uncorrelated diversification. Sometimes admittedly volatile and risky investments, as measured by standard deviation, can be used as a tool to properly diversify a portfolio and potentially reduce standard deviation in the overall portfolio, which sums up several academic conclusions.

Standard Deviation: Markowitz's Measure of Risk

Standard deviation was used by University of Chicago economist Harry Markowitz as a measure of risk in his Nobel Prize–winning Modern Portfolio Theory, and is the basis upon which much of this book's risk measurement techniques are based.[9]

In Figure 1.4, standard deviation is plotted along with past returns. The book's second section explains this graphic and certain alterations to Markowitz's Modern Portfolio Theory. For now, understand that investments nearest the right are considered most risky, based on volatility, and

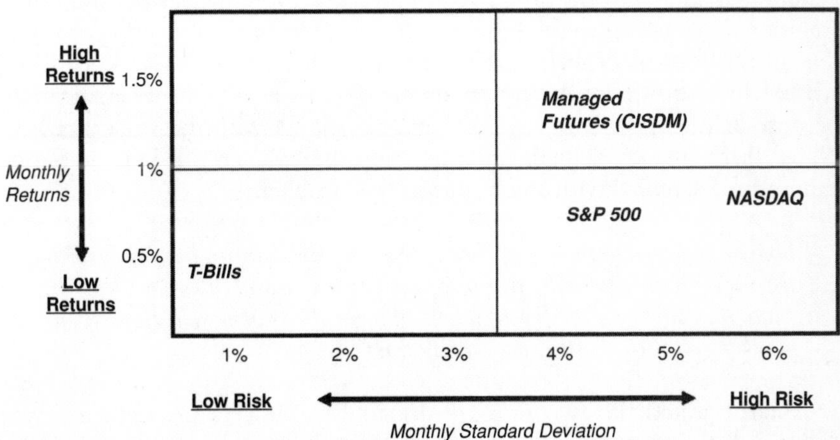

FIGURE 1.4 Graphic Measure of Risk/Reward

investments to the left the least volatile, based on standard deviation; investments nearest the top have the highest expected or past returns and investments near the bottom have the lowest returns. Thus investments in the rarified upper left are most desirable: the lowest risk, highest return.

The stock market's statistical risk is evident when one views a Modern Portfolio Theory graphic on a cold, numeric basis. Investors should take an objective look at where the stock market falls on a risk-adjusted basis. For most traditional investors the fact that their beloved equity market falls in the same risky, unsafe neighborhood as truly risky managed futures can be quite a shock—as when the wrong turn off a city expressway lands the unknowing minivan in a very unsavory and foreboding urban neighborhood.

This is not a comment on the risk in hedge funds or managed futures. They are risky investments and no implication is being made otherwise. The point is to lay the stock market bare with its real risk. While the traditions of society might view the stock market as safe when compared to hedge funds and managed futures, it can look downright risky when viewed on a cold, hard statistical basis.

Investors may have been sold the approach that diversification using only stocks and bonds is appropriate, avoiding managed futures due to its risk. But this stock diversification is fallacy, according to a Nobel Prize winner who proved real diversification cannot be achieved with stocks alone.

The Nobel Prize Winner Who Questioned Stock "Diversification"

For years investors have been indoctrinated with a tonic that leads them to believe they can enjoy the protection of diversification with stocks and other traditional assets tied to the economy at large. However, this popular myth flies in the face of Nobel Prize–winning academic thought and common sense, which shows diversification among equities is not true diversification because of the *systematic* risk, or beta, associated with the stock market. Nobel Prize winner William Sharpe made the call, noting that investors cannot be diversified with stocks due to this problem:

> *Sharpe concluded that systematic (market) risk cannot be eliminated through stock diversification because stocks move more or less in tandem, causing wide fluctuations in price that even well-diversified stock portfolios cannot protect against.*[10]

Sharpe noted the two primary drivers of a stock's price: factors associated with the company itself, such as management decisions, strikes, earnings, and so on, known as *unsystematic* risk, or alpha; and factors associated with the general stock market or economy at large, known as *systematic* risk, or beta. About one-third of the variability of stock prices is due to systematic risk, or the general market factors that affect all stocks. It is this systematic risk Sharpe identified, which again points to the fact that stock diversification is a relative misnomer. This is confirmed by a Brinson study that notes that 92 percent of a portfolio's return is due to asset class selection as opposed to the selection of particular underlying securities.[11]

> *In other words, all that time spent picking stocks would have been better spent diversifying among uncorrelated asset classes.*

Even though stock investors may be diversified among different sectors and geographic regions, they are not really diversified due to the systematic market risk. Said another way, negative economic conditions generally impact all stocks across a variety of market sectors; just ask diversified stock investors in 2008. This leads to a conclusion:

> *True asset diversification is conservative, not the stock market.*

Diversified Portfolio versus Same Old Same Old Take the concept one step further by comparing portfolio results with and without managed futures since 1986 (Table 1.1). The CME expanded on Lintner's academic work in 2008, updating his study of true asset diversification and volatility for modern times. Table 1.1 shows updated results of the same portfolio study the CME conducted. While this is not a complete view of risk, these portfolio statistics tell a very different story than what is being fed most investors.

Table 1.1 is a fascinating study. The "risky investment" with managed futures (B) reduced past overall portfolio risk statistics, which is the message of several academic studies. Consider that when returns go up when managed futures are included, past portfolio risk statistics actually decline. Look at volatility, measured by standard deviation, sink by over 20 percent when a volatile managed futures investment was added. Worst drawdown, for instance, is more than cut in half when the managed futures index is added to the stock and bond portfolio. While the returns when adding managed futures are higher, the significant benefit comes with lowered portfolio volatility in the form of reduced standard deviation, a significantly smaller worst drawdown, and quicker drawdown recovery time. This study's conclusion mirrors several academic findings and does not diminish the risk in managed futures investing, but rather shines light on the real risk in overexposure to stock investing. It is difficult to understand how this information can be so ignored by traditional Wall Street. The indexes utilized in the CME

TABLE 1.1 Advancing the CME Study: Hypothetical Portfolio Results with and without Managed Futures in the Portfolio

	Stocks & Bonds (A)	Managed Futures, Stocks & Bonds (B)
Correlation to Economy	High	Medium
Monthly Standard Deviation	2.7	2.2
Win Percentage	62.59%	64.43%
Worst Drawdown	27.39%	12.94%
Drawdown Recovery Time	3.30 months	2.76 months
Sharpe Ratio	0.40	0.63
Compounded Annual Returns	8.08%	9.15%

(A) Stocks and bonds portfolio included 50 percent stocks (MSCI World Index) and 50 percent bonds (JP Morgan Government Bond Index).

(B) This is compared to similar portfolio components with the addition of 20 percent managed futures as represented by the CASAM/CISDM Equal Weighted Index, 40 percent stocks (MSCI World Index), and 40 percent bonds (JP Morgan Government Bond Index). Past performance is not indicative of future results. Index performance may be different from that of individual investments in single stocks or CTAs.

Source: Barclay MAP.

study were high-performing indexes designed to be a relative reflection of the market in general and individual performance may vary from that of the indexes in both stocks and managed futures. Past performance is not indicative of future results.

This study of past portfolio performance using general indexes is interesting, but the portfolio allocation above is not our ideal managed futures portfolio because, in part, most managed futures indexes are unbalanced and might be difficult to replicate. There is no easily investible managed futures index that accurately replicates the diversity of the strategy. The current managed futures indexes are not the ideal, but a balanced approach that will be revealed through the book as a unique method to manage volatile investments. The simple point of this demonstration is to show a little-known diversification opportunity: Managed futures is an investment that should be considered in risk-appropriate investment portfolios, particularly by those who wish to design their overall portfolio to reduce their debilitating stock market exposure and its related volatility, as measured by standard deviation.

This overview chapter won't waste much more time documenting the obvious risk in the stock market. Throughout the book interesting studies are revealed regarding various markets and how to mitigate stock market risk exposure, providing additional meat on this bone. The only reason any time at all is spent on the topic is because investors have been so effectively brainwashed into thinking traditional buy and hold equity investing was safe, it takes the hard reality of a little intervention to bring reality back.

Academic Reports Consider Managed Futures Risk

A variety of academic reports on managed futures question stock market risk by comparing it to managed futures risk, and this academic discovery should be explored further. In summer of 1998 Thomas Schneeweis, a leading alternative investment academic, penned an article in the *Journal of Alternative Investments* titled "Dealing with Myths of Managed Futures."[12] The article noted that during the period 1990–1997 a single CTA on average had a monthly standard deviation of 6.26 percent, while the average S&P 500 listed stock had a higher standard deviation at 8.08 percent.

Further, in summer of 2004 academics Greg Gregoriou and Fabrice Rouah conducted a study of large CTAs in the *Journal of Wealth Management* noting the positive performance of CTAs during extreme market events and concluded: "... the trend by pension fund managers as well as wealthy individuals toward increasing their exposure to CTAs... makes sense."[13] This general line of thought is echoed by academic Richard Spurgin in his summer 1998 article "Managed Futures, Hedge Fund and Mutual Fund Performance."[14] Another interesting report was written by B. Wade Brorsen and John Townsend in the spring 2002 issue of the *Journal of Alternative Investments*. In "Performance Persistence for Managed Futures" the authors concluded "there could be some advantage to picking CTAs based on past headline performance when a long time series of data is available and precise methods are used."[15] These studies can be categorized as eye opening, but voices exist on both sides of the topic.

Providing Balance: Dissenting Views of Managed Futures Performance

Differences in performance exist between major managed futures indexes, such as the Barclay CTA index and the CASAM CISDM index, similar to differences between the S&P 500, the Dow Jones Industrial Average, and the NASDAQ stock indexes. Further, academic studies have questioned certain aspects of how the managed futures indexes collect and calculate managed futures index performance. Many of these critical managed futures studies fail to recognize the pivotal role that auditing by independent regulatory bodies plays in performance reporting accuracy. These studies fail to make appropriate distinction between different account structures and their impact on governmental regulation, performance auditing, marketing regulations, and transparency. Further, when considering survivorship bias academic studies must not treat stock and equity markets with undue favor. All major managed futures index performance is listed on the *High-Performance Managed Futures* web site, as are all credible and publicly available managed futures studies, both positive and negative, along with a frank review of each study. Sol Waksman of BarclayHedge, one of the industry-leading managed futures performance reporting services notes four primary issues with all managed futures databases that essentially point to the core structural differences between managed futures and stock investments:

1. Managed futures categorization and inclusion is not standard.
2. The index performance is not standard in terms of weighting based on capitalization or equal weighting.
3. Differing methodologies exist for calculating returns and managing administrative methods, such as how they add and subtract CTAs from the index and deal with survivorship bias.
4. All managed futures databases are proprietary.

Further, it is appropriate to wonder why a certification method has not been introduced nor a more consistent and timely profit/loss reporting system for CTAs developed. These industry issues and many more are discussed in detail on the *High-Performance Managed Futures* web site, along with CTA performance reporting and analysis.

The point of mentioning this is to provide balance. There is no perfect investment. This book shows both the pros and cons of what is considered a misunderstood investment, because the belief is all will benefit when the investment, its risk, and its reward are properly understood.

To this point, considerable academic theory has been discussed, but does it have practical application?

IT WORKS IN PRACTICE BUT DOES IT WORK IN THEORY?

Two economists were discussing the successful implementation of a municipal tax levy that was not theoretically analyzed by academia before it was implemented.

"Sure, it works in practice," one academic said to the other, "but will it work in theory?"

This book is more than academic theory. It is practical application that has been working for investors, proving itself day in and day out. And that's the beauty of what is discussed.

Consider Tom O'Donnell.[16] In the early 1990s, as the managed futures industry was poised for significant growth, as Markowitz and Sharpe won the Nobel Prize, and after Lintner released his landmark report, O'Donnell was a portfolio manager at the Virginia Retirement System, a major institutional investor. The chief investment officer of the pension fund asked O'Donnell and one of his colleges to embark on a task that would change the course of his life in an unexpected way.

"Investigate managed futures and see if it is an asset class we should consider," was the request handed down.

Managed futures? "Are you kidding?" O'Donnell said to his colleague, likely with the condescending tone stock investors typically use when discussing the asset class they don't understand. "That's pork bellies, leverage, and shorting!" At the time of the request, O'Donnell might have thought he had all the data he needed to determine that he shouldn't invest; perhaps thinking the fund would have better luck venturing off to Las Vegas and "investing" there.

O'Donnell then conspired with his colleague to write a research paper about managed futures that he thought might be so negative that the chief investment officer would have little choice but to scuttle this foolish idea forever. While the researchers clearly possessed a bias, they also approached the task with the intellectual honesty of a fiduciary. They looked at both the negative and positive claims and then dug deep to get a significant grasp of the issues. All the issues were thoroughly investigated.

And then came the day for the report: judgment day.

The report was honest. It detailed the risks of managed futures investing, which clearly must be understood by all investors. It pointed out the negative aspects of the investment. It considered the strategies and how this very different asset class operated. It pointed to negative stereotypes upon which many unfortunately base their investing decisions, and then it uncovered the naked truth.

Its recommendation?

The Virginia Retirement System, one of the largest pension funds in the country, began diversifying its portfolio with alternative assets and included managed futures in 1991. They followed the path that Markowitz and Lintner had so eloquently outlined, conducted their own research, and made their decisions without undue political interference.

Fast forward to 2009. In a speech about institutional investing, O'Donnell, now firmly engrained and working in the alternative asset investing arena, recalled their interesting experience: Once they got their feet wet in managed futures, they started to feed the data into their computerized asset allocation models. And here is where they ran into problems. The numbers looked so good that the computer program recommended that they place the vast majority of the fund's assets into managed futures, ignoring the stock market and other alternatives, an interesting comment about the nonemotional and bias-free computer-based decision logic.

In fact, O'Donnell said people might have to put artificial constraints in their computer models so that they wouldn't always recommend managed futures.

At first it was also difficult understanding the unique CTA strategies. They worked with Nobel Prize winner William Sharpe, who built a computer model to understand all the equity strategies that their various fund investments employed. With a 93 percent accuracy rate, the computer could decipher the strategies many of the mutual funds were using just by feeding in the stock holdings. However, when the managed futures investment positions were fed into the computer it had no idea how to interpret these rather odd positions, underscoring the complication of the strategies underneath the surface of this asset class.

But here is a truism that you will discover in coming chapters: It is these very complicated strategies and the unique futures and options contract structures that make uncorrelated diversification work. Readers of this book might just be witness to the world's most uncorrelated major asset classes, and perhaps one of the world's fastest growing. (Go to the *High-Performance Managed Futures* web site or www.cme.com to listen to a recent speech given by O'Donnell discussing his experiences in managed futures while at a pension fund.)

WALL STREET'S MOTIVATION FOR KEEPING MANAGED FUTURES A SECRET

The growing attention paid to managed futures is done for obvious reasons. It is rare for an index to perform positively in nine of the last ten stock market declines, have worst drawdown statistics much lower than that of stocks, and to have much quicker index drawdown recovery times. These are key statistics. Past performance is never indicative of future results, but from the perspective of history the past lack of correlation in managed futures performance stands out in all of investing.

The fact that some investors try to diversify with stock investments alone is as ridiculous as the fact that managed futures is misunderstood by all but the most knowledgeable; but this, too, is starting to change. Bright professionals are recognizing investing is about balancing risk and return through true asset diversification. Financial professionals have a duty to understand the latest products and methods of investing; at minimum, they have an obligation to understand an asset class that performed positively in nine of the last ten stock market declines and offers such uncorrelated diversification opportunities. So the question exists:

Why does traditional Wall Street thinking ignore managed futures?

In the recent past, broker–dealers (BDs) who restrict in-house financial advisors generally don't receive compensation on direct managed futures accounts unless they are registered as an Introducing Broker (IB), an effort requiring a new layer of regulatory supervision which few have been willing to undertake. Some Wall Street firms do offer limited selection of managed futures funds (as opposed to direct accounts), but the whisper is these nontransparent investments might be placed on the broker's platform only after the fund manager has agreed to pay a fee to the broker–dealer—a pay-for-play system that might not always be disclosed to the investor. Fund of fund investments in particular can charge an extra layer of fees and net investor performance can be lower. A study of the Barclay MAP database indicated that all fund investments, including funds of funds, reported compounded annual returns 27.26 percent lower than the same study group that included direct managed futures accounts.[17] (This is not to say that fund investments are all bad; there are definitely pros and cons of different direct and fund account structures that are discussed throughout this book and on the book's web site.)

But there is more motivation for a financial advisor not to offer managed futures to investors: It takes extra time and effort.

For a financial advisor, there is significantly more work involved in offering and supervising managed futures, all for what can be the same fee they receive for managing stock investments, where it is comparatively easy for a financial advisor to manage a simple "buy and hold" approach. Managed futures, on the other hand, can require active supervision of many unfamiliar components, including complicated strategies, sophisticated margin-to-equity ratio management techniques and the understanding of market exposure that in some cases is only evident when the strategy risk is understood. Further, with certain account types the advisor can encounter financial risks not associated with traditional stock investments, particularly with aggressive investments. In the past, advisors might have had honest concerns regarding the complexity and volatility of the investment. Managed futures can be a volatile investment and unsophisticated investors who cannot stomach volatility should not enter these waters. But it is also appropriate to raise the same issues regarding stock market volatility.

Even if Wall Street did have the motivation, learning about this investment is difficult. Futures and options are not a part of the normal educational curriculum, even at some of the more advanced institutions of higher learning. What's more, even in their in-house training, financial advisors don't appear to gain futures and options knowledge outside basic risk talking points.

There is more to this story, and investors should not be hypnotized by simple risk definitions or strong returns alone. This book is about balancing risk with reward. Managed futures can be a risky investment, particularly if it is not properly structured and managed. And here is one secret behind managing risk as well as an explanation for a significant degree of the amazing managed futures index performance statistics: diversification.

In Managed Futures Diversification, Not Cash, Is King

The next two points are not widely disclosed in the cloistered managed futures world, but they should be.

1. *Diversification is a primary reason behind the amazing managed futures index performance numbers and alluring risk statistics.*
2. *Investing in an individual managed futures program, or even a single strategy, can expose the investor to more risk than the managed futures index performance indicates, more so than when investing in a truly diversified portfolio of solid managed futures programs.*

The book has strong opinions in this regard, because proper diversification is one key to success in managed futures investing. As you will see from studies throughout this book, proper diversification among solid programs can be vastly superior to investing in a single manager and a key to reducing an important component of risk in managed futures. In part, this book shows investors how to design programs with this goal.

Diversification is important in all investing. Proper diversification could be more important in managed futures than stock investing due to enhanced individual manager risk, or nonsystematic risk. A significant degree of volatility, or risk, in managed futures is on the individual manager level; the often complicated strategies they use, the markets in which they invest, and how they manage leverage, margin, and risk in their trades. All of these will be revealed as methods used to manage risk. But perhaps the most successful method found to mitigate this risk is through diversification among solid investment managers. A deep industry insight, however, is to question the core validity of the diversification within the managed futures indexes, which can be understood in part by considering 2009 index performance.

Managed Futures Waterloo: 2009 Performance Fourth Worst in History

In 2009 managed futures, as represented by the Barclay CTA index, exhibited its fourth worst year in returns performance, down 0.10 percent. The worst year in the history of the Barclay CTA index was 1999, down 1.09 percent. In 2009 major stock indexes crowed gains of 26.46 percent, as highlighted by the S&P 500.[18]

There are financial professionals who proclaimed 2009 "managed futures Waterloo" because "managed futures failed in 2009 while stocks ended with stout gains." These statements are illuminating for several reasons. First, and most obviously, it shows that some, but not all, in financial services are resistant to change and closed to new paradigms for diversification. Second, and most interesting, it potentially points to a future where two camps exist. The first camp of financial professionals and investors is open to new concepts for uncorrelated asset diversification. The second camp will resist change at all costs, finding fault with everything, regardless of the facts or situation. Third, and perhaps most significant, the period from 2008 to 2009 provides perhaps one of the best laboratories to understand a misunderstood asset class. Current times are more relevant to study managed futures for several reasons. Assets under management are much more significant in 2009 than 1999, for instance. The CTAs are much more sophisticated with more diverse strategies, the sheer number within the ranks of CTAs makes study of the current period statistically significant, and current CTA performance auditing and industry regulation provide significant benefits to the investor. While there are many insights that can be garnered from recent times, there is one insight from 2009 that illuminates the investment more than any other—and it is not the obvious insight.

Many consider 2009's illuminating insight that as stocks go up, managed futures go down, thus the negative correlation. But that is wrong. The point isn't negative correlation; it is neutral correlation. In the past as stocks rose, managed futures did its own thing; as stocks fell, managed futures operated independently, apparently to the beat of its own drummer. This lack of correlation shines a light on the real insight from the managed futures negative 2009 performance:

> *Diversification in managed futures is most important because each of the major managed futures strategies performs differently depending on the market environment.*

In 2008, CTA trend-following strategies exhibited some of the best performance in its history, up 17.74 percent among the 443 trend followers reporting to the Barclay MAP database this book follows. While trend followers enjoyed the strong 2008 market environment, volatility strategies posted –14.14 YTD performance as represented by the 119 volatility strategies this book follows. As expected, when overall market volatility dropped significantly from the fall of 2008 to 2009, the primarily short volatility strategies this book follows were enjoying significant 14.30 percent gains in 2009 while trend followers scratched by with YTD performance near −3.33 percent.[19]

Appendix A of this book benchmarks the performance of each primary strategy. Each strategy has very different performance characteristics from one another and that of the stock market, which makes for interesting portfolio correlation considerations. The point is this: One given managed futures strategy can work well when other managed futures strategies may underperform, all based on the market environment. The real insight from 2009 is considering how managed futures strategies correlate to one another, and then designing investment portfolios appropriate to this insight. There are specific reasons for these correlations that provide clarity into the asset class and strategy points. For instance, a trend-following strategy generally has performed best when during a market environment of price persistence and volatility breakouts. The price direction doesn't matter so long as the movement is directionally consistent. This strong trending environment is not always ideal for short volatility strategies, for instance. It is in the understanding of how fairly complex strategies relate to market environments that a degree of success can be found in managed futures. This will be a topic for more detailed analysis in the advanced section of the book, but for this overview chapter consider the impact this performance has on the overall performance of the managed futures indexes and a more interesting fact emerges.

Managed Futures Indexes Are Strategy Unbalanced While the major managed futures indexes are diversified from individual manager risk and markets traded, they are not diversified in terms of strategy. The managed futures indexes significantly favor the most popular strategy, trend following. While the managed futures indices have displayed impressive lack of correlation to the stock market, it might not be as good as it could be because most managed futures indexes are not strategy diversified.

In any given year trend-following strategies can make up roughly 50 to 70 percent of a given managed futures index.[20] In 2009 trend followers exhibited one of their worst performances of all time, hence the major CTA indexes exhibited anemic performance as well. In other words, when trend-followers sneeze, the entire CTA index catches a cold. But the question remains, is this the best representation of the managed futures industry as a whole? It is not uncommon for people to say managed futures had a terrible 2009. But that isn't true. Trend-following strategies had a terrible 2009, but it was a tremendous year for other strategies, including volatility strategies, which might only represent 5 to 10 percent of a managed futures index at any given moment in time.

This points to the fact that while the managed futures indexes are diversified, they may not be diversified enough.

Because the managed futures indexes are so primarily weighted toward trend following, all major reporting services ended the year with relatively negative performance of up or down a small percentage depending on the index. This is a deep industry topic that is explained in the advanced section of the book. The concepts of diversification, risk management, and volatility are the subject of several chapters; a brief overview of this critical component is mentioned here.

Watching Investment History Unfold This chapter has illuminated a limited number of common misconceptions. We live in a free will society where people hold different convictions and beliefs, and different tolerances for change and risk. In an ideal society, as in investing decision making, there should be transparency and proper disclosure so intelligent risk/reward decisions can be made without undue pressure. Thoughts should be freely explored and ideas investigated. All this points to a new investing paradigm unfolding before our eyes.

Note the date Monday, August 3, 2009. That was the day a little-noticed article in the *Wall Street Journal* perhaps identified a milestone, the start of a paradigm shift in investing.

The article noted the rise of investments with the potential for individual investors to make money regardless of stock market performance. Investing uncorrelated to the returns performance of stocks and unhinged from the economy is a powerful concept. The article noted that these alternative investments and their benefits of uncorrelated performance were once an exclusive country club; a gated community for institutional and high-net worth individual investors. But this exclusive club is now being democratized for professional investors and qualified individual investors who understand risk and reward. From major institutional hedge funds launching managed futures mutual funds to futures commission merchants (FCMs) and broker–dealers integrating efforts to offer more seamless service to hedge funds recognizing the value of managed futures, the industry is changing. But this change is not sustained by the industry alone; rather, lasting trends in this industry are sustained by investors.

"These are strategies that should have been offered to retail investors a long time ago," said Morningstar's Papagiannis. Morningstar is a firm the *Wall Street Journal* noted is "typically skeptical of new or seemingly faddish funds."

Papagiannis has observed the motivations for the meteoric rise of managed futures at this moment in history.

> *From the supply side, after 2008 hedge funds and other institutional money managers realized they needed to diversify their investor base," she said. "This is because institutional investors needed liquidity and pulled their money out. Retail investors' money tends to be stickier, and retail investors represent a large untapped market for alternative investments.*
>
> *From the demand side, both retail and institutional investors saw the need for uncorrelated and liquid strategies. They realized managed futures is the most liquid investment in which they could invest and the past diversification opportunity was hard to deny, especially in 2008, when these strategies were the only investments besides government bonds that made money.*[21]

This all highlights a societal shift: A new risk paradigm is on the horizon, forced upon investors by the power of cyclical bear markets, massive government debt, and always-unpredictable economic circumstances. The new risk paradigm understands significant risk exists when real diversification is not in place; it recognizes that investments highly correlated to systematic stock market risk are in fact extremely risky.

On the Book's Web Site

Available to the general public:

- Access to the FINRA document on diversification.
- Download: CME study on managed futures.

Available to registered book readers:

- Updated performance of all major indexes and studies mentioned in this chapter.
- Download: Speech given by Tom O'Donnell.

- Video conversations with the author regarding industry issues mentioned in the chapter.
- Comparisons of managed futures fund performance versus direct account performance.
- Interactive application that assists investors in choosing the appropriate account structure and managed futures investments.
- Weekly commentary on market news as it relates to managed futures.
- Study methodology, software screen shots, and data from all studies in this chapter.

For more information visit www.wiley.com/go/managedfutures.

CHAPTER 2

Define It

Establish Performance and Risk Targets

The headline performance numbers in managed futures can appear stunning—how could they not be captivating at first glance. As readers witnessed in the last chapter, a managed futures index displayed returns double that of the S&P 500 stock index with interesting drawdown and recovery time statistics.[1] The past diversification benefits of the investment are simply unmatched in modern investing. As is detailed in Chapter 5, the performance is audited and supervised by two strong regulatory bodies, which leads to a transparent investment with specific account segregation laws that protect investors to a degree unavailable in most investments: very different from a typical hedge fund investment. These are the sexy headlines, but it is important to understand the whole story.

The high-flying and attractive numbers come at a price: risk. High-performing investing involves risk and managing risk. This is true in stocks, hedge funds, and managed futures.

While the provocative managed futures index returns are enticing, investors should get past the superficial attraction and understand that the substance behind the investment is most important in the long run. Just as managed futures index performance might be different from individual commodity trading advisor (CTA) performance, particularly if the portfolio is not properly diversified, investors looking at the headline numbers can make the investment seem easy, like a dream. But here is the wake-up call, the comedown to reality: As in life, there is no free lunch in investing.

The old truism that strong returns are accompanied by elevated risk is a truism for a reason, as is the worn Midwestern wisdom my father engrained in my head: "If it sounds too good to be true, it probably is." And here is a key insight:

> *Success in managed futures context means a sustainable investment built by understanding risk and then balancing that with potential reward. In fact, when portfolios in managed futures are built, it is done primarily based on risk first.*

This chapter considers basic *targets*, investors' goals for risk and return used for the purpose of building a portfolio. In this chapter, targets are compared to actual past return statistics, after which actual portfolios are built based on these targets in the next chapter. In managed futures investing any consideration of returns should also be balanced with a discussion of risk. Here is the key: Sugar-coating risk and reward should never be the goal in any investment. The best place to start in managed futures is in understanding the risk. Begin by considering the negative portion of an investment as well as the positive; balance risk and reward to make intelligent decisions.

In this chapter readers discover:

- A range of target managed futures past compounded annual returns used for building portfolios:
  - From the conservative returns target of 7 to 15 percent.
  - To the flexible moderate returns target of 15 to 30 percent.
  - Racing to the aggressive returns target of 30 to 60 percent past returns but with increased risk to match.
- Targets are goals and not guarantees. They are opinions and are used only as a benchmark to help select risk reward–appropriate investments and are based on past performance, which is not necessarily indicative of future results.
- Equally important, if not more so, is the range of target risk profiles. In this basic chapter risk is measured by three standards, using average past drawdown:
  - Conservative average drawdown target, 5 to 15 percent.
  - Moderate average drawdown target, 15 to 30 percent.
  - Aggressive average drawdown target, 30 to 80+ percent.

The first step toward understanding comes with a very basic definition of managed futures, which is done below. Chapter 4 further defines managed futures, which leads to Chapter 5, where managed futures performance auditing and regulation is discussed in more detail. Risk is addressed with frank insight in Chapter 11 and throughout the book.

THE SIMPLE MANAGED FUTURES DEFINITION

Managed futures is a $200+ billion investment industry comprised of money managers who invest client capital in worldwide futures and options markets. The industry has grown 700 percent over the last 10 years, making it one of the fastest growing major asset classes.[2]

Managed futures programs often use sophisticated strategies that put this investment in a very different category from traditional investment options. For instance, some managed futures investments can be market neutral where the profits might not entirely be tied to the underlying up or down price movement of the markets in which they invest. More common, the investments can be long or short in various global markets. Investments could take the form of buying or selling commodities such as oil, gold, corn and wheat; financial products such as interest rates, foreign currency, stock indexes and single stock futures; and sophisticated investments can even take place in real estate, pollution and even weather futures. To highlight the product diversity, weather futures contracts are based on the amount of snow in given geographic regions. While this opportunity may sound entirely odd to equity investors, in fact statistical probability software has functionality that considers the past trends in cattle prices based on a single January day's snowfall in Omaha, Nebraska, to provide an exotic and interesting example of sophistication coming from a misunderstood industry. Managed futures is an entirely different animal in some respects and a very sophisticated investment management tool. This is due to the depth of products, their delivery contract structures, and related exchange liquidity.

Managed futures are unique investments facilitated directly by CTAs or through limited liability commodity pool operator (CPO) funds. These "mutual fund–like" investments are tightly regulated by two independent governmental organizations, detailed in later chapters.

Direct CTA investments are highly transparent: Investors can see investments and their portfolio value marked to the market on a daily basis. When direct account investments are regulated by the appropriate U.S. futures regulatory bodies, client capital is placed in a government-mandated segregated account structure, where the investment manager does not have direct access to manipulate investment capital, one of the root causes of so many hedge fund fraud cases.

A RISK DISCLOSURE MADE EASY TO UNDERSTAND

It is unknown who is reading this book, but all should note this book is written for savvy investors. If you are an unsophisticated or new investor, this book's content and its frank discussion regarding risk and managed futures in general might not be appropriate. Before this book reveals past performance or discusses targets, a risk disclosure takes place, with a more inclusive and legally precise risk disclosure in note 7 for Chapter 3 in the Notes section, which investors should read and understand.

Readers are about to be exposed to what can be explosive performance numbers—but if investors are not sophisticated enough to separate themselves from the high-flying, mesmerizing returns to first focus on risk and risk management then this might not be an appropriate investment. Investing should be done with risk capital and decisions to make an investment should never be made under pressure. This book is not making individual recommendations, but rather illuminating broad concepts and providing analysis and opinion, which can be right or wrong and risk/reward targets are opinions. Hypothetical portfolios in this book are built with hindsight and base a portion of their logic on past performance, and investment past performance is not necessarily indicative of future results. If you need a graphic, memorable reminder of past performance look no further than baseball's Chicago Cubs, who seem forever doomed by their futile past performance, a statistical aberration even the brightest hedge fund quant couldn't explain. At some point they will likely break their negative string of bad returns, disappointing past performance. No one can exactly predict the future, which is why as target returns are discussed readers should understand targets are used as a tool to help understand a wide range of past potential; targets are not projections into future performance. Targets are just that, targets, and nothing more: in this case, the author's opinion of a logical goal, one tool used to help design a portfolio, and not a guarantee.

TARGET RISK/REWARD PROFILES

Table 2.1 shows the author's opinion on potential risk and reward targets used for designing managed futures portfolios. In this chapter these performance targets are compared to the actual results of CTAs that reported

TABLE 2.1 Performance Targets Used to Design Appropriately Diversified Portfolios

	Returns Target	Drawdown Target	Recovery Target
Study Group Return Category	Past Compounded Annual Return to Target	Past Average Drawdown to Target	Past Drawdown Recovery Time to Target
Conservative	7%–15%	5%–15%+	1–4+ months
Moderate	15%–30%	5%–20%+	3–8+ months
Aggressive	30%–60%	15%–80%+	5–12+ months

These targets are entirely the author's opinion and are used only as a method to build portfolios based in part on past performance. Past performance is not indicative of future results. The point is to highlight diversification and make clear that investors should consider more than headline performance numbers, and that performance measures are but one tool to consider.

returns in the various study group categories with the goal of gleaning specific insight into the managed futures asset class. In the next chapter, basic managed futures portfolios are built using these targets.

One of life's big disappointments is when the reality of a situation doesn't meet the expectation: a kid not receiving a certain birthday present; a movie not living up to the promise of the book upon which it is based; an investment not living up to its hype. No one can guarantee that disappointment will not occur in any aspect of life, including investing future performance. Investors can, however, attempt to manage expectations so as to strip away the hype and intelligently look at the facts, allowing the cold, hard audited numbers to tell a story. In fact, these target numbers are chosen for specific portfolio design applications and may tend to favor the moderate portfolio type. There are many who might disagree with the opinions expressed regarding the targets listed above, which is part of a healthy dialogue.

"Conservative" Is a Relative Term in Managed Futures

There are many methods available to define a conservative managed futures program, and all definitions could be wrong to varying degrees. It could be argued the word *conservative* is inappropriate in any discussion of managed futures. Nonetheless, in this book, a conservative portfolio risk/return profile targets past compounded annual returns from 7 to 15 percent, targeting past average drawdown from 5 to 15+ percent, as outlined in Table 2.2. The average target recovery time is one to four months or more, meaning that

TABLE 2.2 A Conservative Target Risk/Reward Ideal

	Returns Target	Drawdown Target	Recovery Target
Study Group Return Category	Past Compounded Annual Return to Target	Past Average Drawdown to Target	Past Drawdown Recovery Time to Target
Conservative	7%–15%	5%–15%+	1–4+ months

These targets are entirely the author's opinion and are used only as a method to build portfolios based in part on past performance. Past performance is not indicative of future results. The point is to highlight diversification and make clear that investors should consider more than headline performance numbers. Performance measures are but one tool to consider.

a diversified portfolio on average would be negative for about one to four months before it returned to profitability. This is only a target used for portfolio design, and actual performance can always deviate from a target.

To provide perspective on a new method of investing, contrast the conservative drawdown and recovery times outlined in this chapter to stocks. The worst drawdown for the S&P 500, updated as of July 2009, was 50.95 percent. It is not uncommon for a major stock drawdown to take years to recover. As such, stock investors might salivate at "conservative" target average returns approaching 15 percent and reasonable drawdown recovery times. In fact, many stock investors would likely consider a 15 percent return aggressive. But this is not the case in managed futures and this is critical to understand:

> *Managed futures has a different definition of* conservative *due to the higher range of returns, volatility, and varying risk profiles.*

The risk and reward of conservative investment in managed futures compared with stocks is akin to skiing black diamond runs in Utah and then coming to the Midwest to ski black diamonds. Technically they are both black diamonds, but they are very different ski runs. In fact, from one perspective it could be said there are no conservative managed futures programs, much like an argument could be made there are no real black diamond ski runs in the Midwest. The conservative managed futures programs could be likened to the groomed ski run in Deer Valley, Utah. The skier can choose more exciting and rewarding runs in the Park City area for moderate and aggressive experiences. The investor should know his or her goals and tolerances and understand that even on the conservative ski slopes, as in investing, there is never any guarantee the groomed slopes will not get icy and dangerous. It is all a matter of understanding risk first, then taking steps to manage it.

TABLE 2.3 Actual Average Past Results: CTAs with 7 to 15 Percent Compounded Returns

Actual Average Past Results:

	Returns	Drawdown	Drawdown	Drawdown	Risk/ Reward	Volatility	Managers
Study Group Return Category	Actual Compounded Annual Return	Actual Average Drawdown	Actual Drawdown Recovery Time	Actual Worst Drawdown	Actual Sharpe Ratio	Standard Deviation	Number of CTAs/ CPOs
7%–15%	10.95%	7.45%	1.71	21%	0.61	4.62	283

Source: Barclay MAP. Study conducted 9/09.
Average results and portfolio results are a hypothetical combination of CTAs and these CTAs have not traded together in this fashion in a regulated CPO structure. See the hypothetical risk disclosure in note 7 in Chapter 3. Past performance is not indicative of future results. These numbers can change on a monthly basis. The point is not to highlight individual CTAs or potential portfolio combinations but rather to illustrate the potential power of diversification as a risk-management tool.

Compare the conservative target in Table 2.2 to the actual past performance statistics of CTAs that exhibited annualized average returns in the 7 to 15 percent range in Table 2.3. Throughout this chapter we compare the target portfolio performance with the actual performance and draw interesting conclusions. Later, the chapter also compares the actual performance of the three categories—conservative, moderate and aggressive—and draws insight. All this is done to provide a higher level understanding of the asset class and uncover true fundamentals.

As readers examine the differences between the ideal target (Table 2.2) and the actual reported performance (Table 2.3), note the lowest target compounded annual return is 7 percent.[3] If an investor does not design a program to target at least 7 percent return, the high risk in managed futures is not worth the low reward. Managed futures is a high-performing investment, exhibiting strong volatility, both to the upside and downside. Even at a conservative level, "conservative" can exhibit volatility. The key for investors is to appropriately understand the difference between volatility risk and drawdown risk, because, as investors will discover in this book, they can be different risk types.

In the target (Table 2.2), notice the average drawdown and its upper range target at 15+ percent. This target is near double that of the statistical actual performance of 7.45 percent drawdown (Table 2.3). Also consider the plus sign + at the end of each drawdown target, indicating managed futures loss potential is undefined. The same is true of drawdown recovery time. The target of one to four months recovery time in the target is higher than the 1.71 average months for actual drawdown recovery time. In other words, the targets being established indicate the investor should expect more risk than average past performance numbers indicate. There are several reasons

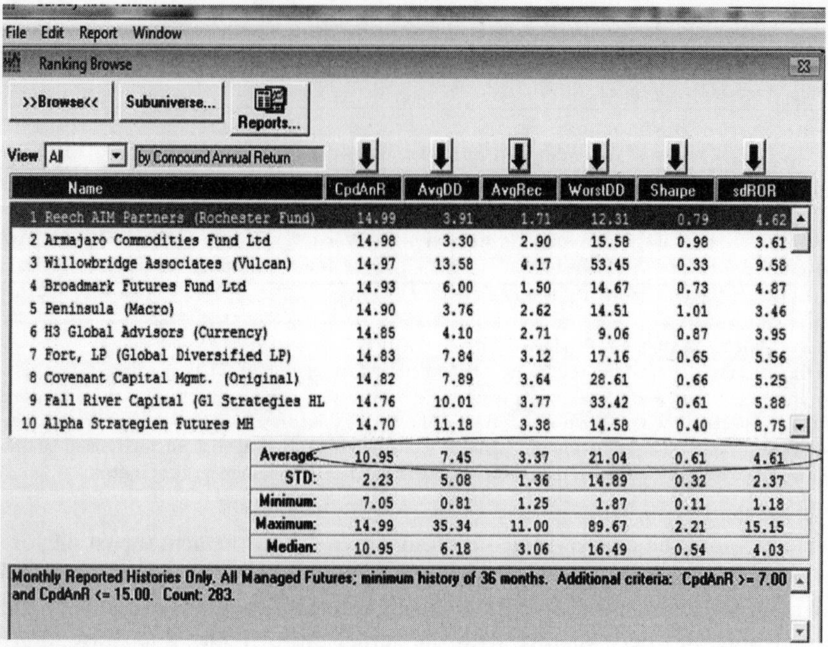

File Edit Report Window

Ranking Browse

>>Browse<< Subuniverse... Reports...

View: All — by Compound Annual Return

Name	CpdAnR	AvgDD	AvgRec	WorstDD	Sharpe	sdROR
1 Reech AIM Partners (Rochester Fund)	14.99	3.91	1.71	12.31	0.79	4.62
2 Armajaro Commodities Fund Ltd	14.98	3.30	2.90	15.58	0.98	3.61
3 Willowbridge Associates (Vulcan)	14.97	13.58	4.17	53.45	0.33	9.58
4 Broadmark Futures Fund Ltd	14.93	6.00	1.50	14.67	0.73	4.87
5 Peninsula (Macro)	14.90	3.76	2.62	14.51	1.01	3.46
6 H3 Global Advisors (Currency)	14.85	4.10	2.71	9.06	0.87	3.95
7 Fort, LP (Global Diversified LP)	14.83	7.84	3.12	17.16	0.65	5.56
8 Covenant Capital Mgmt. (Original)	14.82	7.89	3.64	28.61	0.66	5.25
9 Fall River Capital (Gl Strategies HL	14.76	10.01	3.77	33.42	0.61	5.88
10 Alpha Strategien Futures MH	14.70	11.18	3.38	14.58	0.40	8.75
Average:	10.95	7.45	3.37	21.04	0.61	4.61
STD:	2.23	5.08	1.36	14.89	0.32	2.37
Minimum:	7.05	0.81	1.25	1.87	0.11	1.18
Maximum:	14.99	35.34	11.00	89.67	2.21	15.15
Median:	10.95	6.18	3.06	16.49	0.54	4.03

Monthly Reported Histories Only. All Managed Futures; minimum history of 36 months. Additional criteria: CpdAnR >= 7.00 and CpdAnR <= 15.00. Count: 283.

FIGURE 2.1 Category Averages, Actual Reported Results
Source: Barclay MAP Database. Study conducted 9/09.
Average results and portfolio results are a hypothetical combination of CTAs and these CTAs have not traded together in this fashion in a regulated CPO structure. See the hypothetical risk disclosure in note 7 in Chapter 3. Past performance is not indicative of future results. These numbers can change on a monthly basis. The point is not to highlight individual CTAs or potential portfolio combinations but rather to illustrate the potential power of diversification as a risk-management tool.

for this. On a practical level, it could be difficult for the investor to obtain the exact diversification by investing in all 283 managers that comprise the study; it would require a burdensome asset allocation, even for the largest of hedge funds. Further, it exemplifies the strategy of planning for a higher degree of risk but at the same time striving for the goal of the best performance possible. Plan for the worst, expect the best.

With managed futures, investors can choose to ski the groomed sloops of Utah's Deer Valley through conservative runs or decide to take a helicopter drop for some real risk and reward with the aggressive programs. But the author's favorite portfolios are the moderate versions, because they include a taste of both experiences and might offer the best diversification opportunity.

Moderate Risk/Reward

Moderate doesn't have to be lackluster. In fact, in managed futures moderate is perhaps the most diversified and flexible in terms of its risk profile; and can generate dynamic past returns.

The moderate target return profile in Table 2.4 is 15 to 30 percent past compounded annual returns. The target average drawdown is 5 to 20+ percent depending on the composition of the managed futures portfolio.

The moderate portfolios built from the target in Table 2.4 are more flexible than any other category because they can choose from conservative and aggressive CTAs, dramatically expanding options for diversification. It is the author's opinion that expanded diversification, when properly executed among quality CTAs along five points of correlation, is a superior method of risk management to selecting CTAs based on past returns statistics only. Past performance does not necessarily indicate future results, and for this reason building a portfolio with the understanding of how strategies correlate to market environments and other CTAs might entail understanding the investment beyond simple past returns, focusing on the manager's experience and the diversification benefits of the strategy. Under certain portfolio selection circumstances it might be wise to select a CTA with lower past returns but more significant experience, a strong strategy that provides diversification with good returns distribution. Proper diversification and strong risk management generally rule the day in managed futures.

Comparing targets to the actual performance is interesting, but comparing actual performance of different categories to each other provides additional insight into the personality of any asset class. In fact, in this section compare the actual past results (Table 2.5) and see if you can discover an asset class insight. We will reveal this insight at the end of the section.

TABLE 2.4 A Moderate Target Risk/Reward Ideal

	Returns Target	Drawdown Target	Recovery Target
Study Group Return Category	Past Compounded Annual Return to Target	Past Average Drawdown to Target	Past Drawdown Recovery Time to Target
Moderate	15%–30%	5%–20+%	3–8+ months

These targets are entirely the author's opinion and are used only as a method to build portfolios based in part on past performance. Past performance is not indicative of future results. The point is to highlight diversification and make clear that investors should consider more than headline performance numbers, and that performance measures are but one tool to consider.

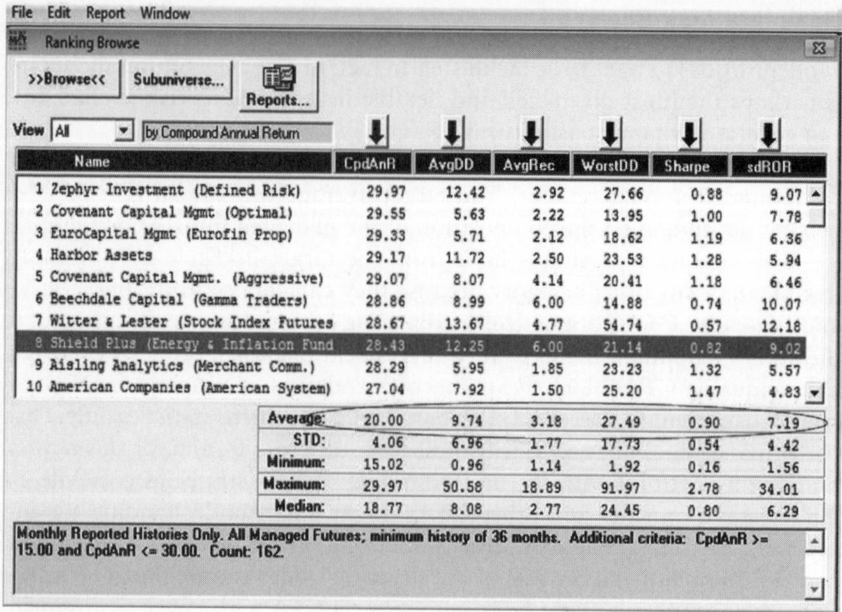

File Edit Report Window

Ranking Browse

>>Browse<< Subuniverse... Reports...

View All | by Compound Annual Return

Name	CpdAnR	AvgDD	AvgRec	WorstDD	Sharpe	sdROR
1 Zephyr Investment (Defined Risk)	29.97	12.42	2.92	27.66	0.88	9.07
2 Covenant Capital Mgmt (Optimal)	29.55	5.63	2.22	13.95	1.00	7.78
3 EuroCapital Mgmt (Eurofin Prop)	29.33	5.71	2.12	18.62	1.19	6.36
4 Harbor Assets	29.17	11.72	2.50	23.53	1.28	5.94
5 Covenant Capital Mgmt. (Aggressive)	29.07	8.07	4.14	20.41	1.18	6.46
6 Beechdale Capital (Gamma Traders)	28.86	8.99	6.00	14.88	0.74	10.07
7 Witter & Lester (Stock Index Futures	28.67	13.67	4.77	54.74	0.57	12.18
8 Shield Plus (Energy & Inflation Fund	28.43	12.25	6.00	21.14	0.82	9.02
9 Aisling Analytics (Merchant Comm.)	28.29	5.95	1.85	23.23	1.32	5.57
10 American Companies (American System)	27.04	7.92	1.50	25.20	1.47	4.83
Average:	20.00	9.74	3.18	27.49	0.90	7.19
STD:	4.06	6.96	1.77	17.73	0.54	4.42
Minimum:	15.02	0.96	1.14	1.92	0.16	1.56
Maximum:	29.97	50.58	18.89	91.97	2.78	34.01
Median:	18.77	8.08	2.77	24.45	0.80	6.29

Monthly Reported Histories Only. All Managed Futures; minimum history of 36 months. Additional criteria: CpdAnR >= 15.00 and CpdAnR <= 30.00. Count: 162.

FIGURE 2.2 Actual Screen Shot, Moderate Statistics

TABLE 2.5 Conservative/Moderate Comparison of Actual Results

	Returns	Drawdown	Drawdown	Drawdown	Risk/ Reward	Volatility	Managers
Study Group Return Category	Actual Compounded Annual Return	Actual Average Drawdown	Actual Drawdown Recovery Time	Actual Worst Drawdown	Actual Sharpe Ratio	Standard Deviation	Number of CTAs/ CPOs
Conservative 7%–15%	10.95%	7.45%	1.71	21%	0.61	4.62	283
Moderate 15%–30%	20.00%	9.74%	3.18	27%	0.9	7.19	162

Source: Barclay MAP Database. Study conducted 9/09.

Average results and portfolio results are a hypothetical combination of CTAs and these CTAs have not traded together in this fashion in a regulated CPO structure. See the hypothetical risk disclosure in note 7 in Chapter 3. Past performance is not indicative of future results. These numbers can change on a monthly basis. The point is not to highlight individual CTAs or potential portfolio combinations but rather to illustrate the potential power of diversification as a risk-management tool.

INSIGHT INTO ASSET CLASS PERSONALITY

When comparing the conservative and moderate statistics (Table 2.5), note the Sharpe ratio, which is a measure of risk and reward. The Sharpe ratio of the moderate actual past returns is a definite improvement, moving up to 0.90 in moderate from the conservative return's category of 0.61and near the relatively elusive 1.0 Sharpe ratio. While returns almost doubled, risk as measured by the average drawdown did worsen slightly from 7.45 percent in the conservative to 9.74 percent in the moderate, which many may consider acceptable risk/reward trade-off given the higher returns. Also consider standard deviation, which provides insight into the asset class. With a strong move higher in returns standard deviation, or volatility, in the moderate portfolio, jumped at significantly higher along with returns. This is a classic risk/reward trade-off: higher returns but increased volatility—a risk truism of managed futures.

A SIMPLE DEFINITION OF THE SHARPE RATIO

Most professional investors are familiar with the Sharpe ratio, developed by Nobel Prize–winner William Sharpe, as perhaps the most popular statistical measure that considers both an investment's risk and returns.*

It could be said the Sharpe ratio is a measure that helps identify the best investment value—the highest returns for the lowest risk—based on measures of volatility and returns.

*Sharpe ratio: Measure of the performance of an investment, computed by dividing the excess return (that is over the return on a risk-free investment such as on Treasury bills) by the amount of risk taken to generate the excess (the standard deviation of the rate of return). A ratio of 1 indicates one unit of return per unit of risk, 2 indicates two units of return per unit of risk, and negative values indicate loss or that a disproportionate amount of risk was taken to generate a positive return. Invented by the Nobel laureate (1990) U.S. economist William Sharpe (born 1934). *Source:* www.businessdictionary.com/definition/sharpe-ratio.html.

(*Continued*)

To provide a simple real estate analogy, imagine when purchasing a home buyers could look at a Sharpe ratio along with housing data when making a purchasing decision. A good value house—high-quality construction, good location at a low price—would have a high Sharpe ratio. A bad home value—in need of repair, volatile past ownership, a bad location at an expensive price—would have a low Sharpe ratio. Thus, the higher the Sharpe ratio, the better the investment's value based on past risk and reward results.

The Sharpe ratio is a formula that divides the excess return of an investment by the amount of risk taken as measured by standard deviation. (This and other managed futures risk measures are defined in more detail in Appendix D.) As mentioned, any Sharpe ratio near 1.00 could be considered very positive; anything over 0.50 is still positive, in the author's opinion. Thus, higher Sharpe ratios are better, meaning a more positive the risk/reward payoff of an investment. In managed futures, of the 1,013 programs reporting to the BarclayHedge database as of this writing, there are two CTAs that have Sharpe ratios over 3.00; there are only 16 CTAs that have a Sharpe ratio over 2.00; there are only 91 CTAs that have a Sharpe ratio over 1.00.** These are lofty numbers, indeed. For a perspective on just how lofty a Sharpe ratio over 1.0 is, consider the indexes below in Table 2.6 and look at the Sharpe for the S&P 500 at a pedestrian 0.34 and the MSCI world stock index at an almost microscopic 0.10:

TABLE 2.6 Sharpe Ratio and Risk Measures of Stock and CTA Indexes: 1/1/1980–7/31/2009

	Sharpe Ratio	Worst Drawdown	Average Recovery Time	STD Mo. (Qtr) ROR
CASAM CISDM CTA Equal Weighted Index	0.57	15.39%	2.75	4.72
Barclay CTA Index	0.41	15.65%	2.94	4.48
S&P 500 Total Return Index	0.34	50.95%	3.5	4.49
MSCI EAFE Index (USD)	0.1	58.23%	5.5	5.1

Source: Barclay MAP Database and CASAM CISDM index. Study conducted 9/09.

**Barclay MAP alternative asset database.

The Sharpe ratio is one performance measure. As we outline later in the book, the blind treatment of upside and downside volatility by standard deviation, used in the Sharpe ratio to measure risk, might not make this the best measure of risk and reward in managed futures, but it is mentioned throughout this book due to the fact of its generally accepted popularity. A more complete analysis of performance measures is available in Appendix D. As readers look at the value in investments, consider the risk/reward profile of the aggressive managed futures target in Table 2.7.

TABLE 2.7 An Aggressive Target Risk/Reward Ideal

	Returns Target	Drawdown Target	Recovery Target
Study Group Return Category	Past Compounded Annual Return to Target	Past Average Drawdown to Target	Past Drawdown Recovery Time to Target
Aggressive	30%–60%	15%–80%+	5–12 months

These targets are entirely the author's opinion and are used only as a method to build portfolios based in part on past performance. Past performance is not indicative of future results. The point is to highlight diversification and make clear that investors should consider more than headline performance numbers, and that performance measures are but one tool to consider.

Aggressive Risk/Reward

A helicopter jump to start a ski run; skydiving at sunset off California's central coast; surfing a monster barrel in Tahiti: These are all risky activities that can have consequences if not properly executed. Aggressive CTAs can be similarly categorized if the investments are not properly designed and managed, particularly investments that are not diversified or investments in a single CTA made at the wrong time, such as after a large profit surge.

To understand an aggressive CTA, consider one managed futures action sequel: 2008 was witness to one highly aggressive CTA reporting a 184 percent positive return in one month—but this performance was preceded by a three-month drawdown of 80 percent.[4] This type of performance is not necessarily an aberration among highly aggressive CTAs. The point is to illustrate that significant and aggressive returns are possible, and so is significant and aggressive risk, particularly if it is not properly managed.

Problem Issues with Aggressive CTAs Aggressive CTA investing can be a roller coaster, particularly if the investor invested in a single CTA or did not properly diversify among CTA managers. The aggressive target return profile in Table 2.7 is 30 to 60 percent, but hang on to your hat. This roller coaster can experience 30 to 80+ percent drawdowns, and higher if the investor is not careful. As a matter of fact, it isn't bad advice to say to aggressive investors: If you desire triple digit returns think about the potential for even bigger triple digit losses first, particularly with an investment in an aggressive single manager.

At the bottom of Table 2.8, consider the actual statistical equal weighted averages for all CTAs in the Barclay CTA MAP database that meet our aggressive return target category of 30 to 60 percent with a minimum of 36 months history.[5] Again, this is all based on past performance and, particularly with aggressive CTAs, the performance can be particularly volatile and might not be indicative of future results. Aggressive CTAs require active portfolio management and, as in all investing, the use of risk capital only.

An average compounded annual return of 44.31 percent (Table 2.8) is a strong headline returns number; given the reward, the average drawdown of 11.18 percent and worst drawdown of 31 percent can appear reasonably attractive, on the surface. However, as we identify in later chapters, investors must move past compounded annual return and consider

TABLE 2.8 Aggressive/Moderate/Conservative Actual Average Past Results

	Returns	Drawdown	Drawdown	Drawdown	Risk/ Reward	Volatility	Managers
Study Group Return Category	Actual Compounded Annual Return	Actual Average Drawdown	Actual Drawdown Recovery Time	Actual Worst Drawdown	Actual Sharpe Ratio	Standard Deviation	Number of CTAs/ CPOs
Conservative 7%–15%	10.95%	7.45%	1.71	21%	0.61	4.62	283
Moderate 15%–30%	20.00%	9.74%	3.18	27%	0.9	7.19	162
Aggressive 30%–60%	44.31%	11.18%	2.49	31%	1.33	10.7	25

Source: Barclay MAP Database. Study conducted 9/09.

Average results and portfolio results are a hypothetical combination of CTAs and these CTAs have not traded together in this fashion in a regulated CPO structure. See the hypothetical risk disclosure in note 7 in Chapter 3. Past performance is not indicative of future results. The point is not to highlight individual CTAs or potential portfolio combinations but rather to illustrate the potential power of diversification as a risk-management tool.

other factors, such as the distribution of those returns, the CTA's business operations, the win/loss percentage, appropriate diversification, National Futures Association (NFA) audit returns, and the CTA's experience, to mention but a few considerations. The aggressive portfolio diversification recommended here is somewhat difficult to obtain, particularly when targeting the high end of the return range. There just isn't appropriate CTA selection, with only 25 potential programs to choose from. Without appropriate diversification potential, the investor is concentrated in his or her investment, which exposes the investor to significant individual manager risk, detailed later in the book. This turns the risk profile into a roll of the dice, which in managed futures investing is not advised. Further, many of the CTAs in the aggressive category would not pass an individual due diligence screening due to a number of factors detailed in part in the chapter on advanced portfolio building. However, the available numeric data is acceptable for the purpose of using this demonstration to better understand insights into managed futures.

Investing in CTAs after a Drawdown

If investors decide to pursue the aggressive route, it is the author's opinion that solid programs are invested in at appropriate timing; namely, investing on a drawdown, not after a profit surge. This strategy was originally validated in the book *Managed Trading: Myths and Truths* (John Wiley & Sons, 1996) by industry legend Jack Schwager, and can be considered a risky strategy not appropriate for all investors. Qualified individuals and professionals can download a professional white paper on the *High-Performance Managed Futures* web site: "Investing in CTAs on a Drawdown: A Statistical Approach" and read more on the topic in Chapter 10 on portfolio building.

Managed Futures Volatility/Returns/ Drawdown Insight

Compare the performance of actual past results (Table 2.8). Earlier in this chapter you were asked to identify an insight by looking at the actual performance of conservative and moderate past return profiles to discover an insight about managed futures. Take a look at the combined past performance and notice this insight:

> *Volatility and returns move up at a similar rate, different from the primary risk measures of average drawdown and worst drawdown, which don't move at the same rate.*

Consider that in Table 2.8 as compounded annual return jumped from 10.95 percent in conservative to 44.31 percent in aggressive, average drawdown slightly budged from 7.45 to 11.18 percent. However, as returns jumped, so did volatility as measured by standard deviation, but other risk measures, such as drawdown, did not follow suit.

This highlights a fact of life in managed futures. Investing returns and standard deviation are correlated to one another, but drawdown, a primary measure of risk, is not correlated to higher returns to the same extent as standard deviation. The fact that the Sharpe ratio for the conservative return study category is actually the worst of all return profiles highlights the fact that the risk reward for low CTAs with the lowest returns is perhaps the least desirable, based on this indicator. Volatility, as measured by standard deviation, increases as returns go higher, emphasizing the naked fact that managed futures returns come with volatility as the price investors pay; a risk consideration. This is an interesting insight that points to what is a different investing animal where the unvarnished reality is that volatility is often the price one pays for returns. The challenge is to try to tame the animal: Understand and manage the risk behind powerful returns without dramatically reducing the reward. And this leads to the start of a formula, a logic that leads to a method of managing risk and CTA portfolios: an environment of risk management through intelligent diversification.

It is fascinating to hypothetically combine well-diversified CTAs with both moderate and aggressive programs. In fact, get ready, because the next chapter and then Chapter 10 pushes the concept of intelligent diversification further to yield very interesting portfolio results.

On the Book's Web Site

Available to the general public:

- Sharpe ratios of all major indexes.

Available to registered book readers:

- Updated performance of all risk categories.
- Professional white paper: "Investing in CTAs on a Drawdown: A Statistical Approach."
- Returns and drawdown statistics of "worst" and "best" CTAs.
- Video with review of the process for establishing the appropriate risk/reward profile.
- Selected CTA performance with author's analysis and power ratings.

For more information visit www.wiley.com/go/managedfutures.

CHAPTER 3

Work With It

Build Basic Portfolios Using Targets

Readers have been introduced to a new investment that on the surface might have amazing statistical appeal, but an investment that must always be understood by balancing risk and reward. For now, look with understanding at targets revealed in the last chapter (Table 3.1) as they will be used in part to build portfolios in this chapter:

Chapter 3 begins to unveil in part what the experience has looked like, a journey extended throughout the book. While the returns on Table 3.1 can be dazzling, the key is managing risk, not only coveting returns. There are risks not seen in these statistics, such as individual manager risk, that require management solutions. The first step in the process should be to build a portfolio recommendation based on knowledge of the investor's risk/reward profile and a high level understanding of financial conditions and ability to invest risk capital (a method to help accomplish this is outlined in Appendix B).

This chapter looks at different investment levels and risk/reward profiles to provide education on different managed futures concepts, and then explains the logic used to arrive at these insights. Readers have started an interesting journey; a path of discovery. It's time to take the experience to the next level by beginning to understand how intelligent diversification impacts past performance.

In this chapter readers discover:

- Single manager performance versus portfolio performance
- Highlighting of three hypothetical portfolios including:
  - Conservative $200,000 portfolio
  - Moderate $300,000 portfolio
  - Aggressive $500,000 portfolio
- Understanding of risk tolerances and issues

TABLE 3.1 Performance Targets Used to Design Appropriately Diversified Portfolios

	Returns Target	Drawdown Target	Recovery Target
Study Group Return Category	Past Compounded Annual Return to Target	Past Average Drawdown to Target	Past Drawdown Recovery Time to Target
Conservative	7%–15%	5%–15%+	1–4+ months
Moderate	15%–30%	5%–20%+	3–8+ months
Aggressive	30%–60%	15%–80%+	5–12+ months

These targets are entirely the author's opinion and are used only as a method to build portfolios based in part on past performance. Past performance is not indicative of future results. The point is to highlight diversification and make clear that investors should consider more than headline performance numbers, and that performance measures are but one tool.

RISK DISCLOSURE

In this chapter a hypothetical portfolio is put on display that utilizes actual returns reported by commodity trading advisors (CTAs) to the Barclay Alternative Database, which is considered by the author to be the leading industry source for CTA information. The performance is hypothetical in part because the CTAs have never traded together in this exact fashion in a regulated commodity pool operator (CPO) structure and the portfolio was built with the benefit of hindsight, all of which is detailed in the hypothetical risk disclosure (note 7 in the Notes section of this book). Further, note that CTA names have been masked because promoting individual performance or highlighting returns is not the point; rather, readers should view the portfolio development process from the standpoint of better understanding the managed futures asset class. Readers who wish to conduct individual research can do so through a variety of independent online industry resources. What follows is the opinion of the author and is based on his investment perspective and research, and is not being represented as a complete view on any elastic topic in managed futures.

PORTFOLIO DIVERSIFICATION VERSUS INDIVIDUAL MANAGER SELECTION

Diversification is a critical underlying tenet of managed futures. Some might say it is the essence of the asset class benefit. While diversification is central to the argument to invest in the asset class, diversification within managed futures is not as common as one might think, even though studies indicate appropriate diversification can greatly assist in managing risk. To understand the benefit of diversification, this section compares an investment in an individual CTA versus a portfolio of CTAs, highlighting at a basic level the risk management benefits of diversification.

$200,000 Minimum: Multimanager Portfolio versus Top-Returning CTA

Individual managed futures programs have investment minimums ranging from $5,000 to $5 million or more. For the point of education, this section looks at an overall investment level from $200,000 to $500,000 outlining a basic method of portfolio diversification, with a more detailed portfolio development and CTA evaluation method outlined in Chapter 10.

Listed in Table 3.2 are three diversified managed futures portfolios: A conservative portfolio was built with a $200,000 nominal investment (Portfolio Cons); a moderate portfolio was built with a $350,000 investment (Portfolio Mod); and an aggressive portfolio was built with a $500,000 investment (Portfolio Agg). Compare the portfolio results against the top returns category leader, a single CTA that would require a $200,000 nominal investment (Top $200K CTA) and notice the difference in risk measures and returns.[1]

The benefit of a diversified CTA portfolio versus a single investment manager is obvious, considering risk factors such as volatility and drawdown and then comparing this to returns. In Table 3.2 compare the moderate portfolio (Portfolio Mod) with the CTA with the best compounded annual returns as of the study date.[2] The real difference between the investments occurs in regard to risk. Worst drawdown, for instance, is very different: 17.16 percent for the moderate portfolio versus 43.10 percent for the high performing individual manager. Also consider standard deviation at 4.56 for the moderate portfolio versus 21.11 for the individual manager. That's a significant reduction in volatility with the portfolio, which is the point. *Portfolio diversification is about risk management and not enhancing returns.* Perhaps the significant risk when investing in a single manager, however, is

TABLE 3.2 Comparison of Portfolio Diversification to Individual Manager Investment

	Returns	Drawdown	Volatility		
CTA	Compounded Annual Return	Worst Drawdown	Standard Deviation	Risk/Reward Sharpe Ratio	Study Start Date
Portfolio Cons	7.65%	6.59%	1.90	0.85	2006
Portfolio Mod	17.71%	17.16%	4.56	0.96	2005
Portfolio Agg	35.16%	32.39%	9.41	1.02	2007
Top $200K CTA	22.61%	43.10%	13.08	0.43	2005

Source: Barclay MAP Database.

Portfolio results are a hypothetical combination of CTAs into a portfolio and these CTAs have not traded together in this fashion in a regulated CPO structure. See the hypothetical risk disclosure in note 7. Past performance is not indicative of future results. The point is not to highlight individual CTAs or potential portfolio combinations but rather to illustrate the potential power of diversification as a risk-management tool.

the investor's exposure to individual manager risk, an often hidden risk in managed futures that is discussed in more detail in Chapter 11.

With a high-level comparison of a portfolio of CTAs versus one individual CTA investment, it is time to consider how the portfolios are built on a basic level.

The Conservative Portfolio: Mixing Moderate and Conservative

Table 3.3 displays the individual CTA composition of the conservative portfolio which is followed by the returns of the hypothetical portfolio generated on a past performance basis.

In Table 3.3, the conservative portfolio included three CTAs, with diversification taking place as best possible over five points of correlation but the reality with only three managers is that sacrifices must be made in terms of true diversification. The portfolio composition in this case included two conservative CTAs and one moderate past performance CTA. It is important to note that a moderate CTA was used in building this conservative portfolio because of the potential power of diversification. The goal is to capture the moderate returns performance but generate conservative portfolio risk statistics. In this study, the portfolio method had the ability to provide interesting risk statistics, with worst past drawdown beating the past

TABLE 3.3 Actual Reported Performance of Individual CTAs Selected by the Author for Inclusion in a Portfolio

	Returns	Drawdown	Volatility	Risk/Reward	
CTA	Compounded Annual Return	Worst Drawdown	Standard Deviation (mo)	Sharpe Ratio	Start Date
CTA 3-1	5.92%	5.93%	1.47	0.66	2006
CTA 3-2	23.41%	34.63%	6.06	0.98	2004
CTA 3-3	8.89%	6.28%	2.74	0.71	Nov. 2006
Combined Portfolio Results	7.65%	6.59%	1.90	0.85	2006

Source: Barclay MAP Database.
Portfolio results are a hypothetical combination of CTAs into a portfolio and these CTAs have not traded together in this fashion in a regulated CPO structure. See the hypothetical risk disclosure in note 7. Past performance is not indicative of future results. The point is not to highlight individual CTAs or potential portfolio combinations but rather to illustrate the potential power of diversification as a risk-management tool.

performance targets for conservative, moderate, and aggressive that was outlined in the last chapter.

Building a conservative managed futures portfolio that consistently generates conservative results can be challenging due in large part to the limited number of conservative programs in managed futures, and the raw risk disclosure that managed futures is not a conservative investment. Programs that appear conservative at first can be deceiving. Intra-month volatility can be bumpier than the reported monthly performance indicates. But another risk disclosure is that managed futures CTAs who appear conservative for several years can take a turn for the worse into a riskier period of life, becoming more volatile, which can particularly be the case with certain managed futures strategies. In fact, in this conservative portfolio one of the CTAs is negatively exposed to the negative price movement of the S&P 500, a risk not evident from the headline statistics. Examples of identifying this risk are outlined later in the book. Investors who wish to target conservative managed futures programs because they can't stomach up-and-down volatility to varying degrees just might not want to invest in this asset class. Drawdowns and volatility are a fact of life in managed futures, often the price required for the potential for better-than-average performance. Liquidating an investment at the first sign of a drawdown can be the wrong approach;

rather, more appropriate might be liquidating managed futures investments due to factors such as strategy drift, unpredictable fluctuations in margin-to-equity ratios, and inconsistent trading behavior, some of just a handful of issues outlined in the advanced section of the book. As readers will discover, managed futures volatility can be a part of the investing formula that has potential to generate interesting returns. One solution outlined in this book is managing volatility through proper diversification to reduce overall portfolio volatility. The concept is including individually volatile but uncorrelated programs integrated together in a diversified portfolio, with the goal of generating smooth overall portfolio performance.

$350,000 Moderate Portfolio: A Wider Variety of Diversification Options

Consider the portfolio results in Table 3.4. It displays strong rewards and reasonable risk, but with a limited number of managers the performance numbers might actually have more risk than headline returns numbers indicate, which is particularly true when an investment is overly dependent on any one individual manager. The point is that when attempting to diversify a portfolio with direct CTA accounts, this is often the sacrifice one makes when asset allocation constraints and CTA investment minimums collide. However, it is the author's opinion that moderate portfolios in managed futures have the best potential for future success due to the wide range of potential selection. Readers of this book, scheduled for release in fall of 2010, can track the actual results online, as this portfolio was built based

TABLE 3.4 Hypothetical Results of Combining Selected CTAs into a Diversified Portfolio

	Returns	Drawdown	Volatility	Drawdown
Portfolio	Compounded Annual Return	Worst Drawdown	Standard Deviation (mo)	Recovery Time (mo)
Results	17.71%	17.16%	4.56%	2.63 months

Source: Barclay MAP Database.

Portfolio results are a hypothetical combination of CTAs into a portfolio and these CTAs have not traded together in this fashion in a regulated CPO structure. See the hypothetical risk disclosure in note 7. Past performance is not indicative of future results. The point is not to highlight individual CTAs or potential portfolio combinations but rather to illustrate the potential power of diversification as a risk-management tool.

on results ending during the early months of 2010. If there is one prediction that has the best chance of occurring, it is that something unpredictable could happen, particularly in light of current market situations. The issue is how these events are managed. Readers can watch this process unfold in real time online, which could offer the most interesting managed futures educational opportunity.

The portfolio study in Table 3.5 uses a $350,000 asset allocation to demonstrate a number of managed futures concepts, adding a few wrinkles to provide insight into the asset class at large. But here is the real twist. This portfolio is designed with portfolio construction errors, detailed in this chapter, showing investors a method of analyzing a managed futures investment that goes beyond headline returns numbers. One problem is that the portfolio does not include proper diversification across all managed futures strategies, which could provide the investor a less-than-optimal risk profile. In this example, a spread trading strategy was not included to highlight the point. (A more ideal portfolio is outlined in Chapter 10 on portfolio building.) The message is clear: Considering investments based only on compounded annual return is short sighted; investors should carefully consider all investment factors, including strategy risk, probability, asset allocation, appropriate investment timing, industry regulation, experience, and more. Targeting risk management first is the top priority in this portfolio-building process. This is accomplished in part, through five-point correlation analysis that includes strategy and market diversification, volatility skewing, and active portfolio management. These topics are mentioned here so readers can begin to connect the cause and effect relationships in managed futures, and are detailed in Chapters 9 through 12.

Take note of the performance of individual CTAs in Table 3.5 and the range of drawdowns, drawdown recovery times, and volatility, and consider that a properly diversified portfolio should generally have lower risk measures than the individual components. When one develops hypothetical sample portfolios as is done throughout this book, investors might think the goal is to create the highest past returns. That is not the case. In fact it is relatively easy to select "hot" CTAs and strategies that have performed well in the recent past. The issue is selecting CTAs that have potential to perform in the future, which involves several portfolio design strategies. For instance, in the moderate and aggressive portfolios, very specific CTAs were selected for investment after they incurred drawdown loss, which can negatively impact the "look" of overall past performance statistics. Several studies have pointed to the concept of investing in quality CTA programs when they experience a drawdown.[3] If the investor believes the CTA is a sustainable program and also believes that performance of markets, strategies and CTAs can be cyclical to varying degrees, with mean reversion potential among

TABLE 3.5 Actual Reported Performance of Individual CTAs Selected for Inclusion in a Portfolio

	Returns	Drawdown	Drawdown	Drawdown	Volatility	Risk/Reward	Experience
CTA Group	Compounded Annual Return	Worst Drawdown	Average Drawdown	Recovery Time (mos)	Standard Deviation (mos)	Sharpe Ratio	Start Date
CTA 3-5	24.52%	35.18%	12.98%	2.45	11.97	0.51	1996
CTA 3-2	23.41%	34.63%	9.86%	3	6.06	0.99	2004
CTA 3-6	13.60%	41.08%	16.66%	2.80	11.68	0.26	2005
CTA 3-7	18.91%	17.62%	6.81%	2.0	5.53	0.84	2005
CTA 3-8	20.46%	31.57%	13.79%	4.0	9.92	0.52	2005
Portfolio Results	*21.61%*	*20.16%*	*7.98%*	*2.28 months*	*4.75*	*1.15*	*2006*

Source: Barclay MAP Database.
Portfolio results are a hypothetical combination of CTAs into a portfolio and these CTAs have not traded together in this fashion in a regulated CPO structure. See the hypothetical risk disclosure in note 7. Past performance is not indicative of future results. The point is not to highlight individual CTAs or potential portfolio combinations but rather to illustrate the potential power of diversification as a risk-management tool.

TABLE 3.6 Returns-Based Correlation Matrix of CTAs in a Portfolio

	BCNDX	CTA 3-5	CTA 3-2	CTA 3-6	SPTR	CTA 3-7
BCNDX	1	0.28	−0.3	0.6	−0.08	−0.17
CTA 3-5	0.28	1	−0.04	0.11	−0.1	0.09
CTA 3-2	−0.3	−0.04	1	−0.35	0.22	−0.05
CTA 3-6	0.6	0.11	−0.35	1	−0.19	0.12
SPTR	−0.08	−0.1	0.22	−0.19	1	−0.07
CTA3-7	−0.17	0.09	−0.05	0.12	−0.07	1

Source: Barclay MAP Database.

In this study, correlation analysis starts from the point of the shortest track record in the portfolio using all periods. The shorter the track record, the less applicable the correlation analysis, in the author's opinion. Past performance is not indicative of future results. The point is not to highlight individual CTAs or potential portfolio combinations, but rather to illustrate the potential power of diversification as a risk-management tool.

sustainable managers, it could be considered better to invest in a quality CTA on a drawdown than after a profit surge. Chapter 10 reveals a method of skewing a portfolio based on the potential for a beaten down strategy to outperform in the future. The point is to illustrate that selecting appropriate CTAs is about more than just selecting hot CTAs with strong short-term performance.

While Table 3.5 displays the headline performance of the CTAs contained within the portfolio, Table 3.6 shows a traditional return-based correlation matrix with the same CTAs, revealing how the returns of the various programs correlated with each CTA within the portfolio and with the S&P 500 (SPTR) and Barclay CTA index (BCNDX). This returns correlation is an indicator of smooth portfolio performance. This correlation matrix is the extent to which traditional correlation analysis is used to measure portfolio diversification, a topic detailed in Chapter 9.

Analysis of Various CTAs and Considerations for Portfolio Inclusion

Tables 3.5 to 3.7 will be referred to in the balance of the chapter, as considerations for various CTAs are examined.

Leverage Adjustment: To illustrate the importance of leverage and margin as a risk-management tool, this portfolio adjusted margin and leverage up and down (Table 3.7), much like one might adjust the temperature of an oven. Here is a key point of risk management, often overlooked: Investors have the option to either dial up or down

TABLE 3.7 Portfolio Asset Allocation with Correlation Considerations

	Allocation	Leverage	Correlation	Correlation	Correlation	Correlation
CTA Group	Cash Investment	Portfolio Margin Usage/ Nominal	Strategy Correlation	Returns Correlation	Markets Correlation	Returns Correlation to S&P 500
CTA 3-5	$50,000	100%	Trend	Med. Correlation	Diversified	Low
CTA 3-2	$100,000	150%	Volatility	Low Correlation	Diversified	Low
CTA 3-6	$100,000	100%	Discretionary	Low Correlation	Diversified	Low
CTA 3-7	$50,000	57%	Counter Trend	Med. Correlation	Stock Indices	Low

Source: Barclay MAP Database.

Portfolio results are a hypothetical combination of CTAs into a portfolio and these CTAs have not traded together in this fashion in a regulated CPO structure. See the hypothetical risk disclosure in note 7. Past performance is not indicative of future results. The point is not to highlight individual CTAs or potential portfolio combinations but rather to illustrate the potential power of diversification as a risk-management tool.

one component of risk by reducing leverage to suit their needs. It is the author's opinion that investors should dial down leverage rather than dial it up.

In this case, leverage was adjusted up with one CTA and down with another others to maintain the same nominal portfolio investment level, but with the goal of skewing risk and volatility. Such activities can be used as a risk-management tool, potentially designing the investment to be more conservative, or used to influence returns, as it has done in the moderate portfolio example, but there are no guarantees any investment will exhibit conservative future performance or increased returns through the use of leverage.

Quicker Recovery Time: As evidenced in Table 3.5, this portfolio was designed so the investment would feature a lower past drawdown recovery time, a critical yet overlooked risk statistic upon which sophisticated portfolios are built in later chapters. The point for this basic chapter is that portfolios can be designed around investor needs, and if the investor desires quick past recovery time as a key attribute, this can be designed in portfolio construction.

Portfolio Diversification and the Miracle on Ice Effect: In 1980 the U.S. Olympic hockey team stunned the world by winning the gold medal, beating a team of much more individually talented Soviet professional hockey players. In perhaps one of the greatest moments in U.S. sports history, a group of relatively moderately talented college hockey players combined their efforts, and when grouped together as a team, performed at a much higher level than their individual performance might indicate. In a managed futures context this refers to the ability of intelligent portfolio diversification to strategically combine CTAs in a portfolio so as to reduce past risk statistics. For instance, in this moderate portfolio aggressive CTAs were utilized due to the diversification effect: It is possible for individually aggressive CTAs to integrate into a moderate portfolio so long as the programs are uncorrelated. In the moderate portfolio, compare the equal weighted risk statistics of the individual CTAs to the combined portfolio results. As a result of this diversification, it is interesting to consider the improvement in worst drawdown, standard deviation of monthly return, Sharpe Ratio, and drawdown recovery time in Table 3.5 and consider the Miracle on Ice. Consider the individual volatility and drawdown performance of the CTAs on an individual basis, then compare them to the smoother overall portfolio performance. This reduction in past risk is the objective behind portfolio diversification.

Volatility Diversification: Also note in the moderate portfolio how a wide range of volatility levels were utilized. In Table 3.5 the volatility (STD) ranges from 5 to 12, but the overall portfolio volatility is low at 4.75—the portfolio volatility is lower than any individual CTA volatility, an important message about proper diversification. This is another measure of proper CTA portfolio development: when uncorrelated volatility is combined in a portfolio with other volatile CTAs with the goal to potentially reduce overall portfolio volatility. Volatility is a key component in managed futures and it is often mistakenly characterized as all bad to the same degree, a topic we touch on later in the book.

While the overall portfolio statistics are interesting, investors should also consider the components within the portfolio and the logic used to build portfolios, and understand potential problems and issues when building portfolios. The portfolio isn't perfect, highlighting the point that *perfect* and *risk free* are word combinations that should never be used in any investing. What's more, each CTA included in the hypothetical portfolio in Table 3.5 has its own story to tell, pointing to unique features in the asset class at large. There are numerous positive and negative features of each CTA and their trading strategy that warrant consideration. For purpose of the book, only features that illuminate insight into the asset class and provide overall education will be discussed, thus all aspects regarding individual CTAs and the selection process may not be included. This chapter touches on several topics in brief fashion, with detailed information contained in the advanced section of the book.

INDIVIDUAL CTA ANALYSIS AND PORTFOLIO CONSIDERATIONS

What follows is entirely the opinion of the author, particularly regarding individual CTA evaluation and selection, and is used to illustrate one method to evaluate CTAs and should not be construed as individual recommendations and opinions should not be confused with statements of fact.

Portfolio Component: Trend Trader

Consider More Than Returns: Experience, Strategy, Risk Management

CTA 3-5 (reported past performance displayed in Table 3.8), is a trend trader and possesses a CTA track record dating back to 1996, which is an unusually long track record for a CTA with a relatively small $50,000 investment

TABLE 3.8 Actual Reported Performance of Individual CTA Selected for Inclusion in a Portfolio

	Returns	Drawdown	Drawdown	Drawdown	Volatility	Risk/Reward	Experience
CTA Group	Compounded Annual Return	Worst Drawdown	Average Drawdown	Recovery Time (mos)	Standard Deviation (monthly returns)	Sharpe Ratio	Start Date
CTA 3-5	24.52%	35.18%	12.98%	2.45	11.97	0.51	1996

	Allocation	Leverage	Correlation	Correlation	Correlation	Correlation	
CTA Group	Cash Investment	Portfolio Margin Usage/ Nominal	Strategy Correlation	Returns Correlation	Markets Correlation	Returns Correlation to S&P 500	Win%
CTA 3-5	$50,000	100%	Trend	Med. Correlation	Diversified	Low	49.41%

Source: Barclay MAP Database.

Portfolio results are a hypothetical combination of CTAs into a portfolio and these CTAs have not traded together in this fashion in a regulated CPO structure. See the hypothetical risk disclosure in note 7. Past performance is not indicative of future results. The point is not to highlight individual CTAs or potential portfolio combinations but rather to illustrate the potential power of diversification as a risk-management tool.

minimum. A study for this book shows the average minimum investment for CTAs with 10 years or more experience is $2.7 million, which is why reasonably strong-performing CTAs with equally lengthy track records could be considered statistically unusual. A CTA is considered experience-positive from the standpoint of undergoing a number of National Futures Association (NFA) due diligence audits, as well as the core human condition that any CTA on-the-job experience and endurance in a fast-paced investment landscape warrants a degree of consideration. Because managed futures has been a rapidly growing asset class, it is not uncommon to see CTAs with relatively short track records. This book generally prefers CTAs with at least three-year track records. While short by equity standards, this length indicates the CTA may have experienced one or two NFA performance audits, his or her strategy and market execution could have been publicly tested in a variety of market environments, and the CTA has experienced one standard deviation of market reporting periods. Another benefit: CTA 3-5 is a trend follower who has exhibited reasonably strong past risk and returns performance and as of this writing the trend trading strategy is experiencing a drawdown, potentially a good time to invest in this strategy. Trend traders tend to capture profits during market environments that feature identifiable price persistence and volatility breakouts.

Some investors might consider simple standard deviation an appropriate measure of risk. CTA 3-5 does have a relatively high standard deviation of 11.97 when compared to the strategy benchmark of 5.48.[4] (The CTA performance benchmark study is available in Appendix A, with monthly updates occurring on the book's web site.) However, volatility as depicted by simple standard deviation may not always be the best measure in managed futures, in the author's opinion. Volatility might not be as big a concern as long as it is uncorrelated to other points of volatility in a fashion that reduces overall portfolio volatility and keeps drawdowns low. This tactic of combining and managing different types of volatility in a portfolio is known as volatility skewing. These ideas are discussed in Chapters 6–12.

More interesting with CTA 3-5 is the positive win/loss size differential of +5.09 compared to the trend trading benchmark of +0.89. As is mentioned in Chapters 6–12, win/loss size differential can be a significant if overlooked performance measure in managed futures, pointing to potential sustainability. While the Sharpe ratio might be relatively low at 0.56 when compared to CTAs with shorter track records, and just above the trend trading benchmark of –0.49, the CTA's length of track record dating to 1996 and their low minimum investment of $50,000 compared to the strategy average of $1.7 million are significant benefits. While performance appears positive, CTA 3-5's correlation is only moderate to the Barclay CTA index, which is not surprising a trend trader is correlated to the Barclay CTA index. While the CTA does have a positive win/ loss size ratio, they do have a lower than average win percentage at 49.41 percent compared with the trend trading benchmark win percentage of 57.89 percent. Let's contrast this trend-following CTA to a short volatility CTA.

Portfolio Component: Short Volatility

Consider Win Percentage as It Relates to Strategy CTA 3-2 (reported past performance displayed in Table 3.9), has a diversified short volatility strategy, and there are several concerns with this strategy. The short volatility option strategy is perhaps most popularly categorized as the S&P options premium collectors, which is too simple a categorization but it is interesting nonetheless to explain the strategy risk from this perspective.

Many short volatility strategies sell put and call options on a single market, such as the S&P 500. Analysis of this strategy can be tricky when only looking at headline performance numbers; it requires one understands what lies beneath the surface. The S&P short volatility strategy can appear conservative during most times, with apparent lack of correlation to the stock market. But this turns rapidly negative during times of significant stock market dislocation, as the strategy can experience significant losses in a short period of time. (This concept is discussed further in Chapter 9 on correlation and Chapter 11 on individual manager risk. Further the short volatility strategy is explained in Chapters 4 and 10.) For this reason, the short volatility strategy has been described as consistently picking up nickels on the street for years and then one day being steamrolled by a bus in an instant when a Black Swan Event causes a volatility spike in a particular market. With strategies such as those of the "short vol" CTA, it is important to understand the potential risk and then form an opinion regarding how different market environments impact true risk. When risk is at its highest is the point investors might discover that a short options contract, now deeply in the money, has similar risk and performance characteristics as a futures contract. Some futures commission merchant (FCM) brokerage firms may institute higher margin levels on short volatility option sellers and have policies that liquidate positions if a margin call indicates a significant amount of account risk. It is important with a short volatility strategy that the manager have strong risk management during the rare moments of market stress. The short volatility strategy can use both covered option spreads or uncovered or naked short options positions, which can possess a similar risk profile to a futures contract if the option sold moves into the money. While the covered strategy can define risk, it is often executed closer to the money

TABLE 3.9 Actual Reported Performance of Individual CTA Selected for Inclusion in a Portfolio

	Returns	Drawdown	Drawdown	Drawdown	Volatility	Risk/Reward	Experience
CTA Group	Compounded Annual Return	Worst Drawdown	Average Drawdown	Recovery Time (mos)	Standard Deviation (monthly returns)	Sharpe Ratio	Start Date
CTA 3-2	23.41%	34.63%	9.86%	3.00	6.06	0.99	2004

	Allocation	Leverage	Correlation	Correlation	Correlation	Correlation	
CTA Group	Cash Investment	Portfolio Margin Usage/ Nominal	Strategy Correlation	Returns Correlation	Markets Correlation	Returns Correlation to S&P 500	Win%
CTA 3-2	$100,000	150%	Volatility	Low Correlation	Diversified	Low	72%

Source: Barclay MAP Database.

Portfolio results are a hypothetical combination of CTAs into a portfolio and these CTAs have not traded together in this fashion in a regulated CPO structure. See the hypothetical risk disclosure note 7. Past performance is not indicative of future results. The point is not to highlight individual CTAs or potential portfolio combinations but rather to illustrate the potential power of diversification as a risk-management tool.

than the uncovered strategy, which could impact the win percentage of the strategy. The book's web site offers a tutorial detailing the primary managed futures strategies.[5]

Compare the 49.41 percent win percentage of the first CTA (Table 3.8) against the 72.10 percent win percentage of the second CTA (Table 3.9). It might be common for the uninitiated managed futures investor to conclude that the high 72 percent win percentage would perhaps make the second CTA a better choice. But the fact is that the win percentage is as much a factor of the CTA's strategy as it is of his individual skill. The average win percentage of option trading CTA's is 74.25 percent, the highest of any of the primary CTA strategies. The book considers higher win percentage a characteristic of many short volatility strategies. In other strategies win percentage is a most common measure; the size of win versus the size of loss is perhaps a more significant yet little known consideration. Option CTAs typically have the most negative win size versus loss size statistics, while discretionary and trend traders have the highest. The trend and volatility strategies also benefit from very different market environments. While the trend trading strategy (Table 3.8) generally benefits from strong, consistent price movement and volatility range breakouts, the opposite can be true with the short volatility strategy, which potentially benefits from range-bound trading and times of decreasing volatility.

When deciding to include CTAs in a portfolio it is constructive to consider individual CTA performance during times of extreme market dislocation. This can provide additional clues as to potential correlation beyond what are the obvious measures of correlation, total returns correlation. Potentially related to low correlation is the CTA's relatively even returns distribution (not shown), which is an important consideration in all CTA selection.

Leverage Usage a Two-Edged Sharp Sword To illustrate a unique aspect of managed futures, in the case of this CTA the leverage amount was increased.[6] (See notionally funded accounts performance table and risk disclosure in note 6.) When leverage usage increases it also increases risk, with the goal of potentially increasing return. As illustrated in Table 3.9 in Allocation Cash Investment and Leverage Portfolio Margin Usage/Nominal, the total investment in the CTA is $150,000: $100,000 nominal investment in the form of a cash deposit, and $50,000 in notional funding or pledged capital that would be deposited by the investor if the CTA were to experience a margin call. Notional funding increases the use of leverage, thus raising the potential for a margin call. In this case leverage was increased by 50 percent and thus loses and gains could be magnified by 50 percent. Notional funding is not recommended to unsophisticated investors and should be used by those qualified investors who clearly understand the risks and use only appropriate risk capital for investing. (Notional funding is explained for demonstration purposes in this section to explain the asset class at a high level, with complete notional funding disclosure in note 6.) Perhaps more significant, the following examples highlight where the leverage was reduced in an effort to design a more conservative investment. It is the author's recommendation that investors first consider utilizing leverage to reduce risk in investments rather than to improve potential reward. The point for this chapter of discovery is to highlight that one method used by investors to manage risk is dialing down and up leverage and margin usage.

Portfolio Component: Discretionary Vol Trader

Strategy Diversification, Low Minimum Investment There are numerous positive and negative features of this CTA that warrant consideration. For the purpose of the book the previous points and insights will not be reiterated, thus certain circumstances surrounding CTAs are not included in the discussion if the concepts have been previously discussed.

CTA 3-6 (reported past performance displayed in Table 3.10) utilizes both a discretionary and directional short volatility strategy and trades in a diversity of markets. The discretionary strategy, as the name implies, is designed and executed at the discretion of the trader. Oftentimes these strategies may combine trend, volatility, and spread trading, which can yield interesting results.

In the instance of CTA 3-6, the compounded annual returns might be relatively low, at 13.60 percent, when compared to the other CTAs in the portfolio, but they are consistent with the discretionary strategy benchmark of 12.6 percent. However, the worst drawdown statistics are high at 41.08 percent, compared to the strategy benchmark of 20.61 percent, making this look like the worst of both worlds: conservative returns with a pretty aggressive worst drawdown. But there are several reasons this CTA is being considered, all of which could be considered subjective opinions. First, the CTA is in a drawdown and now it might be an appropriate opportunity to invest. Using the author's subjective formula, this CTA is a candidate for investing when in a drawdown. Second, the CTA has displayed strong trade management. In the face of drawdowns the CTA has not panicked, changed margin usage, or trading strategy, a subjective consideration not often difficult to determine by looking at just headline performance statistics. Third, their strategy is interesting in the use of its hedging different short and long option spreads and combining short options with a corresponding futures hedge and their markets traded and trade time frame offer benefits relative to overall portfolio diversification. Further, the CTA's low stated

TABLE 3.10 Actual Reported Performance of Individual CTA Selected for Inclusion in a Portfolio

	Returns	Drawdown	Drawdown	Drawdown	Volatility	Risk/Reward	Experience
CTA Group	Compounded Annual Return	Worst Drawdown	Average Drawdown	Recovery Time (mos)	Standard Deviation (monthly returns)	Sharpe Ratio	Start Date
CTA 3-6	13.60%	41.08%	16.66%	2.80	11.68	0.26	

	Allocation	Leverage	Correlation	Correlation	Correlation	Correlation	
CTA Group	Cash Investment	Portfolio Margin Usage/ Nominal	Strategy Correlation	Returns Correlation	Markets Correlation	Returns Correlation to S&P 500	Win%
CTA 3-6	$100,000	100%	Discretionary/ Vol	Low Correlation	Diversified	Low	57.89%

Source: Barclay MAP Database.

Portfolio results are a hypothetical combination of CTAs into a portfolio and these CTAs have not traded together in this fashion in a regulated CPO structure. See the hypothetical risk disclosure in note 7. Past performance is not indicative of future results. The point is not to highlight individual CTAs or potential portfolio combinations but rather to illustrate the potential power of diversification as a risk-management tool.

investment minimum of $25,000, available in some programs, offers flexibility compared with the average managed futures minimum of $1.58 million for an individual managed futures program, and is an important consideration. The reality of CTA portfolio development is that investment minimum is often a limiting factor in the number of CTAs that can be included in a portfolio. While it doesn't necessarily drive a decision, all else being reasonably equal, it is not uncommon to prefer a CTA with a lower investment minimum because additional diversification can be obtained through inclusion of additional managers, as opposed to a single CTA with a higher minimum laying claim to a significant portion of the client portfolio. Further, in this case the CTA's industry experience managing risk and margin is a consideration in the portfolio manager's opinion, as well as the statistical potential to invest in this CTA during a drawdown make the CTA interesting for consideration.

Portfolio Component: Counter Trend

Unique Strategy with Correlation Benefits, Volatility Skewing CTA 3-7 (reported past performance displayed in Table 3.11) is highlighted in this chapter for several reasons, most of which centers on the CTA's strategy. CTA 3-7 utilizes an interesting strategy, the counter trend style, that has potential to provide an interesting correlation benefits when paired with trend traders.

The CTA in Table 3.11 is studied from several standpoints. Most interesting is the CTA's counter-trend strategy and the resulting strategy correlation to trend trading. For instance, as evidenced in the correlation matrix in Table 3.7, the trend trader (CTA 3-5) and the counter trend trader (CTA 3-7) in this portfolio are relatively uncorrelated to the tune of −.18, a slight negative correlation. CTA 3-7 utilizes a shorter-term trade duration than the trend trader CTA 3-5, and this time frame correlation along with differences in strategy and markets traded are points of consideration. CTA 3-7 trades stock indexes and, somewhat troublesome, but perhaps most interesting to note is the short official CTA track record, with a longer proprietary record.

Proprietary Track Record and Portfolio Developer Bias: This CTA was chosen for inclusion for several educational reasons. For instance, investors may find upon detailed examination of the NFA-reviewed disclosure document that portions of the CTA's early track record is proprietary, meaning that audited account traded was the CTA's, perhaps at a time when he was not a regulated CTA. This is an interesting consideration. This CTA has prior trading experience and the portfolio manager is familiar with the CTA's trading

TABLE 3.11 Actual Reported Performance of Individual CTA Selected for Inclusion in a Portfolio

	Returns	Drawdown	Drawdown	Drawdown	Volatility	Risk/Reward	Experience
CTA Group	Compounded Annual Return	Worst Drawdown	Average Drawdown	Recovery Time (mos)	Standard Deviation (monthly returns)	Sharpe Ratio	Start Date
CTA 3-7	18.91%	17.63%	6.81%	2.0	5.53	0.85	2010

	Allocation	Leverage	Correlation	Correlation	Correlation	Correlation	
CTA Group	Cash Investment	Portfolio Margin Usage/ Nominal	Strategy Correlation	Returns Correlation	Markets Correlation	Returns Correlation to S&P 500	Past Probability Win%
CTA 3-7	$50,000	57%	Counter Trend	Med. Correlation	Stock Indexes	Low	54%

Source: Barclay MAP Database.

Portfolio results are a hypothetical combination of CTAs into a portfolio and these CTAs have not traded together in this fashion in a regulated CPO structure. See the hypothetical risk disclosure in note 7. Past performance is not indicative of future results. The point is not to highlight individual CTAs or potential portfolio combinations but rather to illustrate the potential power of diversification as a risk-management tool.

system, which might not statistically validate the CTA but might be an actual consideration in the process, depending on the portfolio developer. Humans being human, sometimes the fact that the portfolio developer is familiar with the CTA's previous professional trading and has witnessed the CTA's performance live as it happens does influence decisions. This is not an endorsement, but it is to point out there are times at which the opinions and personal bias of a portfolio developer come into play. The key is that whoever develops CTA portfolios must disclose all their bias and opinions up front, and any conflict of interest or financial relationship between the portfolio developer and the CTA is completely disclosed in writing to the investor, which is not always industry practice.

Portfolio Component: Trend Trader Gold/ Currency Hedge

We are going to overweight the trend trading component of this portfolio due in part to the fact the strategy has been beaten down and investing in strategies as well as solid CTAs after a drawdown can be an interesting strategy for appropriate investors. There are several different features with this CTA 3-8, (Table 3.12) highlighting educational points of different account structure, the significance of operational depth, low investment minimum, investor communication, and a currency hedging feature, all considerations not apparent in headline performance numbers.

Perhaps most innovative, this is the first known managed futures fund to offer the investment denominated in gold, not a currency that is necessarily tied to any individual economy and a metal that has tended to perform well during times of systematic market stress. On the surface, this program only has a strong four-year track record traded offshore, and it is interesting to note that unlike many trend traders this strategy was recently profitable in part due to the currency hedge. What this four-year track record does not show is that the fund is managed by a firm that offers more than 20 different programs and strategies with a history in the industry dating back to 1996. In fact, this was the first managed futures program to package a system targeted toward the retail investor, allowing qualified investors easy access to establish a managed futures account for as little as $5,000 but also offering significant programs with investment minimums ranging from $50,000 to $1,000,000. What differentiates this program is what cannot be seen in the headline performance numbers. This systematic trend following CTA has strong business operations, with over 250 employees and 14 worldwide offices, an operational depth somewhat unique in an industry often populated by firms with a handful of employees and little operational

TABLE 3.12 Superfund Gold A

	Returns	Drawdown	Drawdown	Drawdown	Volatility	Risk/Reward	Experience
CTA Group	Compounded Annual Return	Worst Drawdown	Average Drawdown	Recovery Time (mos)	Standard Deviation (monthly returns)	Sharpe Ratio	Start Date
CTA 3-8	20.46%	31.56%	13.79%	4	9.92	0.52	Oct-05

	Allocation	Leverage	Correlation	Correlation	Correlation	Correlation	
CTA Group	Cash Investment	Portfolio Margin Usage/ Nominal	Strategy Correlation	Returns Correlation	Markets Correlation	Returns Correlation to S&P 500	Win%
CTA 3-8	$50,000	100%	Trend	Med. Correlation	Low	Low	58%

Source: Barclay MAP Database.
Study conducted January, 2010. Portfolio results are a hypothetical combination of CTAs into a portfolio and these CTAs have not traded together in this fashion in a regulated CPO structure. See the hypothetical risk disclosure in note 7. Past performance is not indicative of future results. The point is not to highlight individual CTAs or potential portfolio combinations but rather to illustrate the potential power of diversification as a risk management tool. Academic researchers are welcome to download exact study details on the book's web site.

redundancy. Another noteworthy aspect of this managed futures program is their investor communications. Most CTAs have little if any communication with their investors, leaving their often complex financial positions unexplained. This is an important consideration, as it is possible that managed futures investors might not understand the true risk or market exposure of some of the more complex positions. This CTA provides regular online market commentary, explaining their positions and market exposure. This fund is available only to foreign qualified investors, and a U.S. version with a shorter track record using a similar trading methodology is also available. This limited liability legal fund structure is important to note, as opposed to direct CTA account, because the fund structure offers a different risk profile as explained in Chapters 4 and 11. Funds such as this are available direct through the fund or financial advisors who carry the fund on their platform, as opposed to a direct CTA account, which are generally available through IBs and FCMs. (However, a recent CFTC letter allows independent RIAs to offer direct managed futures accounts through qualified FCMs with certain restrictions, and funds can be offered through FCMs when the AP making the offering is part of fund ownership.)

$500,000 Aggressive Portfolio: Hang On To Your Hat

Now add a little adrenaline to the situation. Building an aggressive $500,000 portfolio as was done in Table 3.13 is akin to drinking caffeine and then topping off the night with an energy drink. The three-manager hypothetical portfolio was as diversified as possible, given the limited options available—and in fact the investment minimum was raised due to a lack of options in the aggressive returns category.

To show this portfolio (Table 3.13), we employ the standard information originating from portfolio management software:

As Table 3.13 demonstrates, 35.16 percent compounded annual return performance is aggressive as is worst drawdown of 32.39 percent and standard deviation of 9.41—highlighting the risk/reward trade-off. Due in part to the limited selection in the aggressive category, sacrifices were made and the portfolio is not ideal. The three-manager portfolio might not be enough CTAs to achieve proper diversification, particularly with aggressive programs, because of potential heightened individual manager risk.

Always Consider Hidden Risk beyond the Headline Performance Numbers

A trained managed futures eye can identify the risk factors in the aggressive portfolio. First, while it is not visible in the headline performance numbers visible in Table 3.13, the return distribution, skewness and kurtosis, was

TABLE 3.13 Hypothetical Results of Combining Selected CTAs into a Portfolio as Displayed by Barclay MAP Software

Total Return:	166.20	Avg. Monthly	2.96
Cmpnd. An. Rtn.	35.16	STD Monthly	9.41
Last 12 Mo:	5.65	Sharpe:	1.02
Last 6 Mo:	1.45	Sterling:	1.20
Last 3 Mo:	−4.86	Barclay:	2.34
Last Month:	−0.36	Efficiency:	1.08
Winning Mo:	22	Losing Mo:	17
Avg. Win:	8.67	Avg. Loss:	−4.43
STD Win:	8.82	STD Loss:	4.43
% Winning	56.41	% Losing Mo:	43.59
Worst Drawdown:	32.39		

Year	Return
2010 (YTD)	−4.86
2009	11.74
2008	94.44
2007	28.78

Source: Barclay MAP Database.
Portfolio results are a hypothetical combination of CTAs into a portfolio and these CTAs have not traded together in this fashion in a regulated CPO structure. See the hypothetical risk disclosure in note 7. Past performance is not indicative of future results. The point is not to highlight individual CTAs or potential portfolio combinations but rather to illustrate the potential power of diversification as a risk-management tool. Again, there are several circumstances regarding this portfolio's selection, both positive and negative, that are not detailed so as not be repetitive.

uneven, a fact that the compounded annual return statistic does not reveal. It is not advisable for investors to expect that Superman performance year in and year out: Yes, past performance really might not indicate future results. In fact the author would have a difficult time recommending this aggressive portfolio due to its lack of diversification, high exposure to individual manager risk, and the necessity to sacrifice selection. Many times risk management must trump what can appear on the surface as amazing returns. Three managers might not be ideal risk diversification for an aggressive portfolio. The CTA asset allocation was uneven, enhancing individual manager risk, and one allocation occurred to a CTA who shares in commissions, a conflict of interest caution flag that requires further investigation. Further, returns distribution among many of these seemingly high performing CTAs in fact had large returns earlier in their career, not an ideal situation. The investor might discover aggressive CTA returns could come in bunches:

Investors could wait months if not years until witnessing a significant profit surge. When the profit surge does occur it can happen at the speed of light when compared to stock market price appreciation. Further, entering high-performing but risky CTAs at the wrong time, when they are at the top after a profit surge, can be a major mistake. Again, in this portfolio the strategy of investing in CTAs on a drawdown was employed. Investing on a drawdown relies on mean revision and could be considered an aggressive tactic, appropriate with certain CTA and only for qualified investors using risk capital. Many of these risk factors are discussed in the advanced section of the book, and the hidden risk in this portfolio is analyzed in more detail on the book's web site.

Here is the key point:

> *All those risks are not evident by looking at simple past compounded annual return, Sharpe ratio, or the risk measure standard deviation.*

While these exercises have been interesting, the challenge is even more significant when investment minimums drop, because when minimums drop, so does potential CTA selection and opportunity for diversification. The problem at the lower minimum funding level is quality manager selection. For instance, as of this writing there are 33 managers with a $25,000 account minimum and half of these programs have a track record less than three years old—and many have not had their performance and business operation audited by the NFA. As will be outlined in future chapters, the NFA audit and regulation is critical to investor protection, and investors should question any managed futures program that does not have this limited but important degree of scrutiny.

There Is No "Perfect" Financial Investment

In this chapter readers were given an introductory glance at the risk and past returns in managed futures. By many standards the returns were interesting, with high performance past returns and risk profiles to match. Perhaps more interesting is watching the portfolio results in real time on the book's web site, as these portfolios were developed in early 2010.

The point of this chapter is to provide insight into some, but not all, of the considerations that might go into building a diversified portfolio. In fact, the book does not consider these portfolios ideal because of many of the highlighted issues. This section significantly represents the opinions of the author, does not cover all factors, and is done in brief to provide readers an introduction to some of the risk and reward concepts that provide definition to an asset class. Many of these concepts are outlined in further detail later in the book. All portfolios built in this book are considered hypothetical because while the CTA results are those actually reported by the Barclay MAP database, the CTAs have not traded together in this fashion in a regulated environment and the portfolio was built with hindsight. Past performance is not indicative of future results.[7] (The full hypothetical risk disclosure is contained in note 7.)

A major point of this chapter was not the specific performance numbers, but rather considerations that go beyond headline performance numbers. In fact the portfolios in this chapter were not ideal so as to educate investors about potential issues in managed futures investing; a more ideal portfolio building process takes place in Chapter 10. The point for investors to consider is that nothing is perfect. On these pages we have included imperfections to highlight educational points, but these imperfections do not entirely negate an investment, because all investments have imperfections. Significant opinions have been expressed, but the investor must consider that the ultimate opinion is the one they make to invest or not.

On the Book's Web Site

Available to the general public:

- Listing of recommended CTAs with reported performance.
- Online portfolio-building tools.

Available to registered book readers:

- Additional detail and analysis regarding all portfolios, including CTA names and performance history.
- Track the performance of all portfolios mentioned in real time. Step-by-step guide: Build a CTA portfolio using online tools.
- Video: "Understanding CTA Trading Strategies."
- Updated benchmark performance measures of all major CTA strategies.
- White Paper: "Are CTAs worth the incentive fee?"
- Complete listing of all CTAs mentioned in this chapter with ranking and individual analysis.

- White paper: "How to Tell If a CTA Has an Incentive to Overtrade the Account: A Complete Guide to Commission and Fee Sharing and What the Investor Should Understand."
- White paper: "How to Identify the Commission and Fee Structure of Individual CTAs, FCMs, and IBs, along with Insight Regarding Appropriate Fees for CTA Services."
- Professional download: "Performance and Risk Measurement: A Guide to the Best and Worst Managed Futures Performance Measures, and How to Use Them to Build Truly Diversified Portfolios."
- Professional download: "Understanding a CTA's Strategy and Its Correlation to Market Environment and Risk Measures."
- Video from the author on building CTA portfolios.

For more information visit www.wiley.com/go/managedfutures.

CHAPTER 4

Realize It

The Old Way versus High Performance

Both the future and the past point to a need for *High-Performance Managed Futures*, a method of investing not entirely dependent on the stock market or the whims of economic fancy. But here is what is interesting: The investment asset class outlined across these pages has worked well during the good, the bad, and the ugly of economic times, but at the same time has been ignored, neglected, and misunderstood. That is starting to change among open-minded professionals. As a result, managed futures is both an interesting and fast-growing opportunity.

THE FASTEST-GROWING ASSET CLASS?

Look at Figure 4.1. It shows the growth of managed futures, which has grown 700 percent over 10 years.[1] It is amazing that managed futures is one of the fastest-growing asset classes and yet it remains relatively unknown and misunderstood. For this reason the current plateau on the chart could be about to explode into the next leg up.

This chapter and the next provide a brief overview of managed futures. Later chapters provide a more detailed view, specifically addressing investment risk factors. Then the balance of the book applies this knowledge to provide investors real-world examples of how to create portfolios uncorrelated to the stock market.

In this chapter readers discover several key concepts:

- Managed futures involves investing in commodity and financial futures markets from around the world. The asset class has no geographic or time-based investment limitation.

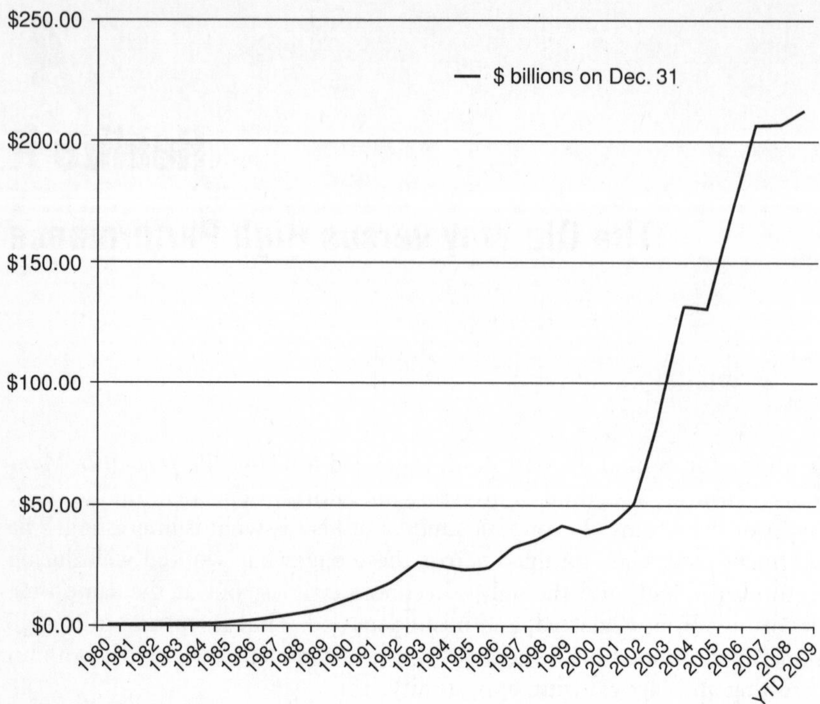

FIGURE 4.1 Managed Futures Assets under Management (in $ billions)
Source: BarclayHedge.

- In fashion similar to a mutual fund, an investment manager with a past track record uses sophisticated strategies to generate audited returns when the commodity trading advisor (CTA) is a National Futures Association (NFA) member.
- Unlike many mutual funds, the strategies can be long, short, or market neutral.

THIS UNIQUE AND VERY SPECIAL ASSET CLASS

On the surface, it would appear the amazing recent growth of managed futures is due to strong return performance. This is significant, but perhaps what makes the asset class most unique is its relative lack of correlation to the stock market and economy at large, and amazingly, the commodity markets in which the programs invest. This investing attribute couldn't come at a better time.

We live in a world where global economies and stock markets are more tightly correlated than at any time in history. This tight correlation is likely to be a trend that continues. What's worse for the qualified investor, many "alternatives," such as hedge funds, are surprisingly correlated with the stock market (as demonstrated in Chapter 9). The need and search for a true alternative—a real uncorrelated asset class—is more important now than at any time in recent history. It is logical that the future holds increased demand for uncorrelation, and the asset class that can demonstrate its independence should emerge as a significant portion of any sophisticated modern portfolio. This is one of several reasons why managed futures could very well be an investment opportunity whose time has come.

Moments like this in history are few and far between, but when they happen it is often generated by a significant and colorful past. In the 1940s Charles Merrill bucked the Wall Street establishment and championed what at the time was a unique concept for the general public: stock investing. Coming off a stock market crash and the Great Depression, Merrill founded Merrill Lynch with the goal of evangelizing stock investing to the general public. He published countless articles and books on investing and held seminars across the country, ultimately growing into the largest brokerage in the country. This paved the way for other pioneers, who were similarly outside the Wall Street establishment.

In the 1960s another new and radically different investing concept was popularized: the mutual fund. Founded and promoted by the likes of Ned Johnson, founder of Boston's Fidelity Investments, the mutual fund was then an interesting concept. Instead of investing in individual stocks, investors could place capital in one fund invested in a diversified portfolio of stocks. The core concept of simplified diversification, the portfolio concept, is driving future trends in managed futures.

Easy and cost-effective access to the stock market was the innovation San Francisco-based Charles Schwab promoted. Schwab, along with many that followed, brought to the investing public cost-effective access to previously cloistered Wall Street opportunity. At each stage of the game, industry pioneers had the vision to see a new opportunity and bring closely held Wall Street investment opportunities to the broader public. Looking at history, there have been those individuals with the foresight to understand a change in trends and how to benefit most.

The corollary between these stories and managed futures is striking. Think about the excitement as an asset class emerges to have a major impact on the investing public. This book is dedicated to helping investors discover new opportunities and understand how they can benefit through the use of intelligent risk management.

For investors, traveling down any potentially historic path and being on the emergence of a new trend can be exciting. Those who first saw the rock band U2 when they were playing small clubs hang on to the concert tickets; people who invested in Microsoft at an early age may still retain the stock certificates; those who supported mutual funds when the concept was first introduced may still hang on to the initial account documentation. Identifying an emerging opportunity and riding a wave from the start can be exciting, but here is an important key you learn when surfing: Before committing to a wave, make sure it is a wave you can handle. All surfers have different skill levels, and sharp reefs and monster barrels can collide to provide a volatile adventure to a surfer who doesn't understand the important variables. What this means to managed futures investors is they should understand that in which they invest.

The previous chapters provided a basic definition of managed futures. Start the discovery in this chapter by seeing more details of the basic definition and comparing the old and new way to invest.

MANAGED FUTURES DEFINED

The old way to invest was for investors to put a large portion of faith in the stock market, pinning their hopes and dreams on things they really couldn't understand or even properly value. For instance, most stocks investors have no idea what is going on behind the scenes in their company; just ask investors in Enron, WorldCom, and Tyco. The value of a particular stock can rise and fall dramatically based on whims in the boardroom and back room that are not known to the general investing public.

The old way is about investors attempting in futility to diversify their portfolios with stocks and bonds, or even stocks, bonds, real estate, and hedge funds: all assets correlated to one another, as later studies in this book will demonstrate. When the economy is chugging ahead at full steam investing seems easy, simple—and stock investors are pure genius. But when the economy moves into a prolonged period of stagnation, with volatile price swings that leave investors bewildered, those once infallible traditional talking heads are exposed. The powerful forces of the economy are not lifting all boats with the same force and conviction.

High-Performance Managed Futures is about knowing the value of something tangible, something whose value is real and in many cases something you can actually touch. It is more of a pure price play: a hard asset traded on an open exchange where there is no discrepancy regarding its value from Paris, Illinois to Paris, France. It might be investing in programs that are selling gold in London in the morning and then buying it back at a lower price in New York later in the day; buying the Australian currency and selling the Swiss; selling wheat in Kansas City and buying it back in Chicago. It might be about a market-neutral options program that sells option spreads in 24 different markets around the world, potentially profiting when the market moves in the investor's favor, sideways, and even profiting when the market moves against the investor at times. It might be about a computerized trend follower who buys in eight markets and sells in ten markets around the world. It is fast paced, it is exciting, and it can be transparent with specific regulated account protections. It does involve risk, as does all investing. The key is understanding and managing appropriate levels of diversification, risk, and reward to fit the individual's needs and situation, and the investment is not right for everyone.

All the things mentioned above are individual investment strategies used by various managed futures programs. Managed futures programs have been likened to the mutual funds for commodity investments because a talented money manager invests client assets in worldwide futures and options markets, sometimes going long, other times short, and sometimes engaging in market-neutral strategies. It is a very different type of investing indeed.

High-Performance Managed Futures is about striving for true balance. It is obviously about managed futures, but in such a fashion to work in concert with stocks, bonds, real estate, and hedge funds, and in proper moderation, proper balance, and appropriate dosages. It is about striving for uncorrelated performance of diversified assets, a state of investing where investment risk is understood then balanced, managed, and planned.

Yes, it is about time for this discovery to be made by most investors: true asset diversification with managed futures, an investing method that has been strangely ignored and overlooked.

Technical Definition

Managed futures programs are run by talented money managers who invest client assets through power of attorney in worldwide commodity futures and option markets. These are markets where buyers and sellers trade *future delivery* of a long list of diversified products, from agricultural items such as corn and wheat to financial items such as gold, interest rate products, and stock market indexes.

Each CTA has an investment strategy to benefit from various markets and the unique future delivery contract structure, with the ability to easily buy or sell in a variety of worldwide markets. The book emphasizes the strategies, the future delivery contract structure, and the ease with which CTAs can go long and short, because they are core reasons the asset class can exhibit such unusual lack of correlation to the economy, the stock market, and even the markets in which they invest. This is what makes this investment unique and somewhat quirky. Some people say that managed futures is a zero-sum game. While an individual futures trade may be zero-sum, on the book's web site the argument is made that many of the unique spread and market-neutral trade strategies are not zero-sum. Further, many types of futures and options transactions are not zero-sum, including hedging activity by farmers and manufacturers.

What Is Managed Futures? or What's In a Name?

At an elemental level, everyone from fathers and mothers to kids and grandparents should understand the investments made by managed futures CTAs.

When people get up in the morning to that warming cup of coffee or the tangy goodness of orange juice, these commodities could be a managed futures investment. When the fashionable adorn themselves in gold jewelry or a rap star's metallic bling makes a statement, these could be managed futures investments. The fuel used to provide warmth to a comfortable house or take a car on a family vacation could be managed futures investments. The interest rates that gauge a mortgage or car loan, or the currency futures that determine exchange rates on a vacation, could also be managed futures investments.

At this level, the argument could be made that managed futures investments are something that people should be intimately familiar with, commodities and financial products that touch the everyday lives of most everyone. While the factors that drive price and the contract structure can be complicated, the products themselves are easy to understand.

Figure 4.2 illustrates the wide variety of products that managed futures programs invest in. It is a dizzying array of everyday household products and services. In fact, if a "name that investment" contest were to take place, the winner might figure out a name that encompasses the concept that managed futures means "things that power everyday human life."

Commodity Trading Advisors Invest in More Than Commodities There is a problem with managed futures. It's the name—it's hard to understand. For starters, the concept that someone could actually "manage" a "future" is somewhat confusing. If the future could be managed, life could get predictably boring. Even the name of the investment manager, the commodity trading advisor, known as a CTA, is somewhat misleading once you understand the investment.

But more than the name, the investment medium itself can be confusing. The investment is *future* delivery of various commodities and financial products. To the casual or uninitiated investor, managed futures sounds complicated, like an enigma wrapped in a quandary. Add to this the foreign

Energy and Oil	Industrial Metals	Precious Metals	Financials
Natural Gas	Aluminum	Gold	S&P
Gas Oil	Aluminum Alloy	Silver	Dow
Crude Oil	Copper	Platinum	NASDAQ
Heating Oil	Lead	Palladium	Russell 2000
Ethanol	Nickel		Interest Rates
Propane	Tin		Bonds
Uranium	Zinc		Treasury Notes
			Currencies
Ag Stock	**Grain Futures**	**Softs**	
Pork Bellies	Corn	Cocoa	
Lean Hogs	Soybeans	Coffee	
Feeder Cattle	Soybean Oil	Cotton	
Live Cattle	Wheat	Orange Juice	
	Oats	Rice	
		Sugar	

FIGURE 4.2 Common Futures Contracts

concepts of leverage and margin and it becomes clear why both individual and even professional investors consider managed futures a complicated and somewhat esoteric asset class.

The CTA is an investment manager of a direct managed futures account and many commodity fund investments. However, this name provides an inaccurate picture of the investment. Dissecting the term and then understanding why it is an inaccurate term paints insight into the larger picture of a managed futures investment.

Start by considering the first and perhaps most important word in the term *commodity trading advisor*: The word *commodity* is often universally used to describe the futures industry. It is not uncommon for professionals to say they are in the commodities business or that they trade commodities. As it relates to managed futures, having the word *commodities* front and center can be somewhat inaccurate. The word implies the products being traded are strictly physical or agricultural in nature. Agricultural commodities are only a portion of the opportunity a CTA has before him, representing only 9 percent of overall futures trading. Managed futures programs can invest in single stock futures, a wide array of interest rate products, as well as foreign currency, real estate futures, and even snow futures, to name just a few. We will address this diversity topic more in a minute, but the point remains: Managed futures is a cornucopia of investment opportunity not just limited to physical commodities.

The industry's storied history in agricultural products has stuck even though the futures industry has since matured. It is this soil and earth agricultural beginning from a bygone era that still is used to define what has become an electronically charged, dynamically linked, and internationally connected industry. But this new reality is also clouded by the second word in the term, *trading*.

Trading, Gambling, or Investing? The term *trading* as it relates to managed futures evokes another interesting image derived from the industry's long-ago past.

Back in the day when egg traders used to casually converge in a back alley just off of Chicago's Randolph Street, trades were recorded in chalk on a blackboard nailed to the alley wall. It was this often rough-and-tumble "trading" activity, executed by interesting characters and questionable personalities, that defined an industry, and even a city. To this day when we think of futures trading, the pit-based image of burly, aggressive men in funny colored jackets trading in a wild-west road show comes to mind. But the reality is today's electronic exchange looks much more like a page out of Silicon Valley than a back-room bar brawl.

This rough history has been used by some to paint trading and the larger futures industry as an unsophisticated, dirty endeavor when compared to the savior that the stock market provides. Not as clean as "investing." But this is a curious topic.

Where is the line drawn between trading and investing? Stocks have been considered investments while futures have always been considered trading, but why is this? At the end of the day, isn't it all just speculation for potential client profitability?

There are those who like to paint the futures markets as nothing short of legalized gambling; something they look down upon while accepting government bailouts. But the fact remains: All investing is a calculated risk, a speculation or a gamble to an extent. Walking across the street is a gamble. For those people to paint futures investing as gambling but stock speculation as exempt from a similar standard is like saying a bank that invests in highly leveraged mortgage products is not gambling. The only difference is that the managed futures investment is relatively transparent and the risks are clearly defined. Don't let the idea peddlers on a little island on the East Coast define your investment world. Managed futures is an investment, it is not just trading or gambling, as some would have you think. It is all a matter of who is providing the advice.

If You Want Advice, You Won't Get It from a Commodity Trading Advisor We have identified two parts of the term *commodity trading advisor* that are somewhat misleading, and more importantly, we have used this to put on display the nature of a managed futures investment. But it doesn't end there. The third word in the term is perhaps most inaccurate, almost to the point of deception. The word *advisor* implies interaction and collaboration to achieve a goal.

But here's the flaw in that logic and the headline at the same time: The CTA doesn't give much, if any, individual trading advice. That's right. The implied "advice" in commodity trading *advisor* doesn't really exist. In reality, the CTA is more like a mutual fund manager in that he generally invests all client capital using the same methodology and rarely, if ever, gets on the phone to hawk trades or sell an individual investment strategy. How often do individual investors speak with a mutual fund manager about investment strategy? Virtually never.

What typically happens is that the investor works with a managed futures portfolio strategist, or broker, if you will, to build a portfolio of managed futures investments. This portfolio manager usually works for a registered futures commission merchant (FCM) or introducing broker (IB), and the broker does not do the actual trading but is more the "manager of managers." The best ones are adept at providing insight to clients relative to the generally sophisticated investments that are being placed on the client's behalf. But, unfortunately, this is often the exception more than the rule. Many clients can be left alone with their investments because there is often little if any regular market commentary from the CTA, fund manager, or broker. For many investors this can be particularly frustrating. Even when the investors have direct visibility into the positions placed on their behalf, they often don't know what it means unless they understand the strategy or have the benefit of someone who is deciphering the strategy. (We address how to solve this problem later in the book.)

So when investors place capital in managed futures they should get advice from their portfolio strategist or broker; it just won't come as implied from the *"commodity" "trading" "advisor."*

The Difference Between a CTA, Commodity Broker, and Trading System

An important distinction needs to be clearly made between the commodity broker trading a client account and the registered commodity trading advisor (CTA) or licensed commodity pool operator (CPO) or fund operation.

Commodity brokers give individual advice and help plan the trades of each account separately. Commodity trading advisors and managed futures funds invest client capital consistently through a power of attorney for all clients without collaborating with each investor before an investment is made.

Another important difference is the broker cannot display a valid past track record, as a CTA or commodity fund can. Here is an interesting test to identify qualified commodity investments. When someone approaches with a commodity investment opportunity, ask this question to separate the wheat from the chaff: "Is this an actual trading record with an overall audit by the National Futures Association?" If the manager can't answer that question properly with a clear "yes," investors should be skeptical. Another powerful tactic is to ask for all communication in writing and invest only in CTAs registered in good standing with the National Futures Association.

Giving advice and the ability to display a valid past track record are two key points of differentiation. But perhaps the most important difference lies in the profit motivation.

Financial advisors/brokers, both the stock and commodity variety, under many circumstances receive compensation from transactional commissions or management fees not tied to client performance, as well as margin interest income. Thus their profit motivation could be based on increased transactional activity, assets under management, and trail fees rather than client profitability. The best CTAs generally receive their primary compensation from an incentive fee: a percentage of the client's net new profits. (Some CTAs do share in the commission revenue, and this potential conflict of interest must be disclosed in their disclosure document, which all investors must review before investing.)

Often investors confuse a trading system with a CTA. A trading system is often a computerized black-box method that generates trades for those that pay a subscription to follow the system's recommendations. Trading systems can be very different from regulated CTAs, perhaps most importantly where regulation and audited performance comes into play. Trading systems are not always officially registered and may not have past performance audited by the National Futures Association (NFA). Any performance that has not been audited by the NFA should be questioned. Sometimes the performance can be audited, but that performance could be based on follow-the-leader methodology, where the trade system's main account is audited but not the performance of all the individual accounts. Such performance is not as valid as that of a CTA in an NFA-audited environment. Systems providers generally receive compensation tied to a monthly subscription fee not based on the performance of the account, another noteworthy difference. Sometimes the system provider can share in commissions if they are also affiliated with the Introducing Broker, a lightly disclosed potential conflict of interest. In general, disclosure requirements of systems providers are less robust than that of CTAs.

Now that we have defined managed futures, understand the structure of the investment.

Buying for the Future

The concept of investing in a "future" can seem strange at first. But think about it. People who shop at store sales often buy what they don't immediately need. The product is purchased for future use because the buyer believes the price will increase significantly over time. The purchaser benefits from the lower price while the store may benefit from increased revenue during specific slow periods.

The same is true with futures investments. Various investors buy and sell items for future delivery, using different contract delivery months. The futures industry was founded near Osaka, Japan in 1697 as a method for farmers and producers to lock in prices to help them run their business more effectively. Thus a farmer who wants to lock in the future price of his summer crop in the cold of January can sell September corn futures. A baking company could manage the future cost of their wheat supplies by buying the March delivery of wheat and selling the September delivery from the next year, depending on their anticipated needs. (The book's web site contains a more complete history with operational details of the futures market.)

A common application of future delivery months is demonstrated by the airline industry engaging in what is known as hedging; helping producers manage fluctuating prices and serving an important economic role. As you might expect, the ramifications can be both positive and negative.

One of the more interesting hedging stories that shows both the risks and rewards of this activity took place in the airline industry. Beginning in 1999, when oil was trading around $20, Southwest Airlines analysis showed strong future oil demand and rising prices. As such, they adjusted their hedging strategy to position themselves to profit from their prediction that future oil prices would substantially rise; they did this via purchasing futures and options on futures. Since the inception of this program through June 2008, Southwest Airlines' hedging strategy successfully saved their company close to $3.5 billion. The hedging strategy they utilize effectively locks in their operating costs on a going forward basis, and alleviates any additional costs that might arise from spikes in oil, such as the 2008 spike to close to $150 a barrel. For example, Southwest hedged about 70 percent of their full needs for the year 2008 prior to 2008 at approximately $51 a barrel. They do this on an annual basis and are essentially locking in their future costs, which helps define one of their largest costs and potentially makes them money as well: profits from the appreciation on their purchased futures contracts. However, where there is reward there is often risk lurking in the shadows. Oil has risen substantially from when Southwest began their program and purchasing contracts now for future hedging at these elevated levels could put profits in jeopardy if oil prices were to retrace. The key focus for a business considering a hedging strategy is the notion that they are locking in operating costs, and so long as their strategy is sound and well thought out and executed, hedging is doing its job.

It is this ability to create investments that are little correlated that makes managed futures interesting as an asset class, and this is particularly true during times of significant stock market dislocation. The ability to create amazingly uncorrelated investment strategies is made possible by the core derivative contract structure, which enables some very interesting and unique investment strategies.

Examples of How CTAs Invest Client Capital In managed futures, categorization of CTAs is often less than standard. This book puts forth the concept that CTAs should be categorized first by strategy, as this determinant of how and why trades are executed can be the most important feature impacting diversification considerations. After strategy, categorization should take place based on markets traded, trade time frame, and volatility, in that respective order. There are four primary managed futures strategies: Spread/Arbitrage; Options/Volatility; Systematic/Trend Following; Discretionary. Each strategy can have sub strategies, such as the countertrend trader or the long volatility option strategy. As you consider the following limited examples of how CTAs invest client capital, understand how these strategies can benefit regardless of the underlying price direction of the markets in which they trade, and then begin to understand how this asset class can be so strangely noncorrelated to just about every market, including the markets in which the CTAs invest, which is quite significant indeed. The following is for illustrative purposes only, and the CTA names and circumstances have been changed to illustrate larger points.

Spread (Arbitrage)Trading: The spread trader starts his decision-making process by eying what he considers price discrepancies in live cattle and feeder cattle. Based on experience in both cash and futures markets, the trading manager makes a determination that the price for feeder cattle for delivery in September is high relative to the low price of the live cattle for delivery in March of the following year. Feeder cattle and live cattle are essentially different variations of the same basic commodity. The trading manager would place the following trade in your account and all other accounts under his management:

- Buy (long): One March live cattle contract (to potentially take advantage of a low price, hoping the price moves higher relative to the sell he will initiate below.)
- Sell (short): One September feeder cattle contract (to potentially take advantage of a high relative price, hoping the price moves lower relative to the buy above.)

While both trades occur within the cattle market, there are variations on the product type, live versus feeder cattle, and the delivery month, March versus September. This trade is profitable when the March live cattle (long) contract increases in price relative to the September feeder cattle (short) contract. It doesn't necessarily matter if the underlying cattle market in general moves up or down in price; all that matters is the differential in price between the March live cattle futures contract and the September feeder cattle contract.

This CTA will generate client profits when the spread between the contract he bought and sold tightens; the contract he bought moves higher in price relative to the contract he sold, which moves lower in price or even moves higher in price but at a lower rate. The CTA will make his money from an incentive fee, a percentage of the profit from his trading capabilities. For example, if this trade results in the account value, or liquidation value (LV), moving from $50,000 to $55,000, the CTA will take a percentage of the $5,000 profit generated, which is his incentive fee, one of his primary methods of compensation for managing the account.

This spread trading strategy with different variations of the same commodity and different delivery months is just one example of how the unique contract structures available in the futures and options markets make possible the powerful uncorrelated performance of managed futures to the markets in which they invest. Highlighted here is one trading manager to give the story life, but there is a list of quality trading managers who utilize this strategy.

While agricultural CTAs may come to mind when one thinks of commodity traders, in fact the strategy can be executed across a wide variety of markets, not just ags. According to a study conducted for this book, "ag" traders have posted compounded annual return of 15.59 percent and average drawdown of 5.47 percent.[2]

Options/Volatility: Moderate investors are often attracted to short volatility options programs, but anyone considering this strategy must understand the risks, particularly during times of severe market crisis, when these option-selling programs that appear so conservative can get volatile. The better CTAs in this sector generally have mathematical minds for understanding statistical probability. An emerging subcategory is the diversified premium collector who executes the premium collection strategy in 15 to 20 different markets, from gold and oil to wheat and interest rate products.

The concept is that the trading manager looks to identify a trading range and then sells near expiration options above or below the trading range. For instance, if oil is trading at $50 per barrel, a volatility strategy might initiate a position that sells a put option spread with the sell at $30 per barrel with the put option expiring in 30 days or less. This strategy can be profitable if in 30 days the oil market moves higher, stays the same in price, or even moves lower against the position—so long as the price of oil stays above $30 at expiration and the option that was previously sold expires worthless. Think about this strategy from a pure statistical standpoint. Unlike stocks, which benefit only when the price moves higher, this options premium collection strategy can potentially benefit when the price moves higher, when the price stays the same or even if the price moves lower to a degree, potentially putting the odds of a successful trade in favor of the option seller, which could explain why winning months outnumber losers by three to one in many strategies. But the option-selling strategy, like all investing, has risk. When market volatility increases substantially, such as when a Black Swan Event hits a given market, the CTA can experience significant losses in a short period of time. This hidden strategy risk is detailed later in the book.

There are several successful CTAs that trade options. Although Barclay does not have an index for the options category, this book follows a diversified group of options traders who execute strategies both long and short. The overall category has a compounded annual return of 12.39 percent and average drawdown of 10.23 percent.[3]

Systematic/Trend Following: The most common managed futures strategy is trend trading. Trend traders generally use computers to analyze mountains of data, such as trading volume, price velocity, and other technical measures too numerous to mention here. Confidential computer algorithms then identify potential emerging trends in different markets worldwide. Once a trend is identified, the trend trader either buys or sells futures contracts in over 100 different products or markets and holds that trade until the CTA identifies a trend change. The systematic trend trader could receive a computer-generated indication to sell coffee and gold futures while at the same time receiving a buy signal on the Swiss franc and U.S. ten-year note futures. Thus, trend traders are not necessarily correlated to the upward price movement of any market in which they invest. There are also several counter trend traders that operate as a foil to the trend-trading strategy. Unlike the trend trader, the counter trend trader attempts to identify when a trend has ended and then attempts to execute a strategy that benefits from the end of a trend. Combining these complementary CTAs in a portfolio yields interesting results. The average annual return for trend traders is 10.99 percent with average drawdown of 9.34.[4]

Discretionary: This method of trading often relies on the CTA's subjective decision making to enter and exit trades, may not always involve the same interpretation of a market indicator or it may include different execution strategies. It might be a long volatility spread trader purchasing a put spread in gold options then selling silver futures, but when he receives the exact market conditions again he may have a different result. It could a trader who combines short volatility and trend following methods to sell options and go long futures. Or it could be a trader who simply looks at a chart and makes decisions on entry and exit points based on "experience" or "market feel," difficult to quantify decision making processes.

Account Structure Decisions Impact Risk A little-known insight into managed futures is that account structure can impact the investor's risk profile. When making a managed futures investment, there are four general choices:

Single CTA: The investor could allocate all his or her capital toward a single CTA and open a direct account with a registered FCM. This can be accomplished through the FCM, or the IB, or even certain independent Registered Investment Advisors (RIAs) who are affiliated with FCMs. Investors who concentrate their entire managed futures investment with a single manager should only use risk capital they can easily part with. While allocating to individual CTAs is an industry practice, this could be the riskiest of strategies in an already risky investment, in the author's opinion.

CPO/Fund of Funds: A good option for qualified investors might be a commodity pool account structure (CPO) and its associated limited liability investor protection. With a fund of fund structure investors can dip their toe in the water with investments ranging from $5,000 to $250,000 to obtain manager diversification that would equal a direct investment of several million. However, just like all investing, there are risks, rewards, and trade-offs. The CPO often adds an extra layer of fees on top of the individual manager's fees. Here is a brief comparison: With the CPO investment the investor could experience a 2 percent management fee and a 20 to 30 percent incentive fee on top of the fees charged by the CTAs contained within the portfolio. While the CPO is fee heavy in an industry that can have the highest fees in financial services, it can also lack transparency and might not provide the full benefits of the limited protection of government-mandated account segregation. Further, investor capital is placed in the name of the CPO. CPO investors must weigh these cons against the significant benefits of theoretical limited liability protection and the ability to invest a relatively small amount of capital and receive diversification benefits of a much larger portfolio. An investment in any fund or CPO requires the investor to establish an account with a registered securities broker only (unless working with CPO ownership). Investors are always advised to only conduct business with those firms and individuals in a regulated environment.

Direct Account Diversified Portfolio: Instead of investing in a single manager or a CPO, the investor could invest in a diversified portfolio of direct managed futures accounts with lower account minimums. There are several problems and benefits with this approach. First, the problems. Perhaps the most significant applies to those investors allocating under $100,000: The limited choice for diversification and the practical restrictions that lower account minimums sometimes mean the individual investor must accept shorter track records, higher fees or some other pimple on this otherwise interesting-looking face. Further, the direct account may expose the investor to a more significant degree of individual manager risk and risk of a margin call, particularly if the investment was not properly designed or managed. These risk issues are discussed in more detail in Chapter 11. The benefits of a direct account should also be considered: With a direct account, investors receive the protection of account segregation. The investment capital is in the name of the investor, so as not to be manipulated by the CTA trading manager. There is daily transparency into the generally liquid account, transparency into the positions and the daily liquidity value of the investment, an almost unheard-of notion in the hedge fund world that we explain in the next chapter. The direct account can have the lowest fees, but often lower fees are accompanied by a lower level of actual knowledge and service. In a direct CTA account investors do not need to meet "qualified" status but the investment must be appropriate. It is the author's advice that investors should use only risk capital, money they can afford to lose, when investing in managed futures.

Hedge Fund, Mutual Fund, or ETF: A growing investment category is the managed futures mutual fund or exchange-traded fund. This emerging investment type will likely become one of the most popular investment methods in the future, due to the low potential initial investment and the ability to invest through a financial advisor. At this point, what investors may gain in convenience they may lose in performance, as many of the managed futures mutual funds have not lived up to the standards set by direct CTA investments. However, as the industry matures, and many of the mutual funds recognize the value of strategy diversification within managed futures, this investment may offer better performance.

What account structure should investors choose? To provide a general rule to choosing the appropriate account structure, the author has a multitiered approach that ranks the importance of different factors, much like that food pyramid we all grew up with. At the top of the pyramid is diversification. Other people may have different priorities at the top, but it is the author's individual belief that diversification should be the number one concern when establishing a managed futures investment. The second level is important, and in fact has some conditions in it that would not even allow the investment for consideration. One example is regulation and registration. If a CTA were not a member of the NFA or could not provide audited results of some type, this investment would be significantly questioned. That is not to say all investments of this type are out of the question: It is to say there might be better alternatives available. Another tier is solid management, of which there is a 14-point checklist. Readers can visit the book's web site to download the granular report.

Much of the information used to make appropriate investment decisions can be found in the disclosure document, which is designed to be a legally informative and inclusive tool.

DECODING THE D DOC

Perhaps the most important document in managed futures is the CTA's disclosure document (D Doc), with emphasis on the word *disclosure*.

The disclosure document is designed as a tool to help investors understand the risks of investing in various CTAs. The disclosure document must reveal any material information that could impact the investment. Civil, criminal or disciplinary proceedings in which the CTA was involved must be disclosed. The CTA's past business background and, most important, his past trading history must be disclosed. This is important from several standpoints. If the CTA traded client accounts in an NFA-regulated environment, that past performance must be reported. Further, CTAs can't close down their operations after poor performance and start again with a clean slate—their managed futures track record follows them in this regulated environment.

Disclosure documents can seem daunting, and this guide is designed to help you understand a legal document that might not be easy to read.

Although the NFA requires that all D Docs contain the same basic information, they might vary to certain degrees. The following general components are included in most disclosure documents. While D Docs are required to be reviewed and approved by the NFA before they are distributed to investors, it is important to note that this review is not any sort of endorsement by the regulatory body.

The following are highlights, a brief overview of the most important items in the D Doc but by no means a complete list of components. For the NFA's complete publication "Disclosure Documents: A Guide for CTAs and CPOs," visit www.nfa.futures.org or this book's web site.

Opening Pages: The D Doc generally starts with the CTA's contact information, location of records, and the location from which trading activity is conducted, as well as the date of the document, which must be updated every nine months according to NFA regulations. After this follows the mandatory CFTC risk disclosure statement, followed by the table of contents.

Advisor Background, Conflicts of Interest, Brokerage Arrangements: D Docs often start with information on the advisor. Look for details of their background that point to industry experience. Consideration of the manager's background should be accompanied by consideration of any potential conflicts of interest or any litigation in which the CTA has been involved, which must be disclosed in this document. Conflicts can occur in the brokerage arrangement section, and it is good to confirm the CTA does not receive unusual compensation from an FCM or IB, and likewise the FCM and IB to not receive undue compensation for recommending an investment. Ideally you want to keep these two entities separate, like church and state.

Trading Strategy, Fee Structure, Principal Risk Factors: The trading strategy is usually interesting to consider, and should be outlined in detail in this section. However, understand that often, because these are legal documents, the strategy is usually written from the perspective of not legally limiting the manager and can be very broad.

The fee structure discusses specifically how the CTA will take his or her fees: monthly or quarterly, for instance. Often in the fee section the CTA also discloses the commission rate to be charged by the FCM or the IB. Brokerage firms make their primary income through commissions, interest rate float, and other fees, sometimes sharing in CTA incentive fees. It is advisable that all fees and commissions are disclosed to the investor up front. There is a tug of war of sorts between CTAs, who generally want the lowest commissions possible so their profits are highest, and FCMs and IBs, who make their money from commissions. Watch to make sure the CTA does not share in the commission, because this can create a conflict of interest. While there are examples of highly successful CTAs who share in commissions, this practice should be generally frowned upon by the investor as it might provide the individual making trading decisions incentive to excessively trade the account. Further, it is not uncommon for some CTAs to share their incentive and management fees with the FCM. This is not as significant a conflict of interest as CTAs sharing in commissions—it puts the broker in the same boat with the CTA and investor, to a limited degree—but it is nonetheless a conflict. On the book's web site readers will find a disclosure form that investors can use with brokers to make sure any conflict of interest or financial relationship between the CTA and FCM is fully disclosed, included with a list of questions to ask brokers and CTAs or commodity pool operators (CPOs).

Generally close to the fee section is the principal risk factors section, which describes in detail the risks in futures and options investing and at times can be filled with difficult-to-read but important legalese that describes risks in futures and options investing in general. Again, because this is a legal document, it is going to outline any and all potential risks and will not pass an opinion on the probability of that risk. The D Doc may also include information on notionally funded accounts, which is a method to increase leverage and risk that only applies to those who use this funding method, which is detailed in the next chapter. Past performance is calculated based on the nominal investment level, not the notional funding level.

Past Performance: The past performance capsule must disclose relevant and accurate information relative to the CTA's past performance using standard account methods. This reporting is to include all client trading the manager conducted on behalf of clients while registered in the NFA. Past performance capsules include more than just monthly performance; the capsule shows how many accounts the CTA manages, his or her assets under management, worst drawdown statistics, and the number of accounts that opened and closed with profits and losses, which is interesting. The D Doc must also clearly disclose that "past performance is not indicative of future results."

Signature Documents: Signature documents typically include acknowledgement that the investor has received the D Doc; limited power of attorney that gives the CTA the sole right to trade the account;

a fee payment authorization notice that allows the CTA to take out his or her incentive and management fees that have been approved by the FCM; the commodity advisory agreement, which describes how business is to be conducted; oftentimes a client questionnaire, which is used by some CTAs to make sure the investment is appropriate for the investor; an arbitration agreement; and potentially a notional funding agreement, if this risk-enhancing direction has been chosen by the investor.

This has been an abbreviated description of the CTA/CPO disclosure document. More information is available at www.nfa.futures.org, and on the book's web site readers can download actual D Docs and view an educational video detailing the D Doc.

On the Book's Web Site

Available to the general public:

- Link to NFA publication "Disclosure Documents: A Guide for CTAs and CPOs."

Available to registered book readers:

- Download: Example CTA D Docs.
- Interactive discussion: "Is managed futures really a zero-sum game?"
- Updated performance of all major trading strategies with related analysis of market environments.
- Interactive Guide: "Selecting the Appropriate Account Structure."
- Video: "Understand the Disclosure Document."
- Download: Conflict of interest disclosure form.
- White paper: "How to Conduct a Cost-Free Background Check of Your CTA, CPO, FCM, IB, and Even Your Portfolio Manager Using NFA's Online Tools."

For more information visit www.wiley.com/go/managedfutures.

CHAPTER 5

Don't Be a Victim

Leverage Managed Futures Regulation and Account Structure to Avoid Hedge Fund Fraud

The armchair quarterbacks among us might say that Bernie Madoff's 2008 $50 billion Ponzi scheme, the most massive deception of its kind to date, should have been detected. It seems almost absurd that hedge fund fraud of that size had no real assets or investments but paid investors amazingly consistent 10 to 12 percent a year every year, regardless of the market environment. It was classic, indeed—perhaps the financial scandal of the decade. Not only for the size of the fraud, but more interestingly the complicity displayed by investors, who apparently gave Madoff capital with a wink and a nod, many thinking his deep connections and past role as non-executive chairman of the NASDAQ stock exchange put their investment on "the inside" of a Wall Street game of fastball.

This chapter dissects limited aspects of Madoff's Ponzi scheme as it relates to managed futures, highlighting the account structure and regulation that provide a very different investor environment. It matters not who perpetrates the fraud, Madoff or future would-be scam artists; the principles of how to avoid fraud outlined in this chapter are timeless because of their focus on the core levels of transparency, control of client capital, having different eyes monitor investor capital, and intelligent yet firm industry regulation.

This chapter defines the book's unique take on a hedge fund scandal, used as an example to illustrate larger points and not as a definitive account of events.

Madoff's scheme is really a tale of investor manipulation with unique twists, but it was similar in important respects to many hedge fund frauds. There was a lack of transparency and the investment manager had complete control over client capital with very little active oversight. Investors cannot protect themselves until they know what to look for, and this is where they should keep their eye on the ball.

As readers stare with curiosity at the underbelly of Madoff's fraud scheme, this chapter will show how the regulation and structural components of the managed futures investment can be very different. Readers will see how the industry is regulated and how client accounts are protected by this government regulation. This section identifies truisms and insights that apply across all hedge fund fraud, and then applies these standards to the managed futures industry. When reading this overview chapter understand it is just that, an overview, a condensation of information and not a complete view of the topic. For more information readers are encouraged to visit this book's web site or view the key regulatory web sites: www.nfa.futures.org or www.cftc.gov.

In this chapter readers discover:

- Key differences between direct managed futures accounts and hedge fund accounts, including:
  - Transparency: the ability to see your investment on a daily basis.
  - Liquidity: the ability to easily exit a program without fees.
  - Segregated account protection: designed to reduce the investment manager's direct access to investment capital with the goal to make typical hedge fund fraud and Ponzi schemes difficult to perpetrate.
  - Regulation: operated by putting the investor's needs first.

MANAGED FUTURES REGULATION, ACCOUNT STRUCTURE, AND PROTECTION

As an asset class managed futures often gets lumped in with hedge funds as an alternative investment. But this is a lazy categorization. In fact, the managed futures investment can be very different in so many respects from a hedge fund and a stock mutual fund. The key differences between a hedge fund and a direct managed futures account are outlined next. Direct account is stressed because many of the protections described below are not available in a managed futures fund, which has different benefits as outlined in the previous chapter, including varying risk considerations and benefits of limited liability fund structures. For now consider perhaps the most interesting oddity in a direct managed futures account, something unheard of in the hedge fund world: transparency, the ability to clearly see an investment in the light of day.

TRANSPARENCY: THE ABILITY TO SEE AND UNDERSTAND AN INVESTMENT

One of the benefits of a direct managed futures account is transparency, the ability of the investor to see his or her investment on a daily basis. If investors in the Madoff Ponzi scheme could have seen their investments with clarity—understood the positions that were established and watched the daily account balance in a regulated third-party FCM as profit and losses were (or were not) actually accumulated—the Madoff Ponzi scheme would not have gotten to first base. With a direct managed futures investment in a brokerage firm separate from the fund, investors can see exactly what investments are being placed in which markets, and the exact account balance is visible on a daily basis. Even more unique, investors can see the decisions the trading managers make on a daily basis. Investors have right before their eyes all the positions, and thus they can peer into the execution of the trading strategy, even though the trade decision logic may not be apparent. This transparency is practically unheard of in the hedge fund arena, as the fund's strategy is kept a well-guarded secret.

Think about the transparency of stocks or even a stock mutual fund. At the end of the day, the average investor really doesn't have visibility into this investment. They really don't know what goes on in the corporate boardrooms or the company executive meetings. Consider major scandals of our time: Enron, WorldCom, or Tyco. Investors had no clue, no visibility into these ticking time bombs they held in their portfolio. In many cases, even the employees of these companies didn't have visibility into their own company. The same is true with hedge funds. The Bernie Madoff hedge fund Ponzi scheme could not have been perpetrated with a direct managed futures account in large part due to transparency and the fact that investors can see how their money is invested and view their actual account balance on a daily basis. Transparency is important in an investment because it leads to accountability and the ability for investors to adjust strategies and portfolios based on real-time information. The fact that stock or hedge fund investors don't always have visibility into their actual stock investment can lead to a poor decision-making process.

When transparency is discussed, investors need to consider the ability to see a position and get a real-time view of the strategy, but also the ability to price assets marked to the market. This successful concept extends past the managed futures industry.

Think for a minute about one of the largest financial meltdowns in world history: the U.S. credit crisis of 2008. Mortgages were being packaged as investments in veiled and deceptively complicated wrappers. While few Wall

Street wizards will admit it, there were professional investors who didn't have complete visibility into the combination of mortgage loans in which they invested, from prime to subprime. Importantly, investors didn't always know the value of this investment in real time as the market fluctuated, which is in part why the crisis caught some by surprise. It wasn't like the investments were traded on a regulated futures exchange, which provides daily price discovery into an investment's value.

In fact, it's interesting to consider what would have happened if these mortgage-backed assets were publicly traded on an open, regulated futures exchange. Investors could have seen the value of their asset in real time—it would be marked to the market on a daily basis. They might not like what they saw, as their empires crumbled and the ever more socialist U.S. government was called to the rescue of the Wall Street establishment like a mother coming to the aid of a favorite son. But as an investor, it is better to have transparency into an investment, to understand the value of an investment as it is rising and falling, good or bad, than to be surprised and caught flat-footed. This is important, because Mother Government isn't likely to come to the aid of alternative investors who invested in the wrong nontransparent assets.

While transparency is one reason perpetrating a Bernie Madoff "hedge fund–like" Ponzi fraud scheme would be difficult with a direct managed futures account, so too is the power and protection of the segregated account.

The Limited Protection of a Segregated Account

With a direct commodity trading advisor (CTA) account, here is a key reason why Madoff-like hedge fund fraud would not exactly have been perpetrated: The investment manager, the CTA, is not allowed to directly hold or manage customer investment capital. This is a critical difference between a direct managed futures segregated account and most of its alternative investment brethren.

In managed futures there is a constant three-way trifocal standing watch over client capital: The CTA eyes the futures commission merchant (FCM) brokerage firm where the capital is held, the FCM watches the CTA, and the investor watches the capital on a daily basis through the Internet. All this is supervised by the National Futures Association (NFA) and Commodity Futures Trading Commission (CFTC), who conduct regular audits of member firms and enforce strict business management practices. In part, this transparent control of client assets is due to segregated account rules with which all direct managed futures accounts are required to comply.

One of the benefits of investing in a direct managed futures program is that the investor's capital is placed in a segregated account, which by CFTC mandate provides a high degree of investor protection and transparency. The account is segregated at the FCM in the name of the investor. (The FCM then deposits this money in a financial institution under its name.) This is very different from hedge funds. For instance, Madoff's fund took client capital and deposited that capital in a bank account controlled by the hedge fund, hidden from the view of investors.

As part of the Commodity Exchange Act, the CFTC, one of two regulatory bodies that serve as a commodities industry watchdog over the managed futures industry, mandated that all client funds used for investments in futures and options, including managed futures, must reside in a segregated account. A segregated account is an account separate from that of the investment manager or the brokerage company who coordinates the investment. Investor funds cannot be commingled with funds of a brokerage or investment manager. This is important because the CFTC regulations mandate that no one is allowed to unduly manipulate the investor's capital for his or her own purposes.[1] This is a significant difference between general hedge fund regulation and direct managed futures account regulation.

There are several primary benefits to the investor of this segregated account structure, which is available for direct managed futures accounts. For the purpose of this overview chapter, primary features and benefits are mentioned and readers can refer to the NFA or CFTC web sites for granular detail.

As an investor, this segregated account structure is designed with the idea of preventing fraud and misappropriation of assets. In the Madoff scandal, for instance, if regulators at the NFA audited Madoff's books and saw that he was commingling client assets with his own capital, both he and the FCM holding the accounts could be in serious trouble.[2] It is unfortunately all too common to learn about fraud as it relates to hedge fund investments. In fact, much of what happens with hedge fund fraud regarding misappropriation and unseen manipulation of client assets would be difficult to duplicate in managed futures due to the account segregation requirements and managed futures regulation regarding the transparency of a direct segregated account. Simply put, in hedge fund investments you can't see your investment and the investment manager can easily manipulate the capital. With a direct managed futures account investors can have transparency into their direct account and the investment manager does not have the ability to manipulate the funds.

In the author's opinion, much of the secrecy and lack of transparency in fund investments is unnecessary to varying degrees and a major issue that investors should consider (discussed in an open forum on the book's web site).

Many funds claim they can't provide any degree of transparency to investors because they wish to keep the fund's strategy a secret. However, the fact is only the positions and account balances are visible—the core logic, timing, and algorithmic formulas that drive such decision making remain a secret. Even the most sophisticated investor would still have difficulty understanding the finer details of the strategy without understanding the strategic logic driving trade execution. But the real question is that of what is more important. Is investor protection and transparency valuable enough to allow investors even a degree of transparency into a fund's investments? The logic behind the direct segregated account system seems to determine that investor protection and transparency is more important than strategy secrecy. But this is not the only point at which the segregated account may provide investors limited degrees of protection.

Consider the unfortunate case of a bankruptcy of the CTA or brokerage, which can get complicated. If something were to happen to either the investment manager or the FCM/introducing broker (IB) brokerage firm that established an investment, neither company has legal claim to investor money in a segregated account, according to CFTC mandate. Investors who place their money in a segregated account are said to retain certain rights to their investment capital, even during a bankruptcy. Those clients who invest in the unregulated foreign exchange markets and various hedge funds might not enjoy such account protection.

Here is an important and somewhat amazing fact: Since 1988, there has not been an instance where the client segregated account system at an exchange member FCM has failed an investor, according to the NFA.[3] Legal issues can obviously become sticky, and there are no guarantees relative to the future performance of anything in investing, but this fact speaks volumes to the industry account structure and regulation.

There have been cases that have tested the resolve of the industry. The REFCO bankruptcy, where in 2005 one of the largest FCMs at the time was ensnarled in scandal, is arguably one of the most contentious cases to date that tested the stability of the account segregation process. Even in this instance, clients who invested in direct managed futures accounts ultimately received 100 percent of their investment capital back, while clients in unregulated accounts could have been subjected to fraud and misappropriation of assets.[4] Having said this, the segregated account is not like an FDIC-insured bank account, there is no guarantee relative to speculative loss or bank failure, and in all investing there is no guarantee something that didn't happen in the past won't happen in the future. There have been other issues that have tested the resolve of the account segregation process, but the futures industry has thus far withstood what could be categorized as significant challenges to the core of futures account segregation, which can be considered a foundation of industry stability. More details regarding these tests of industry resolve are available on the book's web site, but for the purpose of this overview chapter it is important to understand the basic concept of account segregation.

True Liquidity Means Investors Get In and Out Quickly and Easily

When investing in an alternative asset class like a hedge fund, it is not uncommon for that fund to have restrictions on when money can exit the program. In fact, many funds not only restrict when investors can take money out of the program, but also impose heavy exit fees to leave their programs early.

With many direct managed futures accounts it is much more uncommon to see severe or restrictive lock-up periods or exit fees. In their disclosure documents, the various programs are required by regulators to clearly spell out their redemption policies. While redemptions can vary from program to program, exiting a direct managed futures program can be a relatively quick and effective process, as can certain commodity pool fund accounts. In a direct managed futures account, investors simply revoke the CTA's power of attorney by faxing and e-mailing this revocation to the FCM and CTA. The book's web site contains a form for investors to use to accomplish this goal.

The length and exact process for exiting a managed futures program can vary, and it is often described in the CTA's disclosure document. The process of exiting a program starts by the investor providing their portfolio manager or CTA a revocation of the power of attorney and trading authorization. Often times the CTA is allowed a reasonable amount of time to unwind the positions he or she may have established in the course of an investment cycle. When an account is closed it may be subject to one last billing cycle by the CTA, collecting any management or incentive fees that have not been paid. Management and incentive fees are paid directly from the client's account upon approval by the FCM where the account is being held.

All else being equal, smart investors often don't like to work with programs that have overly restrictive exit programs and instead opt for programs with little or no penalty for withdrawal of capital. If a managed futures program includes restrictive or expensive exit policies, investors should have a clear understanding as to why the restrictions exist.

AUDITING PERFORMANCE AND MONEY FLOW

One of the critical roles of the NFA is their auditing of the FCM brokerage firms that hold investor capital, as well as the CTAs and commodity pool operators (CPOs) that invest client assets and the IBs that advise and service the investor.

Perhaps the hot topic for some investors is the validity of the returns reported by the CTA or CPO. Importantly, each CTA and CPO is subject to a detailed NFA audit on a periodic basis. Regarding profit reporting, the auditors examine CTA investor accounts, calculating profits based on an industry formulation that requires all costs, including fees and commissions, to confirm the actual profit the investor received. The auditing of performance is done by averaging the performance of all accounts and looking at the starting liquidating value of the account and the ending liquidating value of the account at month end. Any trading cost the account incurred during the month, such as fees and commissions, is reflected in the net liquidating value. It is the difference from the starting liquidating value to the ending liquidating value that makes up the profit and loss the CTA reports. If a CTA is found to have audit performance discrepancies that the NFA considers fraudulent, the CTA could face a disciplinary hearing and be barred from the industry.

The frequency of audits can vary. Generally the CTA or CPO will receive an initial audit within the first year of operation. Another significant point of contact is the full follow-up audit where a sample of performance information is verified by the NFA and the CTA is given a complete audit of his or her business activities. This audit occurs on a periodic basis: If the NFA's risk analysis system points to a normal profile, that audit could take place every three to four years. If the NFA analysis points to a higher risk profile, then the audit could take place more frequently, according to the NFA.[5] Items that would move a CTA to a higher risk profile might include the background of their principal, bookkeeping, performance reporting different from norm, and customer complaints, to name a few. "We have a robust risk-management system that helps NFA identify factors that assist in scheduling the audits," said Patricia Cushing, Associate Director of Compliance at the NFA.

At the conclusion of the audit, the NFA sends an audit report, or what is known as a "No Comment Letter," to the CTA, in the case where the CTA passes the NFA audit. This report summarizes the NFA's findings in generally frank terms. This NFA audit is critical when considering a CTA for an investment. While the report says it is confidential—for the member's eyes only—here is a little-known insight: It is up to the NFA member (CTA) to determine if he or she wants to send that audit report to the investor. Some CTAs may simply say no, which sometimes might be the attitude of a trader or more ominously, this could indicate more significant issues. If the NFA does find significant discrepancies in their audit, they make the results of their enforcement actions public. An astute and experienced FCM or IB portfolio manager may sometimes attempt to decipher the actions the NFA has taken as an indication of the issues underneath the surface.

While the audit is significant, it is important to understand that an old NFA report may not be as valid or reflective of the current situation. "Investors need to be careful of looking at dated material," said Larry Dyekman, Director of Communications and Education, who has been at NFA since its inception in 1982.

The audit effectiveness can be enhanced when the CTA or CPO is also having his or her performance audited by a third-party, independent accountant. There are a handful of accounting firms experienced in the industry and generally well regarded that can provide a further layer of protection, particularly with smaller emerging CTAs.

Fees and Performance Reporting

In compensation for managing a client's investment, managed futures programs generally charge an incentive fee and a smaller management fee. Separately, commissions for trades executed are charged by the brokerage, and some but not many CTAs share in these commissions, as previously outlined.

Incentive fees generally range from 15 to 35 percent of the investor's net new profits, depending on the CTA as outlined in the D Doc. Once an investment manager takes the incentive fee, he or she can only take further incentive fees on net new profits above the previous high water mark. Generally speaking, incentive fees are what drive the investment manager to generate profits. The 2 percent management fee is generally used to cover account overhead, particularly with the smaller managed futures programs. For now, perhaps the most important issue to understand is when a managed futures program reports performance, that performance is net of all fees. Individually, comfort can also be found in knowing that most registered managed futures programs' performance has been audited by an independent regulatory body. It is important to remember that a new CTA could be operating several months before receiving an audit, which is why the author recommends when investing in new CTAs to wait for the conclusion of a CTA's NFA audit. Further, it is important to remember NFA audits are not regular or yearly. There are instances when an initial audit might not generate a routine follow-up audit for another three years.

The net reporting of performance is a handy tool for investors, and differs from what some investors might have experienced in the equity world. Mutual funds, for instance, report performance without taking into account fees and commissions. This mutual fund reporting seems a little deceptive. Performance reporting should be true to the concept of showing exactly the past returns less any fees and expenses. This is one reason why reporting performance after commissions, fees, and expenses, as is done in managed futures, is generally a more honest representation. This is not to say that managed futures performance reporting is without its own issues.

There are issues under which the investor may experience different performance from that which the CTA officially reports. This can be due to several reasons. For example, a CTA reports performance that is actually a compilation of all the individual accounts he or she manages. In many cases, different individual CTA accounts can experience different performance because all investors may not be charged the same incentive fees, commissions, and variance in "fills," the price at which the CTA buys and sells. These concepts are explained in detail on the book's web site. Another reason for differing performance could be due to the investor utilizing notional funding, a method of partially funding an account that magnifies gains as well as losses, explained later in the book.

But here is the important point:

If the investor feels his or her performance is significantly different from that which the CTA officially reports, he or she should immediately contact the CTA, FCM, or IB portfolio manager and demand a written explanation. Investors could also report this directly to the NFA, but the process will likely move most efficiently when the NFA has in its hands an explanation of any profit and loss disparity from a knowledgeable industry professional.

TIGHT REGULATORY CONTROL: MEET THE NFA AND CFTC

The exact details of the Madoff Ponzi scheme would be very difficult to pull off in managed futures due to the structure of the investment. This is not to say that scams and fraud can't happen in managed futures. This is why the industry regulators come into play.

The managed futures regulatory agencies are aggressive in their pursuit of industry scams, which benefits the investor. The managed futures industry is tightly regulated by two organizations. The NFA is a nonprofit self-regulating industry organization that is an interesting model for regulation. The regulator is self funded through a fee on each trade executed on the futures exchanges and is not beholden to the industry it regulates. The CFTC is the governmental regulatory agency, reporting directly to the president, that helps shape and enforce regulations. Note that the Securities and Exchange Commission (SEC) and Financial Industry Regulatory Authority (FINRA) regulate securities such as commodity pools and other hedge funds that may trade futures and options. Any direct managed futures program or managed futures fund is subject to the watchful regulatory eye of these generally thorough and powerful regulators.

Regulation occurs on many fronts in managed futures. Already discussed have been regulations designed to protect investors relative to how their investment capital is managed, and importantly, who does and does not have control of the investor's capital. In addition to tightly controlling how client assets are handled, regulators also focus on how managed futures products are marketed and advertised, what can and cannot be said to the investor. Perhaps most important is the audit process, which ensures that the performance advertised correlates with the actual return investors received. Any violation of the rules of the governing agencies can lead to being discredited and disbarred from the industry. The book provides additional detail about each of these critical functions next, but the very detailed information can be obtained on this book's web site.

It is important to note that every CTA must be a member of the NFA in good standing. Professionals in the futures industry who knowingly conduct futures business with a non-NFA member could themselves have their membership revoked. Having one's NFA membership revoked is for most practical purposes an industry death sentence and would likely require that person to leave the industry. Another issue that could land an NFA member in trouble is glossing over risk, which unfortunately sometimes occurs with unregulated entities. CTAs registered by the NFA and CFTC can advertise past results so long as those results are accurate, balance risk in the discussion with reward, and mention that past performance is not indicative of future results. Many fund investments, on the other hand, cannot advertise performance to the general public.

Does Regulation Work?

In testimony before congress on September 8, 2005, NFA President Daniel J. Roth commented on the impact the NFA has had on cleaning an industry that at one point could be argued represented more of a Wild West road show than a sophisticated financial marketplace.[6]

"Since NFA began operations in 1982, volume on U.S. futures markets has increased by over 1,200 percent—a great testament to the innovation and value of our futures markets," Roth said. "What most people don't realize is that during that same time period customer complaints in the futures industry are down by almost 75 percent."

In most cases when an industry expands, complaints increase. It is a powerful comment that when any investment industry has grown at an unprecedented rate that customer complaints are down by a whopping 75 percent.

When considering the NFA's disciplinary complaints it is also interesting to note that complaints are generally not centered on managed futures or CTAs. The NFA regulates IBs, FCMs, individual brokers (known as associated persons or APs) as well as CTAs and CPOs. Of the complaints the NFA handles, managed futures complaints against CTAs are among the lowest.[7]

"In the history of NFA disciplinary cases, a very small percentage of them relate to CTAs," said Dyekman. "CTAs are not normally an area where we see a problem with behavior."

This is not to say anything is perfect or that an investment in managed futures is guaranteed against loss or deceptive practices. There will always be deviously clever individuals who attempt to manipulate situations. But it is to say that intelligent industry regulation works more often than not. While some inside the futures and options industry may consider regulation somewhat onerous, it is clear regulation has cleaned what was at one point considered a dirty industry and made the investment legitimate by protecting the investor. The benefits of such intelligent regulation touch the investor but also benefit the industry at large. When the investor benefits, the entire industry benefits.

On the Book's Web Site

Available to the general public:

- Checklist for avoiding investment fraud.

Available to registered book readers:

- White paper: "The Subtle yet Important Differences between NFA-Registered CTAs and CPOs, Trading Systems, Full-Service Brokerage Accounts, and Unregulated Educators."
- White paper and interactive tool: "Guide to Appropriate Account Structure."

For more information visit www.wiley.com/go/managedfutures.

CHAPTER 6

Recognize It

Volatility + Volatility and Lintner's Message*

When can "bad" be "good"?

When someone rides a roller coaster he or she does so with the goal to be "excited." At what point does exciting transform into "scary"? It all becomes clear with an understanding of individual volatility tolerance. Anyone physically fit who works out endures the physical pain of exercise with a goal: Transform the pain into the gain of a lean body and a fit mind.

In investing there are pain and gain, risk and reward trade-offs, as well. Unfortunately, the truth behind real risk is often hidden from investors. This is true with stock market volatility, and even volatility itself.

Societal norms to which investors have been indoctrinated teach that investing risk, as measured by volatility and standard deviation, should be avoided; you can avoid the pain, yet expect the gain. In the fall of 2008 stock investors learned the truth about risky investments: Stock market volatility is the price to play a game of high risk/high reward poker. It is traditional for financial professionals to measure investment risk based on volatility using an antiquated standard deviation formula, which leads to a question:

Is all volatility the same degree of bad?

Standard deviation is a formula that measures volatility by considering the differential between a mean and the variance from that mean. For instance, a CTA that exhibited (monthly) returns ranging from +5 percent to −5 percent would have a lower standard deviation, thus less perceived risk, than a CTA that exhibited (monthly) returns from +25 percent to

---

*Past performance is not indicative of future results. This book is significantly based on the author's opinions and these opinions are not appropriate for all investors and should not be construed as individual advice.

−5 percent. The problem with the formula is that it treats positive return performance the same as negative return performance. An investment with a year of +5 percent returns each month would be considered to have the same risk as an investment with a year of −5 percent monthly returns. This may sound absurd for a risk formula, particularly one so commonly used through financial services, and it raises this question:

Is volatility that generates positive returns the same degree of risk as volatility that generates negative returns? Said another way: Should an investment that delivers a positive 25 percent return be considered equally risky as an investment that delivers a 25 percent drawdown? This is particularly true in managed futures, where volatility can be the risk one pays to achieve return.

It seems obvious that a negative return represents higher past risk than a positive return, but that is not the case according to standard deviation, which treats upside and downside volatility of returns as equal. This book echoes that of other academic voices and puts across a concept that professional and individual investors should recognize. This chapter addresses risk as defined by volatility and standard deviation, then draws the opinion:

All volatility is not the same degree of "bad": There is upside and downside volatility and they are both risky, but to different degrees.

It is for this reason that standard deviation may not be the best measure of risk. This chapter considers the work of Harvard University professor John Lintner, who conducted a study that combined two risky and volatile investments into a portfolio and the overall portfolio volatility in that investment was reduced. Readers unfamiliar with this work should first read a brief explanation of the work of Harvard's Lintner and Nobel Prize winner Harry Markowitz in Appendix F.

In this chapter the concept is taken to a new level: Uncorrelated yet volatile investments have the potential to be combined in such a fashion as to reduce overall portfolio volatility.

In this chapter readers learn:

- The academic concept that adding risk and volatility to a portfolio can actually reduce risk and volatility, using a specific formula.
- This theory is tested using the following models and using a variety of risk measures:
  - Standard deviation
  - Sharpe ratio
  - Worst drawdown

VOLATILITY USED TO REDUCE VOLATILITY

The common industry wisdom and analysis regarding Lintner's work centers on the value of adding *managed futures* to a portfolio to create diversification and lower past risk statistics. In fact, this has become a point of validation for this asset class with certain investors. But is that really the main headline? Is managed futures really the most important aspect of the story, which is the common perception in the industry? This question may sound odd coming from a book admittedly supporting the industry, but here is my unvarnished opinion:

> *It could be argued the key to Lintner's work is an interesting concept that should be taken to the next level: Properly integrating solid, strong-performing, uncorrelated yet risky asset classes into a portfolio has the potential to actually reduce overall portfolio risk and improve returns on a past performance basis—regardless of the asset class or investment.*

Investors should put in perspective different types of risk and their meaning in individual situations. Too many people consider all volatility, as measured by standard deviation (STD) of returns, equally "bad" as other risk measures, such as drawdown. It is not uncommon to hear investors discuss volatility in singular terms. But should risk, measured by standard deviation, be a singular concept? Warren Buffett, speaking to Berkshire Hathaway shareholders in 2007, observed:

> *Volatility is not risk. The whole concept of volatility as a measure of risk has developed in my lifetime and isn't any use to us.*[1]

ALL VOLATILITY IS RISKY... TO DIFFERENT DEGREES

Certain types of volatility can be better than other types of volatility in the author's opinion. While all volatility represents risk, it does so based on degrees. There are occasions when risk can be required to yield appropriate return: circumstances when a risky/volatile investment can generate positive overall results in a portfolio, such as providing uncorrelated higher returns or contributing to quicker drawdown recovery time. Likewise, there are instances when unwanted volatility and risk can generate negative results:

drawdown and loss. This is not to diminish the risk in investing, and what is revealed on these pages is not for all investors.

Lintner's central finding was that when managed futures was added to a stock and bond portfolio, the overall investment portfolio exhibited higher returns and lower portfolio volatility. For the most part that is the end of his initial conclusion. The phrase *initial conclusion* is used because no one really knows how Lintner would have advanced his theory or to what higher insight his thoughts would have gone. Months after he presented his initial landmark findings his life was cut short in a car accident.

At its core, Lintner took two very risky but uncorrelated asset classes (stocks and managed futures) and combined them to actually reduce portfolio volatility. The bond exposure is important, but it remains consistent in its conservative nature and thus is not an active consideration in this chapter.

Ignoring managed futures in Lintner's study and considering the real point, the formula might apply to other noncorrelated investments. When noncorrelation, solid risk management, and proper performance exists:

Volatile Investment
+ Uncorrelated Volatile Investment
+ Uncorrelated Volatile Investment
= Potentially Less Volatile Combined Portfolio Investment with Higher Past Returns (based on statistical measures)

This should be the headline, and the next step in Lintner's work.

It was important that Lintner chose for his study what can arguably be the world's most uncorrelated asset, managed futures. This is the important component many asset allocation models generally miss: Uncorrelated assets that perform independent of one another, particularly during times of stock market dislocation, should be a key consideration in modern asset allocation. Ignoring this truth is generally done by the same people who ignore Lintner's work. For the point of this chapter, we scale back the concept to prove the formula confining ourselves to the smaller world of managed futures.

Proving the Concept

To prove this point the author engaged in three studies, with more available on the book's web site. This formula can be independently proven because it can be considered a mathematical truism. Researchers can combine any three uncorrelated but high-performing and volatile investments into a portfolio and the overall portfolio risk statistics should improve more often than not.

To prove out this concept the first study considers core differences in performance among CTAs with high levels of risk in standard deviation, drawdown, and drawdown recovery time. In all the studies, CTAs with the highest standard deviation had much better risk/reward profiles than did CTAs with highest drawdown statistics. The concept behind the next two studies in this chapter is to consider the "worst" CTAs and determine if this formula can make them better in a diversified portfolio. The studies consider the riskiest investments based on standard deviation, worst drawdown, and longest average drawdown recovery time and then consider the risk and reward balance between volatility, as measured by standard deviation, and drawdown risk. The second and third studies consider the average statistics of two lists of CTAs, taking the most uncorrelated subgroup among the lists, placing them in a hypothetical portfolio together, and observing risk measures improve as the volatility formula is in place, which is always the case. It is important to note the point of this formula is not to improve returns among these high-performance investments, but rather to reduce past risk statistics.

RISK DISCLOSURE

This chapter is not appropriate for all investors. The chapter addresses volatility, a complicated and unpredictable topic, showing a technique for identifying and differentiating between upside and downside volatility. The book peels away thought that has not been entirely explored in a public display or academic forum, and what is presented is for illustrative purpose only. All study conclusions are based on past performance. It is important to note that while the studies in this book show how properly adding and managing risky but high-performing assets such as managed futures to a portfolio can improve traditional statistical risk measures such as standard deviation, Sharpe ratio, and worst drawdown, past performance is not indicative of future results. There is significant risk of loss when investing in volatile assets and only risk capital should be utilized. Additionally, this is not for everyone. The risks are always unpredictable and can be different in high-performing asset classes. Risks are outlined in part throughout this book, but this book is not being represented as a complete look at the unpredictable, elastic, and constantly changing topics of risk and volatility.

Study #1: How "Bad" Is Volatility?

The first study (Table 6.1) identified the 20 "worst" CTAs based on highest standard deviation, highest worst drawdown, and longest average drawdown recovery time.[2] The performance of the 20 "worst" CTAs was averaged and then observations were made about the volatility differences relative to performance measures.

Thus begins a discussion on investing risk as consideration is given to two primary measures of risk: drawdown and volatility, as measured by standard deviation. One risk measure, drawdown, is bottom line risk. Drawdown is the ultimate negative investing consequence: loss. Drawdown could be the definition, the poster boy of risk. Standard deviation, on the other hand, might be considered a symptom of risk, to varying degrees, a concept that runs counter to popular Wall Street dictum.

Take an objective look at Table 6.1, the average performance of a list of the 20 "bad" CTAs based on the highest standard deviation (STD), highest worst drawdown (DD), and longest drawdown recovery time. Many might consider standard deviation and drawdown as equal risk measures, but do they tell the same risk and reward story?

In this study (Table 6.1) the most pronounced difference between standard deviation (STD) (Line A) and drawdown (DD) occurs in past compounded annual returns. The group of the 20 worst CTAs based on STD provided investors compounded past annual returns of 22.33 percent. The 20 worst CTAs with the highest worst drawdowns (Line B) and longest drawdown recovery time (Line C), provided investors minuscule 1.03 percent and 8.95 percent respective returns, but most significantly, investors were required to endure significant drawdowns and long recovery times to achieve these paltry returns. Thus, when risk was measured by standard deviation it achieved what could be considered a significant positive 22.33 percent return while risk as measured by drawdown achieved a minor 8.95 percent and even a 1.03 percent return. It could be concluded from this study that "bad" drawdown statistics indicate a poorly performing past investment, but "bad" standard deviation statistics indicate a high-performing investment, in this instance.

But further, consider line C in Table 6.1: those 20 CTAs with the highest average drawdown recovery time. This group had an extremely low compounded annual return of 1.03 percent. But it is interesting to note how low the standard deviation is. When standard deviation was low, so were returns. Further, consider the spread between the upside and downside deviation, another potential key insight. In Table 6.1, the group of CTAs with the highest spread between upside (Up Dev) and downside deviation (Down Dev) also were the largest among high-performing investments, a key

TABLE 6.1 Negative Managed Futures Information: Average Performance of 20 Worst CTAs in Three Categories: Highest Standard Deviation, Highest Worst Drawdown, and Longest Drawdown Recovery Time

Study Group	Compounded Annual ROR %	STD	Worst DD	Loss %	Average Recovery	Average DD	Up Dev	Down Dev
A. Bad 20: Highest STD	22.33%	18.88	64.20%	41.55%	5.42	28.11%	16.51	9.46
B. Bad 20: Highest Worst DD	8.95%	13.64	77.04%	40.37%	6.53	25.71%	10.55	8.45
C. Bad 20: Longest DD	1.03%	5.7	22.97%	50.57%	13.72	20.85%	4.33	3.57

Source: Barclay MAP Database.

Results are averages of CTA category performance and these CTAs have not traded together in this fashion in a regulated CPO structure. These statistics change on a monthly basis and the current month's performance analysis is on the book's web site. Past performance is not indicative of future results.

insight we will utilize when developing advanced managed futures portfolios in Chapter 10. This is just one study, with more posted on the book's web site, with this point:

> *High standard deviation generated risk, but this very volatility might have been required to generate high past return and quick drawdown recovery time, which is an important difference because large worst drawdown or long recovery times are generally not associated with positive performance.*

This leads back to the key question: Are investments that deliver positive returns more risky or less risky than those that deliver negative returns? It would appear that negative performance is riskier than positive performance to varying degrees. For this reason, drawdown statistics are a better measure of risk than standard deviation. This is because the standard deviation formula punishes volatile but strong performing investments, ignoring the difference between upside and downside performance.

This section has demonstrated how standard deviation and drawdown are very different measurements of bottom line risk. While drawdown could be considered a pure measure of risk, standard deviation is more a measure of risk and reward, a key concept we address over the next two chapters. This book is not alone in its assessment of standard deviation.

Study #2: Worst Drawdown—Using Correlation and Portfolio Development to Tame the Beast

The point of the next studies (Tables 6.2 to 6.5) is to show how uncorrelated but volatile investments can be integrated into a portfolio and result in a potential reduction in risk statistics.

Table 6.2 is a negative list highlighting bad behavior from the worst of the worst from one perspective: the top 20 riskiest CTAs in the notorious "worst drawdown" category. This study takes the most uncorrelated from the list and combines them into a portfolio. The study then compares the average statistics of all 20 of the worst drawdown CTAs and the portfolio of uncorrelated CTAs from within this group, with the goal to prove the concept that uncorrelated risky investments can be combined into a portfolio to reduce past risk measures.

The average statistics in the lower line in Table 6.2 from the 20 CTAs based on worst drawdown will be compared to an uncorrelated subgroup portfolio comprised of eight CTAs from this list. CTA selection is based on nothing other than the CTAs' correlation to each other based on an average of the correlation numbers. For the purposes of this study a basic returns

TABLE 6.2 Highest Worst Drawdown CTAs: Actual Reported Performance of the 20 Individual CTAs with the Highest Worst Drawdown

CTA NUMBER	Worst Drawdown	Compound Annual Return	Sharpe Ratio	STD Mo. (Qtr) ROR	Start Date
1	89.66%	14.14%	0.24	12.38	Jul-92
2	89.66%	14.08%	0.23	12.69	Apr-93
3	82.7%	16.65%	0.26	12.34	Jan-81
4	80.6%	−8.12%	−0.27	11.59	Aug-04
5	78.21%	32.26%	0.5	17.09	Sep-03
6	77.79%	23.32%	0.22	24.6	Jan-86
7	74.86%	10.16%	0.24	7.92	May-93
8	74.75%	11.06%	0.27	7.91	Oct-92
9	73.99%	16.7%	0.24	15.29	Sep-94
10	71.63%	−1.08%	−0.11	10.14	May-05
11	69.6%	4.59%	0.05	10.14	Nov-99
12	69.54%	21.18%	0.58	9.28	Oct-01
13	69.48%	23.08%	0.36	13.85	Jan-75
14	68.84%	11.07%	0.16	12.01	Jan-85
15	68.45%	22.25%	0.43	12.52	Nov-93
16	65.28%	−20.95%	−0.88	7.49	Dec-06
17	65.13%	−1.09%	−0.12	8.61	Jun-04
18	64.76%	−18.73%	−0.81	7.38	Nov-06
19	64.03%	−19.19%	−0.83	7.39	Dec-06
20	63.97%	−17.48%	−0.86	6.67	Jun-06
Average	73.15%	6.7%	−0.005	11.37	

correlation analysis is used, which only uses one of five correlation points that are explained in Chapter 9 on correlation and could be considered a handicap.

Table 6.3 is a correlation matrix of the eight most uncorrelated CTAs in the subgroup of the list of 20 CTAs with the worst drawdown. It is these CTAs who are combined in an equal weighted portfolio with the goal to observe how uncorrelated, diversified, risky investments have the potential to reduce overall past portfolio risk measures.

The statistics in Table 6.4 are powerful.

The first line in Table 6.4 shows the statistical averages of the 20 CTAs based on highest worst drawdown: in this case, 73.15 percent worst drawdown, a standard deviation of 11.37, and an average recovery time of 6.7 months.

TABLE 6.3 Returns-Based Correlation Matrix of the Eight Uncorrelated CTAs' Worst Drawdowns

	CTA 6-1	CTA 6-2	CTA 6-3	CTA 6-4	CTA 6-5	CTA 6-6	CTA 6-7	CTA 6-8
CTA 6-1	1.00	0.11	−0.34	−0.05	−0.04	0.29	−0.08	0.13
CTA 6-2	0.11	1.00	0.05	0.21	0.01	0.10	0.24	0.09
CTA 6-3	−0.34	0.05	1.00	0.57	0.13	0.03	0.11	0.52
CTA 6-4	−0.05	0.21	0.57	1.00	0.11	−0.12	0.05	0.45
CTA 6-5	−0.04	0.01	0.13	0.11	1.00	−0.06	0.04	0.06
CTA 6-6	0.29	0.10	0.03	−0.12	−0.06	1.00	−0.13	0.25
CTA 6-7	−0.08	0.24	0.11	0.05	0.04	−0.13	1.00	−0.09
CTA 6-8	0.13	0.09	0.52	0.45	0.06	0.25	−0.09	1.00

Source: Barclay MAP Database.
Results are averages of CTA category performance and these CTAs have not traded together in this fashion in a regulated CPO structure. Correlation is done from the point of the CTA with the shortest track record for all periods. Correlation statistics may be unreliable regarding CTAs with a short track record. These statistics change on a monthly basis and the current month's performance analysis is on the book's web site. Past performance is not indicative of future results.

TABLE 6.4 Average Reported Performance of the 20 Individual CTAs with the Highest Worst Drawdown Compared to a Subportfolio of Eight Uncorrelated CTAs Taken from the List of 20 Worst Drawdown CTAs, Followed by the Portfolio Improvement When Relative Uncorrelated Diversification Is in Place

CTA Name	Compound Annual Return	Worst Drawdown	STD Mo. (Qtr) ROR	Sharpe Ratio	Average Recovery Time
A. Statistical Average, 20 Worst DD CTAs	6.70%	**73.15%**	**11.37**	0	**6.7**
B. Subportfolio Results, 8 of 20 Uncorrelated CTAs	23.00%	**25.85%**	**6.32**	0.94	**3.94**

Source: Barclay MAP Database.
Results are averages of CTA category performance and a hypothetical portfolio. These CTAs have not traded together in this fashion in a regulated CPO structure. These statistics change on a monthly basis and the current month's performance analysis is on the book's web site. Past performance is not indicative of future results.

TABLE 6.5 Hypothetical Portfolio Performance of the Eight Uncorrelated Individual CTAs from the List of the Highest Worst Drawdown

Total Return:	271.06%	Avg. Monthly Returns	1.94%
Cmpnd. An. Rtn.:	23.00%	STD Monthly Deviation	6.32%
Last 12 Mo:	5.57%	Sharpe:	0.94
Last 6 Mo:	−0.63%	Sterling:	0.56
Last 3 Mo:	−6.70%	Barclay:	1.62
Last Month:	−1.79%	Efficiency:	1.05
Winning Mo:	49	Losing Mo:	27
Avg. Win:	5.41%	Avg. Loss:	−4.36%
STD Win:	5.37%	STD Loss:	3.85%
% Winning Mo:	64.47%	% Losing Mo:	35.53%
Worst Drawdown:	25.85%		
Year	**Return**		
2009	5.57%		
2008	29.00%		
2007	6.07%		

Source: Barclay MAP Database. Calculated values are for the period 09/01/2003 to 12/31/2009; statistics based on monthly data.
Results are averages of CTA category performance and a hypothetical portfolio. These CTAs have not traded together in this fashion in a regulated CPO structure. These statistics change on a monthly basis and the current month's performance analysis is on the book's web site. Past performance is not indicative of future results. See the hypothetical risk disclosure in note 7 for Chapter 3.

The second line in Table 6.5 shows a portfolio using the subgroup of eight most uncorrelated CTAs taken from the group of 20 worst drawdown CTAs, all with significant improvement in risk statistics. It shows this equal weighted portfolio had a compounded annual return of 23 percent, a worst drawdown of 25.85 percent, STD of 6.32, and an average drawdown recovery time of 3.94 months, a substantial improvement. Consider the power of uncorrelated diversification as these performance numbers were generated from a list of CTAs with the worst drawdown statistics.

Typically the portfolio diversification method will reduce returns slightly while dramatically improving past risk measures. Past performance is not indicative of future results. Table 6.5 shows the hypothetical results as generated by the portfolio software.[3]

PROVE IT YOURSELF

Here is what is most interesting. Investors can prove this theory on their own. First, make a list of 20 top negative or volatile performing CTAs (or even 20 randomly selected CTAs) with a reasonably long track record. Then pull out the eight most uncorrelated and build an equal weighted portfolio. Based on the mathematics, it is more than likely than not the resulting uncorrelated portfolio will display a lower risk profile than the averages. In other words, take past uncorrelated volatility and add it with past uncorrelated volatility and the resulting portfolio will more often than not exhibit lower past volatility.

Study #3: Standard Deviation—Using Correlation and Portfolio Development to Tame the Beast

Take a look at the same study (shown in Table 6.6), but instead of using worst drawdown consider standard deviation, or volatility, asking which is the best measure of risk.

Considering the CTAs on the list of worst drawdowns in Table 6.2, there are very few, if any, that would make the author's recommended list. But considering the CTAs with the highest standard deviation in Table 6.6, there are several CTAs that are commonly recommended in volatile portfolios. The author's experience in selecting CTAs is not a statistical argument in favor of an academic concept, but the frank, unvarnished risk insight is that volatility is the price one pays for returns in managed futures—and

TABLE 6.6 Average Performance of 20 Worst CTAs in the Category of Highest Standard Deviation

CTA Name	STD Mo. (Qtr) ROR	Compound Annual Return	Worst Drawdown	Sharpe Ratio	Average Recovery Time
CTA 1	35.38%	38.13%	61.72%	0.28	2.8
CTA 2	27.6%	−9.85%	86.39%	−0.13	3.7
CTA 3	25.36%	24.46%	65.21%	0.25	2.75
CTA 4	24.64%	23.55%	77.79%	0.22	19
CTA 5	21.95%	56.93%	55.42%	0.71	3.8
CTA 6	21.13%	16.78%	91.97%	0.18	7.14
CTA 7	21.11%	41.16%	49.72%	0.52	1.9
CTA 8	20.88%	−15.46%	63.44%	−0.24	3.87
CTA 9	20.19%	40.61%	60.72%	0.53	2.66
CTA 10	17.2%	32.13%	78.21%	0.49	3.93
CTA 11	15.76%	20.47%	53.16%	0.32	2.93
CTA 12	15.33%	17.05%	73.99%	0.25	3.63
CTA 13	15.31%	50.6%	39.66%	0.9	2.73
CTA 14	15.15%	−12.13%	90.44%	−0.28	9.5
CTA 15	15.08%	8.7%	56.79%	0.11	8.66
CTA 16	15.07%	27.99%	61.77%	0.45	4.5
CTA 17	14.63%	20.59%	54.6%	0.36	3.86
CTA 18	14.6%	24.09%	45.15%	0.39	5.87
CTA 19	14.57%	−6.94%	76.95%	−0.18	17
CTA 20	14.27%	15.27%	65.88%	0.25	2.91
Statistical Average 20 Highest STD CTAs	20.52%	22.49%	72.47%	0.29	7.91

Source: Barclay MAP Database.
Results are averages of CTA category performance. These CTAs have not traded together in this fashion in a regulated CPO structure. These statistics change on a monthly basis and the current month's performance analysis is on the book's web site. Past performance is not indicative of future results.

standard deviation unjustly penalizes the upside volatility component of that volatility to an incorrect degree. From this we see a managed futures insight. CTAs with consistently high upside deviation and low downside deviation potentially indicate a strong risk management program. For instance, a CTA who "lets his winners run while cutting losers" would have a high upside deviation because fewer controls over the upside, positive returns would be in place. But when the investment turns negative the CTA's risk management program might take control, eliminating losing positions through stop losses or predetermined exit strategies based on certain risk statistics. Thus, it is not uncommon to see good CTAs with high upside deviation and low downside deviation numbers; but in the eyes of standard deviation, this letting the upside winners run while cutting downside losses would be viewed as the same degree of risk as a CTA who lets his downside drawdown run uncontrolled while cutting his winners short. It just doesn't make sense, but that is how the mathematical measure of standard deviation treats upside and downside deviation.

In this study, the "riskiest" 20 CTAs based on those with the highest standard deviation are first identified, then the study overlays a basic returns correlation matrix to identify the most uncorrelated to one another. Table 6.7 shows how the eight most uncorrelated CTAs in the risky standard deviation category correlate to one another as well as to the S&P 500 stock index and the Barclay CTA index. As a reminder, CTAs with correlation closet to 0.00 are the most uncorrelated, which is the goal.[4]

Consider that Table 6.8 shows the uncorrelated CTAs chosen from a list of the 20 CTAs with the highest standard deviation. The CTAs are similar in high standard deviation, the measure of risk, but very different from the list of worst drawdown in terms of the sweet measure of reward, strong returns. Compounded annual returns run from a low of −14.05 percent to a high of 57.66 percent with an equal diversity of Sharpe ratios. But unlike the list of CTAs based on worst drawdown, the list contains the likes of high-performing well-known CTAs alongside low-performing unknown traders. It is an interesting lot, sort of like strolling through Chicago's Wicker Park neighborhood, L.A.'s Silver Lake, or New York's Upper West Side: edgy yet creatively trendy urban neighborhoods that contain a complete diversity of people; from the high-performing money machines to the out-of-luck homeless, who can be volatile and negatively powerful when prodded, similar to investing in the wrong CTA.

The statistical average line on the bottom of Table 6.8 provides the average of the individual CTA results. To illustrate the potential power of noncorrelation and diversification, witness how the results differ when placed in a portfolio, as is done in Table 6.9. Considering this portfolio of CTAs with high STD in Table 6.9 yields interesting results. While the returns drop slightly, risk statistics improve significantly. The last line in Table 6.9 shows investments combined and placed in a single portfolio, integrating CTAs with equal asset weighting and viewing the combined CTAs from the perspective of a hypothetical single investment.

For the point of this study on standard deviation, consider standard deviation itself was almost cut in half as a result of uncorrelated diversification, to 10.67 from 20.52; a significant improvement.

TABLE 6.7 Correlation Matrix of Most Uncorrelated in the Group of High Volatility (STD)

	Barclay CTA Index	CTA 6-1	CTA 6-2	CTA 6-3	CTA 6-4	CTA 6-5	CTA 6-6	CTA 6-7	S&P TR Index	CTA 6-8
Barclay CTA Index	1.00	0.06	0.12	0.09	0.06	−0.21	−0.11	0.08	−0.13	−0.12
CTA 6-1	0.06	1.00	0.12	0.00	0.00	−0.30	0.08	0.13	−0.25	0.08
CTA 6-2	0.12	0.12	1.00	0.04	0.29	0.14	0.11	−0.05	0.20	−0.22
CTA 6-3	0.09	0.00	0.04	1.00	−0.10	0.10	0.02	−0.04	0.14	0.08
CTA 6-4	0.06	0.00	0.29	−0.10	1.00	0.04	0.22	−0.16	0.20	−0.09
CTA 6-5	−0.21	−0.30	0.14	0.10	0.04	1.00	0.21	0.09	0.46	0.00
CTA 6-6	−0.11	0.08	0.11	0.02	0.22	0.21	1.00	−0.18	0.14	−0.21
CTA 6-7	0.08	0.13	−0.05	−0.04	−0.16	0.09	−0.18	1.00	−0.16	0.05
S&P TR Index	−0.13	−0.25	0.20	0.14	0.20	0.46	0.14	−0.16	1.00	−0.05
CTA 6-8	−0.12	0.08	−0.22	0.08	−0.09	0.00	−0.21	0.05	−0.05	1.00

Source: Barclay MAP. Correlation Matrix (November 2005 through May 2009).

TABLE 6.8 Individual and Average Performance of Eight Uncorrelated Subgroup CTAs within the Group of 20 Worst CTAs Based on Highest Standard Deviation

CTA Name	Compound Annual Return	Worst Drawdown	STD Mo. (Qtr) ROR	Sharpe Ratio	Sortino Ratio	Average Recovery Time
CTA 6-1	−14.05%	86.39%	26.99%	−0.18	−1.05	3.5
CTA 6-2	23.28%	77.79%	24.76%	0.22	2.26	18.83
CTA 6-3	57.66%	55.42%	22.21%	0.71	5.08	3.7
CTA 6-4	16.67%	91.97%	21.11%	0.17	1.24	7.03
CTA 6-5	45.21%	60.72%	20.41%	0.59	4.27	2.5
CTA 6-6	0.71%	93.34%	18.68%	−0.07	−0.55	9.06
CTA 6-7	52.47%	39.66%	15.41%	0.93	8.96	2.66
CTA 6-8	−2.06%	74.49%	14.62%	−0.09	−0.41	16
Statistical Average	22.49%	72.47%	20.52%	0.29	2.48	7.91

Source: Barclay MAP Database.

Results are averages of CTA category performance. These CTAs have not traded together in this fashion in a regulated CPO structure. These statistics change on a monthly basis and the current month's performance analysis is on the book's web site. Past performance is not indicative of future results.

TABLE 6.9 Average Performance of 20 CTAs with Highest Volatility versus an Uncorrelated Subgroup Portfolio of the Eight CTAs from the List of 20 Worst CTAs in the Category of Highest Standard Deviation

	Compound Annual Return	Worst Drawdown	STD Mo. (Qtr) ROR	Sharpe Ratio	Average Recovery Time
Statistical Average 20 Highest STD CTAs	22.49%	72.47%	20.52%	0.29	7.91
Portfolio Results 8 of 20 Uncorrelated STD	15.92%	52.45%	10.67%	0.35	4.5
Statistical Average 20 Worst DD CTAs	6.65%	80.18%	14.7%	0.08	6.64
Portfolio Results 8 Worst DD Uncorrelated	18.78%	25.29%	6.45%	0.72	3.11

Source: Barclay MAP Database.

Results are averages of CTA category performance and a hypothetical portfolio. These CTAs have not traded together in this fashion in a regulated CPO structure. These statistics change on a monthly basis and the current month's performance analysis is on the book's web site. Past performance is not indicative of future results.

Worst drawdown and drawdown recovery time were also impressively reduced. While average portfolio returns did drop from 22.49 percent to 15.92 percent, the point of the portfolio diversification management system is to reduce risk and retain close-to-significant results. As you will see, when a more complete complement of risk filters are in place through an intelligent diversification process, the past risk and reward statistics can change in even more dramatic fashion, but understand past performance is not indicative of future results.

This is really a payoff study highlighting how when risky investments are relatively uncorrelated it can reduce overall portfolio risk statistics.

At this point you might be wondering, "Why are uncorrelated portfolio results different from the statistical averages?" Answering this question starts to reveal a mathematical equation that is the core reason why a diversified portfolio method can be so potentially powerful. In part it illustrates how combining uncorrelated assets into a single portfolio can reduce past overall investment volatility and risk measures. This is due to the very nature of uncorrelated assets. All things being equal, on a pure mathematical basis when returns of risky assets are uncorrelated, overall portfolio risk statistics will be reduced when these uncorrelated assets are placed in a portfolio together. The way this uncorrelated diversification is designed to work is that at any given period of time a handful of CTAs may have posted negative results while a different group of CTAs may have posted positive results. The idea is that when high-performing, volatile yet uncorrelated assets are properly combined in a portfolio, the individual components of the portfolio may be volatile, but the overall performance of the investment can be designed to be less volatile. The goal is to smooth overall portfolio volatility and drawdown risk while retaining the high performance. This in part explains the results of Lintner's work and points to the next step.

STANDARD DEVIATION AS MEASURE OF VOLATILITY

It is important to differentiate what standard deviation really measures. It is popular to consider standard deviation a pure *risk* measure, but is this true? Standard deviation measures differentials between upside and downside returns behavior. Is deviation to the upside a clear measure of risk? This leads to the book's conclusion:

> *Standard deviation in and of itself is a measure of volatility, and when upside and downside volatility is blindly packaged together it measures both risk and reward to a degree, not just risk, which is the common perception.*

The Sharpe ratio is not only a measure of risk; it is a measure of risk and reward. Standard deviation should be considered in the same light to a certain degree. This is because with high performing investments, degrees of "bad" volatility exist.

Degrees of "Bad" Volatility Exist

According to standard deviation, all volatility is an equal degree of "bad, representing the same level of risk. The point is this: that might not be the case in managed futures, an investment built on volatility. Managed futures can be a volatile investment and no attempt is being made to diminish the risk. The key is to break apart what one might consider more "positive volatility" or more appropriately "less negative volatility" and separate it from truly negative volatility.

The concept of utilizing volatility to reduce volatility is explored further in the next chapter, as a risk/reward measure is designed with the goal to separate upside volatility from downside. The concept of utilizing uncorrelated volatility to reduce volatility but maintain positive returns is further detailed in Chapter 10 when actual managed futures portfolios are built.

On the Book's Web Site

Available to registered book readers:

- The chapter's volatility + uncorrelated volatility formula is further tested.
- Additional portfolio examples where volatility is used as a tool to generate interesting past results.
- Professional white paper: "How to Use Volatility as a Tool in Building Risk-Appropriate Portfolios."
- Author's video regarding volatility in managed futures and all investing.

For more information visit www.wiley.com/go/managedfutures.

CHAPTER 7

Use It

Reward-Adjusted Deviation (RAD) Considers Past Probability and Rewards Success*

Can you take the work of a great artist and make it better? Improve upon the Mona Lisa? Make Beethoven's Fifth Symphony more compelling? We can always strive to improve as sure as the New York Yankees will no doubt pull out their endless wallet in attempts at improving their lineup, despite having already acquired a plethora of World Series rings.

What about Markowitz's formula? Can an updated and useful formula be derived from what is Nobel Prize–winning lineage? Can we reach back over 60 years and revisit the harsh, windswept shores along Lake Michigan to the same place Markowitz developed his masterpiece and craft something that perhaps works better on LaSalle Street than it does on Wall Street? Perhaps a new formula better suited for high-performance managed futures because it attempts to measure past probability of success alongside the potential to receive the associated highs and lows involved in all investing?

In this chapter readers witness the development of a formula to measure risk and past probability of success; a mathematical calculation that is capitalistic, almost "American" because it rewards success over failure, as much as that might sound unusual in light of current societal conditions.

In this chapter readers walk on sacred ground laid by Harry Markowitz, slightly altering his Nobel Prize–winning formula to measure risk. (Readers unfamiliar with the work of Markowitz should read the background Appendix F.) The alteration takes place in the standard deviation component

*Past performance is not indicative of future results. This book is significantly based on the author's opinions and these opinions are not appropriate for all investors and should not be construed as individual advice.

of the formula. This book's premise is that standard deviation is not the best measure of risk, particularly in managed futures. This is primarily because standard deviation does not differentiate between upside and downside deviation. Upside deviation can be *less negative* than downside deviation to the extent of past probability, and negative downside returns performance is riskier than positive upside performance, in the author's opinion.

While this may sound obvious, the current standard deviation formula used to commonly measure risk bases its output on the notion that all deviation is equal. Hence, a new formula to measure deviation is required, particularly when analyzing high-performance assets.

$$\text{RAD} = \text{Probability of Past Success} + \text{Correctly Weighted Volatility}$$

The Reward-Adjusted Deviation (RAD) model recognizes the difference between upside and downside volatility, assigning a *lesser degree of negative weighting* to upside volatility to the extent of past probability. The formula is:

$$\text{RAD} = (\text{Upside Deviation} \times \text{Loss }\%) + \text{Downside Deviation}$$

The formula treats all deviation as a negative, a measure of risk. It is just done so at different degrees based on the probability of past success, represented by loss %. In addition, the formula points to degrees of even returns distribution.

STUDY 1: EXPLORING RAD WITH MATH

For the point of understanding the formula, start with a pure mathematical demonstration. Control numbers are established in the first line of Table 7.1 (Control).[1] This control contains random numeric values, where upside and downside deviation are equal at 6 and loss percentage is equal at 50 percent. The study then independently changes the numeric values to identify how the change impacts the RAD indicator.

In the second line (Higher Up Dev) upside deviation (Up Dev) is increased by three points from the control, from 6 to 9. As a result of this increased upside deviation, RAD increases from 9 to 10.5—worsening the RAD indicator by 1.5 because RAD indicates higher past risk as it increases in value, just like standard deviation. This increase represents an indication

TABLE 7.1 Changes in RAD Indicator Resulting from Changes to Upside Deviation

	Up Dev	Down Dev	Loss %	RAD	Change
Control	6	6	50%	9	
Higher Up Dev	9	6	50%	10.5	1.5
Lower Up Dev	3	6	50%	7.5	−1.5

of higher risk in upside deviation similar in a conceptual fashion to standard deviation used in the Markowitz formula that assigned higher risk when volatility increased. When upside deviation is lowered from the control, from 6 to 3, the RAD is bettered by 1.5.

Now consider similar changes to downside deviation, because it generates different weighting (see Table 7.2).

In the fourth line of Table 7.2, downside deviation (Higher Down Dev) increased from 6 to 9, the same amounts as upside deviation was previously increased. However, the RAD indicator changed in a more significant fashion, moving up 3 points rather than just 1.5 points as was the case when upside deviation changed by the same amount. This is one of the significant premises of the reward-adjusted deviation theory:

> *The formula recognizes that all deviation/volatility represents risk, but treats upside deviation different, to a degree, than downside deviation.*

Now consider what happens when loss percentage, considered a measure of probability to a degree, enters the formula (see Table 7.3).

TABLE 7.2 Changes in RAD Indicator Resulting from Changes to Downside Deviation

	Up Dev	Down Dev	Loss %	RAD	Change
Control	6	6	50%	9	
Higher Up Dev	9	6	50%	10.5	1.5
Lower Up Dev	3	6	50%	7.5	−1.5
Higher Down Dev	6	9	50%	12	3
Lower Down Dev	6	3	50%	6	−3

TABLE 7.3 Changes in RAD Indicator Resulting from Changes to Loss Percentage

	Up Dev	Down Dev	Loss %	RAD	Change
Control	6	6	50%	9	
Higher Up Dev	9	6	50%	10.5	1.5
Lower Up Dev	3	6	50%	7.5	−1.5
Higher Down Dev	6	9	50%	12	3
Lower Down Dev	6	3	50%	6	−3
High Loss %	6	6	75%	10.5	1.5
Low Loss %	6	6	25%	7.5	−1.5

When loss percentage is increased by 25 percent, from 50 percent to 75 percent losing months, indicating a lower level of past probability on a random walk basis, the RAD measure increases to 1.50, indicating higher risk, assuming that past probability indicates a degree of risk, which is a component of the strategic logic behind the formula. Likewise, when loss percentage is reduced by 25 percent the RAD indicator indicates less risk by 1.5.

These are simple theoretical examples using equal numeric values to prove the formula at a basic level.

THE TEST OF SUCCESS

The success of the RAD measure relative to standard deviation (STD) can be judged to a large degree based on how the new indicator performs when real risk in high-performing investments both increases and decreases. When real risk increases, does the RAD indicator more effectively indicate this risk? When risk decreases, such as when investments are profitable with strong probability and win percentage, does the RAD indicator indicate less risk than STD? Here is the concept that readers can independently test:

Among high-performing, credible commodity trading advisor (CTA) investments, create a situation where real risk both increases and decreases in terms of worst drawdown. More often than not the RAD measure will more accurately indicate the change in real risk than will STD. For instance, create a situation where actual worst drawdown increases and see which indicator best illuminated this actual risk

Moving to the real-world analysis of CTAs proves somewhat more interesting. In the studies that follow, RAD's success, when compared to

STD, is measured by how it more accurately reflects past risk based on worst drawdown and average drawdown of high-performing investments.

Considering High Performance: RAD versus STD

The purpose of the RAD formula is to more accurately identify the degree of past risk. The RAD formula operates on the premise that volatility is a potential symptom of risk, not risk itself. The most tangible risk in investing is drawdown, bottom line negative return performance. Because it is built from the assumption upside returns are less risky than downside returns to the extent of a loss percentage, the measure is designed to more accurately identify risk and does not penalize high-performing assets. A study proving this concept compares two risk measures, STD and the new risk measure, RAD. As risk increases, observe how the two measures accurately reflect the true mathematical risk conditions. Likewise, as returns increase, as in done in Table 7.4, consider which of the two measures, RAD or STD, best identifies this potential reduction in risk, assuming that positive performance is less risky than negative performance.

We start by establishing an appropriate control study group: those CTAs that might be considered high performing and credible.[2] The criteria for selection in this high-performance study group were a six-year track record,

TABLE 7.4 Study Control Group of 41 Top-Performing CTAs

Study Group	STD	RAD	RAD/ STD	Loss %	Avr Rec	Avr DD	Worst DD	Cpd An RoR %	Sortino Ratio
Control									
Av	6.76	5.6	1.16	38.81%	2.4	7.84%	23.60%	23.90%	8.14

Key: STD = Standard deviation of monthly returns; RAD = Reward-adjusted deviation; RAD/STD = Differential between the RAD and STD formula; Loss = Percentage of monthly losses; Avr Rec = Average recovery time in months; Avr DD = Average drawdown; Cpd An RoR% = Compounded annual rate of return from BarclayHedge software; Sortino ratio = Ratio measuring the risk-free rate of return relative to downside deviation—the higher the ratio the more positive the risk profile.
Source: Barclay MAP Database.
Average results and portfolio results are a hypothetical combination of CTAs into a portfolio and these CTAs have not traded together in this fashion in a regulated commodity pool operator (CPO) structure. See the hypothetical risk disclosure in note 7 for Chapter 3. Past performance is not indicative of future results. The point is not to highlight individual CTAs or potential portfolio combinations but rather to illustrate the potential power of diversification as a risk-management tool.

at least $20 million under management, at least 15 percent compounded annual return, average drawdown recovery time under three months, and an up/down deviation ratio of at least 1.50. The goal of this study is to determine the best risk measure with high-performing investments, comparing RAD and STD as it relates to actual risk: average drawdown, worst drawdown, and loss percentage.

The study first established a control: the average statistics for all 41 top-performing CTAs in the group.[3]

Study Expectations: Now that a study control of high-performance investments has been established, two studies are conducted: The next study takes this control group and adjusts circumstances to decrease risk to consider how the RAD and STD indicators measure these adjustments. After this the study considers the characteristics of the RAD and STD to provide insight into the better measure of overall risk. The expectation is that among high-performing investments the RAD will be a more accurate measure of actual past risk when compared with STD. The study will create a situation where actual CTA performance and risk increases and decreases and then compare the resulting actions in the RAD and STD indicators.

STUDY 2: AVERAGE DRAWDOWN: RAD VERSUS STD WHEN ACTUAL RISK IMPROVES

The first study (Table 7.5) compared the average statistics of the control group of 41 CTAs relative (A. below) to a top 10 subgroup of CTAs who had the lowest average drawdown (B. below).[4] The 10 CTAs with the lowest average drawdown are compared to the control group because this should create a situation where actual risk in terms of drawdown is reduced. As readers witness below, as drawdown risk statistics improved from the study group of 41 CTAs (A) to the lower-risk top 10 CTAs based on lowest average drawdown (B), the RAD measure more accurately reflects this reduction in risk.

In Table 7.5, the first line, (A. Control Group Av 41 CTAs) shows the average statistics of the control group of 41 high-performing CTAs.[5]

Line A is compared with the second line (B. Lowest Average DD), the less risky subgroup of 10 top CTAs based on lower past average drawdown. As can be expected, the top 10 CTAs had a very low average drawdown (Avr DD), at 4.10 percent, relative to a higher average drawdown for the control group of 7.84 percent, and worst drawdown (Worst DD) moved dramatically lower to 12.56 percent in the top 10 list from 23.60 percent in the control group of 41 CTAs, a significant reduction in risk in real risk. Loss percentage (Loss %) also moved lower while drawdown recovery time

TABLE 7.5 Performance Improvement: Control Study Group of 41 Top-Performing CTAs versus Subgroup of 10 CTAs with the Lowest Drawdown

Study Group	STD	RAD	Loss %	Avr Rec	Avr DD	Worst DD	Cpd An RoR %	Sortino Ratio	RAD/ STD
A. Control Group Av (41 CTAs)	6.76	5.6	38.81%	2.4	7.84%	23.60%	23.90%	8.14	1.6
B. Lowest Average DD (Top 10)	6.8	5.28	36.96%	2.44	4.10%	12.56%	29.64%	12.96	1.52
Differential from Control	−0.04	0.32	2%	−0.04	4%	11%	−6%	−4.82	0.08
% Differential from Control	−1%	6%	5%	−2%	48%	47%	−24%	−59%	5%

Key: STD = Standard deviation of monthly returns; RAD = Reward-adjusted deviation; RAD/STD = Differential between the RAD and STD formula; Loss = Percentage of monthly losses; Avr Rec = Average recovery time in months; Avr DD = Average drawdown; Cpd An RoR% = Compounded annual rate of return from BarclayHedge software; Sortino ratio = Ratio measuring the risk-free rate of return relative to downside deviation—the higher the ratio the more positive the risk profile.

(Avr Rec) exhibited a slight increase. As a side note, compounded returns and Sortino, the measure of risk and reward, improved in the top 10 list relative to the study control group.

All this confirms one point: The Line B group of top 10 CTAs has much better performance statistics—better returns, lower drawdowns. As risk performance lessened, how accurately did the RAD and STD risk measures reflect this lowering of actual risk?

In this study (Table 7.5), the RAD indicator moved lower from 5.60 to 5.28, correctly indicating that CTAs with the lowest past average drawdown and worst drawdown in fact had a lower degree of past risk. However, here is the surprise. STD was expected to move lower, but it actually indicated a higher degree of risk, moving from 6.76 in the control example to 6.8 among the top 10 average drawdown statistic. This highlights a major difference between the indicators.

In this study, when high-performing investments exhibited lowered past risk statistics, the RAD indicator correctly reflected this reality in the study group, while STD did not accurately reflect the improvement in actual past risk.

This study can be independently replicated using high-performing CTA groups and current performance numbers (see Figure 7.1). Such study updates will be posted periodically on the book's web site.

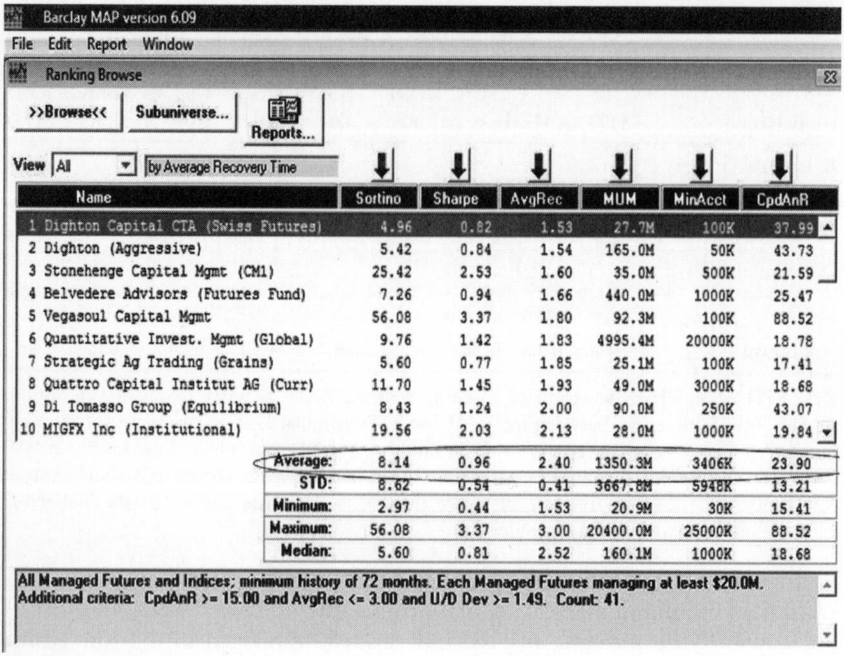

Barclay MAP version 6.09

File Edit Report Window

Ranking Browse

>>Browse<< Subuniverse... Reports...

View All by Average Recovery Time

Name	Sortino	Sharpe	AvgRec	MUM	MinAcct	CpdAnR
1 Dighton Capital CTA (Swiss Futures)	4.96	0.82	1.53	27.7M	100K	37.99
2 Dighton (Aggressive)	5.42	0.84	1.54	165.0M	50K	43.73
3 Stonehenge Capital Mgmt (CM1)	25.42	2.53	1.60	35.0M	500K	21.59
4 Belvedere Advisors (Futures Fund)	7.26	0.94	1.66	440.0M	1000K	25.47
5 Vegasoul Capital Mgmt	56.08	3.37	1.80	92.3M	100K	88.52
6 Quantitative Invest. Mgmt (Global)	9.76	1.42	1.83	4995.4M	20000K	18.78
7 Strategic Ag Trading (Grains)	5.60	0.77	1.85	25.1M	100K	17.41
8 Quattro Capital Institut AG (Curr)	11.70	1.45	1.93	49.0M	3000K	18.68
9 Di Tomasso Group (Equilibrium)	8.43	1.24	2.00	90.0M	250K	43.07
10 MIGFX Inc (Institutional)	19.56	2.03	2.13	28.0M	1000K	19.84
Average:	8.14	0.96	2.40	1350.3M	3406K	23.90
STD:	8.62	0.54	0.41	3667.8M	5948K	13.21
Minimum:	2.97	0.44	1.53	20.9M	30K	15.41
Maximum:	56.08	3.37	3.00	20400.0M	25000K	88.52
Median:	5.60	0.81	2.52	160.1M	1000K	18.68

All Managed Futures and Indices; minimum history of 72 months. Each Managed Futures managing at least $20.0M. Additional criteria: CpdAnR >= 15.00 and AvgRec <= 3.00 and U/D Dev >= 1.49. Count: 41.

FIGURE 7.1 Average statistics of 41 Top-Performing CTAs and Study Methodology
Source: Barclay MAP Database.
The results of the study are listed in Table 7.6 on the first line (A. Control Av Top 41 CTAs) with the point considering the RAD indicator as it relates to STD in this direct comparison with the high-performing group of CTAs. Testing among the high-performing CTAs is the point of the RAD measure, because if it works properly it should work best with high-performing past investments. Past performance is not indicative of future results.

This study (Table 7.6) took the control group of 41 high-performing CTAs (A) and sorted them by the best RAD (B) and STD (C) measures. The 10 CTAs with the lowest RAD and STD measures were compared.[6] As is evidenced from Table 7.6, the RAD measure exhibited higher returns and lower risk measures in every comparable category in the study. The top 10 CTAs based on RAD had a quicker average recovery time, lower average drawdown, lower worst drawdown, and lower loss percentage than STD. As you should expect, the CTAs with the best RAD measure also exhibited the highest past return performance and best Sortino ratio.[7]

This study is revealing and can be particularly useful as a guide to the effectiveness of the RAD measure and can be independently confirmed

TABLE 7.6 Performance Improvement: Top 10 CTAs with the Lowest RAD and Lowest STD versus Control Group of 41 Top-Performing CTAs

Study Group	STD	RAD	Cpd An RoR %	Loss %	Avr Rec	Avr DD	Worst DD	Sortino Ratio
A. Control Av (Top 41 CTAs)	6.76	5.6	23.90%	38.81%	2.4	7.84%	23.60%	8.14
B. RAD (10 Lowest)	3.9	2.8	24.82%	31.96%	2.15	10.47%	29.06%	16.03
C. STD (10 Lowest)	3.66	2.89	17.70%	33.95%	2.26	10.86%	29.92%	11.03
D. Differential from Control	3.1	2.71	6%	5%	0.14	−3%	−6%	−2.89
E. RAD/STD Differential	0.24	−0.09	7.12%	−2%	−0.11	−0.39%	−0.86%	5

Key: STD = Standard deviation of monthly returns; RAD = Reward-adjusted deviation; RAD/STD = Differential between the RAD and STD formula; Loss = Percentage of monthly losses; Avr Rec = Average recovery time in months; Avr DD = Average drawdown; Cpd An RoR% = Compounded annual rate of return from BarclayHedge software; Sortino ratio = Ratio measuring the risk-free rate of return relative to downside deviation—the higher the ratio the more positive the risk profile.

Source: Barclay MAP Database.

Average results and portfolio results are a hypothetical combination of CTAs into a portfolio and these CTAs have not traded together in this fashion in a regulated CPO structure. See the hypothetical risk disclosure in note 7 in Chapter 3. Past performance is not indicative of future results. The point is not to highlight individual CTAs or potential portfolio combinations but rather to illustrate the potential power of diversification as a risk-management tool.

with current monthly data when the following criteria are used: Among CTAs assumed to be high-performing, credible and NFA-audited, when real average drawdown and worst drawdown is reduced the RAD measure should better reflect the reduction in this risk more often than not.

STUDY 3: WHERE CTAs FALL BASED ON RAD

The point of the study in Table 7.7 is to observe how the STD and RAD risk indicators react when actual performance changes both positively and negatively. The better risk measure should indicate less risk when actual risk decreases and should indicate higher risk when actual risk increases.

This study consisted of only CTAs with a 36-month track record, a time frame under which those NFA members have likely undergone at least one NFA performance audit. The study group was broken down into two "good" CTA groups and two "bad" groups. The goal is to watch the STD and RAD indicators to see how they react when performance and real risk has increased and decreased. Instead of looking at a numeric table, this time we consider the view on a risk/reward graphic.

TABLE 7.7 Performance Differential, Good and Bad: Study Groups of CTAs Based on Good and Bad Recovery Time, Drawdown, and Compounded Annual Returns

CTA Study Group	Up Dev	Down Dev	Losing % (mo)	Standard Dev	Comp. Annual Return	Sortino Ratio	Reward-Adjusted Deviation
A. Good: 30+% Cpd An Ret	10.24	4.82	34.20%	10.7	44.31%	12.43	8.32
B. Good: Rec Time 15% Performance	5.82	2.57	30.91%	5.91	29.99%	16.56	4.37
C. Bad: Worst Drawdown 30+%	7.46	5.72	42.66%	9.43	10.33%	1.43	8.9
D. Bad: Rec Time <7% Cpd >30% DD	5.73	5.89	45.50%	5.3	−1.74%	−0.74	8.5

Source: Barclay MAP Database.
Average results and portfolio results are a hypothetical combination of CTAs into a portfolio and these CTAs have not traded together in this fashion in a regulated CPO structure. See the hypothetical risk disclosure in the Notes section. Past performance is not indicative of future results. The point is not to highlight individual CTAs or potential portfolio combinations but rather to illustrate the potential power of diversification as a risk-management tool.

Figure 7.2 graphically illustrates how these study groups would be plotted on a RAD portfolio graphic. Note how when the statistics were positive the RAD did a better job of indicating lowered past risk (top 25 percent returns, top recovery time) and when the statistics were negative RAD did a better job of indicating increased risk (worst recovery time). There is one exception: When return performance was poor (worst drawdown), the RAD and STD were very close in terms of risk measurement, which is part of the point—RAD rewards positive performance because negative performance is assumed riskier to a degree.

Notice in Figure 7.2 that when performance was good the RAD indicated lower risk, and generally when performance was bad the RAD indicated higher risk (with the exception of worst drawdown, with the indicators ending very close to one another.)

The first line in Table 7.7 (A. Good: 30+% Cpd An Ret) is a grouping of all CTAs with at least a 36-month track record with a compounded annual return in excess of 30 percent.[8] On the date of this study this netted a total

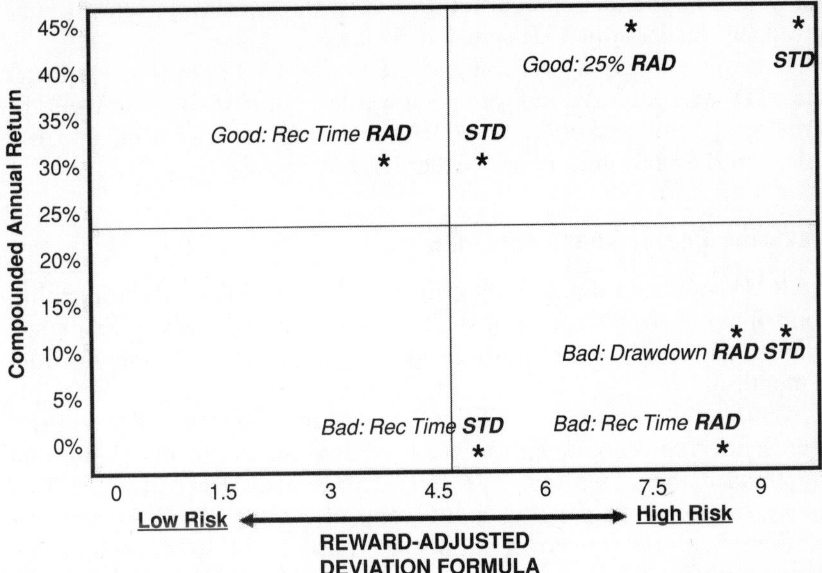

FIGURE 7.2 Performance Differential, Good and Bad: Study Groups of CTAs Based on Good and Bad Recovery Time, Drawdown, and Compounded Annual Returns

of 26 CTAs. The average performance statistics for this group are listed in line A of Table 7.7. It is interesting to note the difference between STD and RAD with high past performance, as evidenced by an average compounded annual return of 44.31 percent. Standard deviation indicated the highest degree of risk in the study (10.7) when returns performance was highest. The RAD indicator treated high performance very differently, indicating that the highest returns performance in fact indicated low relative risk, in the third risk position at 8.32.

The second line in Table 7.7 (B. Good: Rec Time 15% Performance) is a grouping of all CTAs with at least a 36-month track record with compounded annual return of at least 15 percent and drawdown recovery time of at least under two months. This netted 42 CTAs.

The third line in Table 7.7 (C. Bad: Worst Drawdown 30+%) is a grouping of all CTAs with at least a 36-month track record with worst drawdowns exceeding 30 percent. This netted 188 CTAs.[9]

The fourth line in Table 7.7 (D. Bad: Rec Time <7% Cpd >30% DD) is a grouping of all CTAs with at least a 36-month track record, under a

7 percent compounded annual return and with drawdown recovery time exceeding four months. This netted 105 CTAs.

Note, in the "good" grouping of CTAs the RAD indicator was lower than STD, with the RAD indicating a lower level of past risk than the STD. In the "bad" grouping of CTAs the RAD indicator was higher on a relative basis than the STD, indicating a higher level of past risk.

Widen the Performance Measure

The RAD indicator significantly outperformed the STD indicator with a group of high-performing, credible CTAs. But what happens when the study sample is widened by lowering the length of track record to 36 months from 72 months?

This study, documented in Table 7.8, widened the range of the control to only filter based on length of track record (36-month minimum) and compounded annual return (15 percent). This yielded 188 total CTAs. This study group was compared to a subgroup of the top 10 CTAs with the best (lowest) worst drawdown out of the group of 188. In other words we are comparing a subgroup of the least risky CTAs to the overall control group. This group of "good" drawdown CTAs had much better average drawdown, worst drawdown, and recovery time than the control group of

TABLE 7.8 Performance Differential, Good and Bad: Study Group of "Good" CTAs Contrasted with a Subgroup of the 10 Top CTAs with the Lowest Worst Drawdown

Study Group	STD	RAD	RAD/ STD	Loss %	Avr Rec	Avr DD	Worst DD	Cpd An RoR %	Sortino Ratio
36 Months 15+%, 188 CTAs	7.6	6.3	1.3	36.52%	3.08	9.94	27.92	23.36	8.49
Top 10 (Worst DD)	2.41	1.28	1.15	23.82%	1.96	1.65	4.03	19.7	34.28
Differential from Control	5.19	5.02	0.17	12.70%	1.119	8.29	23.89	3.66	−25.79
% Differential from Control	68%	79.76%							

Key: STD = Standard deviation of monthly returns; RAD = Reward-adjusted deviation; RAD/STD = Differential between the RAD and STD formula; Loss = Percentage of monthly losses; Avr Rec = Average recovery time in months; Avr DD = Average drawdown; Cpd An RoR% = Compounded annual rate of return from BarclayHedge software; Sortino ratio = Ratio measuring the risk-free rate of return relative to downside deviation—the higher the ratio the more positive the risk profile.

Source: Barclay MAP Database.

188 CTAs. Further, the Sortino significantly improved, jumping to 34.28 from 8.49. This move could be due to the low degree of negative returns, drawdown months, in the top 10 list and how the Sortino ratio prizes low negative drawdown. Most significant to this study, the RAD indicator was lowered 11.76 percent more than the STD measure, indicating that RAD better measured the actual risk of worst drawdown in the "riskier" control group of 188 CTAs. However, the gap in measure improvement is closing. In part this could be due to the compounded annual return. Note how the returns dropped from the broad average control group to the top 10. And this highlights an interesting component of the RAD measure: It works best at identifying high-performing assets, which is as it should be.

The studies presented in this book scratch the surface of the RAD indicator. Additional studies must consider high-performing investments, which is the point of the RAD indicator.

Negative Return Performance Is the Ultimate Risk

The fact that CTAs with low standard deviation exhibited significantly lower returns than CTAs with a low reward-adjusted deviation demonstrates how standard deviation punishes positive returns performance. This leads to an observation:

Performance to the downside is significantly riskier than performance to the upside. A proper risk measure should understand this fact, particularly as it relates to managed futures. This is why the RAD indicator was developed.

RISK "INDICATORS" DON'T INDICATE RISK

People often identify formulas such as the Sharpe ratio, standard deviation, Calmar ratio, and others as *indicators*, but really they are measuring past performance. Such formulas do not "indicate" as much as they *measure* past performance. For this reason, no risk measurement formula is perfect because in part the formulas are based on past performance, and past performance does not always indicate future results; further, numbers have limited ability to convey the human component in risk.

This chapter does nothing more than begin to highlight the study of a new risk measure. Visit the book's web site for complete due diligence, a white paper providing additional detail on the risk measure's development, and significant testing using the indicator.

On the Book's Web Site

Available to registered book buyers:

- RAD ratings for major CTAs, updated on a monthly basis.
- Download: Further studies of the RAD indicator.

For more information visit www.wiley.com/go/managedfutures.

CHAPTER 8

Protect it

Principal-Protected, Conservative, and Risky Investments*

It has been demonstrated how a Harvard University Professor combined volatility with volatility to theoretically reduce overall volatility. In this chapter the discussion is advanced with a unique twist and a practical application:

Volatile but High-Performing Investment
+ Conservative, Principal-Protected but Low-Performing Investment
= High-Performing Investment with Principal "Protection"

Stock market alternatives, such as managed futures, are accurately categorized as risky investments. Many investors rightfully have difficulty investing in risky assets due to the potential for volatility and drawdown. This chapter reveals a method designed to transform risky assets by adding a principal-protection feature, a rather unique conceptual twist: high-performing uncorrelated volatility and performance surrounded in a conservative principal-protection wrapper.

Sophisticated investors may be familiar with principal-protection products and structured notes. This is because a principal-protected product is marketed as protecting the investment principal so as not to lose more than the initial amount invested while at the same time enjoying upside profit potential; the worst-case scenario is that at the end of the investment period the initial principal invested is returned to the investor. The best-case

*Past performance is not indicative of future results. This book is significantly based on the author's opinions and these opinions are not appropriate for all investors and should not be construed as individual advice.

scenario is that the investor receives significant returns while maintaining the ability to sleep soundly at night with the knowledge his or her principal is protected.

While principal protection can sound like a dream, some protection products might be more a mirage. It is important for investors to understand who is backing the guarantee, as well as understanding factors of inflation, the time value of money and upside profit caps. This is not to say principal-protected products do not have value. In fact, there are rather interesting principal-protection methods revealed in this chapter that enable investors to "do it themselves" without significant fees and upside caps. The key is to enjoy the theoretical peace of mind, which could be viewed as protection's most important benefit, while generating reasonable performance.

In this chapter readers discover:

- Key points in principal protection
  - Source of protection
  - Returns generator
- Do-it-yourself strategies to develop principal-protection products without significant fees or profit caps
  - Step 1: Determine investment minimum
  - Step 2: Determine lockup period and liquidity
  - Step 3: Determine source of protection
  - Step 4: Determine returns generator
- Strategies to maximize returns
- Pure mathematical examples of principal protection

DON'T BE FOOLED

Some principal-protection programs offered on Wall Street give up significant protection money to the issuer of the protection in the form of lost upside potential and fees. Those packaging the principal protection design programs where much of the upside is captured by the provider of the protection by leveraging two factors: perception and the math.

Perception: The protection of an investor's principal is a high-level concept, a comforting and powerful desire. What investor wants to experience the pain of loss? But the question one must consider is who is providing the perception of protection and how "guaranteed" is that protection? For instance, Wall Street titan AIG is a primary guarantor of such investment insurance. While they may have been sold at the time as a powerful Wall Street player, their protection was only as good as a government bailout could provide. This book recommends what are considered solid guarantees that stem from U.S. Treasury debt. But even this seemingly safe guarantor could encounter difficulty in the form of default risk in our debt-laden world.

Math: The second reason returns from many principal-protection products don't find their way into investor hands is due to math. Many of the principal-protection notes are structured with terms that, like insurance tables, state lottery tickets, and Las Vegas odds, are mathematically calculated to benefit the house more than the investor. They are packaged with significant fees and, importantly, carry clauses that limit the investor's upside potential, capturing upside profits for the issuer of the protection. For example, some programs are tied to the stock market and are structured to limit the maximum profit an investor can capture on the risky stock investment, but the losses have no cap. Say the maximum monthly profit an investor is allowed is 3 percent, with unlimited loss provisions. If the risky investment delivered a 6 percent return in a given month, the investor would only receive 3 percent of that gain. In managed futures, with potentially explosive monthly volatility in both directions, this, in particular, would not benefit investors.

The question investors should ask is simple: why?

Why pay the fees and give away the upside potential of an investment? Once the interior of the investment is made transparent, investors can create principal-protection products on their own (with a little help).

How It Works: Like the Wizard of Oz

Looking behind the curtain of principal protection, investors should understand that with a small dose of professional guidance they can create their own principal-protected products without going through the fees and upside caps associated with prepackaged products. To build the program, investors must first understand how principal protection works and break it down to its basic level by understanding the following:

Principal-protected products often consist of two components: the source of the protection and the returns generator, often a riskier investment.

Source of Protection: An interest-paying government-backed bond or corporate note is quite frequently used as the source of protection. If the investor desires to improve returns, he or she can choose alternatives delivering higher returns, but this may also increase the investment's risk profile, potentially compromising the protection guarantee.

Returns Generator: In most principal-protection products, the risky investment is often a long equity or equity derivative investment, but can also be alternative investments such as hedge funds, real estate, venture capital, private equity, or managed futures—any investment that is structured so as not to be subject to more risk than the initial capital invested, which means careful selection of the appropriate limited liability managed futures commodity pool operators (CPOs), if this is the direction for the returns generator. If 100 percent principal protection were an absolute need, this would exclude real estate investments where a mortgage is issued, or certain types of private equity that could require a "capital call," venture capital, or certain direct managed futures accounts that do not offer a limited liability structure.

Returns Generator Derives Its Value from Source of Protection

The risky investment often derives its value from the protected investment. For instance, if the source of protection is a government coupon bond, the interest on the coupon would be utilized as the source of the risky investment capital.

Consider an example using nothing more than illustrative mathematical values:

Assume a total investment of $1,000,000 and a 10-year term of investment, as in Table 8.1 later in this chapter.[1] This investment might include the $700,000 purchase of an interest-bearing note paying 5.75 percent annually. This would be a high interest rate and is optimistic in light of current circumstances but is nonetheless valid for the purpose of explaining the generic academic concept, which is how the examples at the end of the chapter are structured but may not be valid depending on the interest rate environment. This $700,000 principal-protection allocation serves the purpose of providing the guarantee because it could have a value in excess of $1,000,000 in 10 years' time, leaving $300,000 available for the risky returns-generating investment. Assuming the risky investment compounded annual return was 15 percent, to again provide an optimistic mathematical example, the value of the protected investment could grow to near $2,316,167 in 10 years depending on a number of factors including compounding investment returns, fees and commissions, and current interest rates.

Structuring a Principal-Protected Note without Massive Fees or Upside Caps

It is exciting and fun to design a new house in which you plan on living. Homeowners can plan a house to exactly fit their needs. "The allure of the blank page is our best salesperson," an architect once said.

The same can be true with an investor structuring his or her principal-protected investment. The investment can be structured with the underlying principal protection exactly to fit an investor's needs, ranging from a coupon note to a bank guarantee. However, perhaps more significant, the alternative investment can be customized as well. The investor can choose the exact alternative investment portfolio, from hedge fund market neutral to managed futures and more.

FOUR STEPS TO CREATING PRINCIPAL-PROTECTED PRODUCTS

There are four primary steps to developing a principal-protection program, which generally works best when interest rates are higher and the source of protection can generate enough revenue to provide a significant amount in the returns generator.

Step 1: Investment Minimums—Structuring Your Investment

The first step in structuring your own principal-protected investment is to determine the investment size as this will drive the available options.

Investors might be surprised to learn they can structure a principal-protected investment with as little as $150,000, but ideally a custom-designed principal-protection program utilizes a $500,000 investment minimum.

Step 2: Determine the Lockup Period—Consider Illiquidity

Principal-protection products have a lockup period defined by the investment vehicle. For instance, if the source of protection is a seven-year coupon bond, then the duration of the investment is seven years. The interest rate paid is relative to the duration of the investment, with short-term, liquid investments often accompanied by low returns. If the investment product utilized was a 10-year Treasury note, for instance, the investor could sell the note before the note was due and thus receive liquidity of the investment when he or she desired. Investors should consider that liquidating the investment before the redemption period could result in a loss of a certain amount of principal.

Lockup periods can also be determined by the risky investment portion of the investment. If the investment is made in certain hedge funds or venture capital programs that have lockup periods or minimum investment levels, the liquidity of the investment product would be driven by the risky investment.

Step 3: Select a Guarantor—A Guarantee Is Only as Good as the Guarantor

A primary issue with principal-protection products is selection of the conservative interest-rate driven investment. Principal protection might not work well in economic environments where interest rates are low. The lower the interest rate the lower the amount available for the returns generator portion of the investment. As this book is being written, the United States is in a low interest rate environment likely moving to a higher-rate environment, which might not be an optimal point in time to structure such an investment. From a practical standpoint, an interest rate under 5 percent may not provide an appropriate environment, a concept demonstrated in Table 8.2 later in the chapter.

Sometimes principal-protected products are marketed as guaranteed principal protection. However, the term *guarantee* can be misleading. When investing in principal-protected products, remember the investment is only as good as the organization guaranteeing the investment. Any organization can default on its debt obligation—including the U.S. government!

Corporate bonds, real estate structured notes, and foreign debt products can be used for protection, as well as interest-bearing products offered by investment banks. For instance, Goldman Sachs offers principal protection on various investments for a fee. The investment is backed by the Goldman name. The risk is that the organization who issued the guarantee may default.

Consider foreign government bonds. When this is the source of protection, the investor is exposed to what is known as sovereign risk, the risk of the country defaulting on its debt. This common wisdom appears to be the case particularly with emerging markets. Countries have defaulted on their foreign-denominated debt, so this is not out of the realm of possibility. In fact, if you look at emerging market debt from January 1991 to September 1999, the emerging market debt exhibited greater volatility than emerging market stocks. Further, depending on the investment structure, the investor may be subject to foreign currency risk that might need to be hedged.

Consider for a minute U.S. government-backed debt. The common wisdom is that these investments are considered to have no credit risk. However, is that really the case? Can any investment have no risk? While it may seem odd to consider the United States defaulting on its debt, stranger things have happened. In fact, any source of protection, including U.S. government debt, should be considered by the investor to carry a degree of risk.

Step 4: Determine the Returns Driver—High-Performance Managed Futures is One Choice

Now that the "guarantee" component of the investment has been selected, it is time to select the returns driver. This component of the investment is generally a smaller percentage than the entire investment but delivers the significant source of the past returns. This need for significant returns is why stock investments are a likely candidate, but more to the point, it is why managed futures might be a more significant candidate. One consideration here is working with the appropriate managed futures limited liability account structure so that the theoretical protection is not subject to margin calls or leverage issues that theoretically could lay claim to the source of protection if the investment experienced significant drawdowns.[2]

With the basics of the program outlined, it is time to inject adrenaline into this formula with strategies designed to boost returns.

STRATEGIES TO MAXIMIZE RETURN

As was mentioned at the beginning of this chapter, there are methods to improve the returns of a principal-protected product that involve adjustments to the investor's risk profile. These adjustments can have dramatic impacts on performance. As you will see in the studies listed at the end of this chapter, past returns can jump from 6 percent to as much as 20 percent or more if the investor is willing to accept an incremental level of additional risk. Like all investing, the issue is making intelligent risk decisions and understanding the past does not indicate the future.

There are three primary methods to improve returns of the principal-protected product, and all involve adjusting the investor's risk profile. This chapter will outline the adjustments and the level of acceptable risk, and then provide the author's opinion on the appropriate risk/return payoff.

Amount of Protection: Perhaps the most significant method to improve results of a principal-protected product is to make adjustments to the amount of protection being offered. A small change in the amount of protection, from 100 percent to just 80 percent can have the result of doubling or even tripling total returns of the investment, studies show. In this case the investor should ask: Is the doubling of a potential return worth the risk of accepting 80 percent protection rather than 100 percent protection? Of course there are no guarantees regarding any investment performance, which is part of the risk/reward judgment.

Invest in High-Risk Assets: The strategy being set forth is one in which the investor has the potential to achieve significant returns in a principal-protected environment. The intelligent use of certain high-risk assets such as stocks, hedge funds, and managed futures funds can generate significant returns. For certain investors the comfort of principal protection allows them to invest in higher risk/reward assets. It is important to note that appropriate diversification in uncorrelated high-performing assets is recommended along with the appropriate limited liability account structure—keys that can be easily established.

Source and Term of Protection: There are varying sources of protection available to the investor. Some sources provide higher return but also carry with them higher risk. Some terms of protection can provide quick liquidity but also provide very low returns, while other sources of protection provide more significant returns, but carry with them longer-term commitments and are relatively illiquid. But perhaps most significant, some sources of protection can be used as collateral to increase the level of the risky investment. This potentially has a significant impact on returns. As the chapter points out, all sources of protection carry a degree of risk; even government-backed notes. The key is for investors to understand their individual risk tolerance and accept only risks they understand and for which they are being properly compensated. One interesting method to improve returns is to utilize the source of protection as a margin deposit. This component is demonstrated in Table 8.4, but investors must understand that this can theoretically compromise the source of protection depending on margin and leverage issues.[3] (This concept is outlined in Chapter 11 on risk.)

The Largest Factor Impacting Returns

The amount of capital available for the risky investment is perhaps the single most important factor in determining the level of return of the principal-protected investment. The larger the allocation of capital made available for the risky investment, the more dramatic the returns in the sample study. To understand the impact of varying levels of investment, do a little experiment.

Tables 8.1 to 8.4 are hypothetical charts from a mathematical principal-protection calculator. It shows various calculations illustrating how different investment level inputs impact overall returns, only changing the amount of principal protected and the returns for the purpose of making the academic principle clear. All inputs are determined by the investor.

The first example in Table 8.1 mathematically demonstrates how a hypothetical investment of $1 million at the term of the 10-year investment works in a principal-protected environment. The "protection allocation" of 70 percent means that $700,000 is devoted to the source of the principal protection, in this hypothetical case an interest rate product yielding a hypothetical 5.75 percent. Obviously this example can change depending on the interest rate and compounding. The lower the interest rate, the higher the percentage required for the protection allocation and thus the lower the overall return. In this case the aggressive allocation is determined at $300,000, delivering hypothetical compounded annual returns of 15 percent over the term of the investment, which could be considered an aggressive

TABLE 8.1 Hypothetical Principal Protection Example Calculation: Conservative Return 5.75%; Aggressive Return 15%

Principal-Protection Return Calculator		Year	Protection VAMI	Aggressive VAMI
		Start	$ 700,000	$ 300,000
Principal Protection Level	100%	End Yr 1	$ 740,250	$ 345,000
		2	$ 780,500	$ 396,750
Total Investment	$1,000,000	3	$ 820,750	$ 456,263
Term of Protection	10	4	$ 861,000	$ 524,702
Protection Allocation %	70%	5	$ 901,250	$ 603,407
Aggressive Allocation %	30%	6	$ 941,500	$ 693,918
Conservative Return %	5.75%	7	$ 981,750	$ 798,006
Aggressive Return %	15.00%	8	$1,022,000	$ 917,707
Value at End of Term	**$2,316,167**	9	$1,062,250	$1,055,363
		10	$1,102,500	$1,213,667

Note: The purpose of this pure mathematical calculator is to educate investors on how different allocations and return allocations impact performance, and does not infer specific investments. This calculator assumes no compounding on the Protection value-added monthly index (VAMI) but does assume compounding on the Aggressive VAMI, which may or may not be based on any actual example. Calculation Logic: The Protection VAMI calculates interest by multiplying the Start amount by the Conservative Return to obtain a potential amount of interest earned on a yearly basis, the interest amount. This interest amount is added to the previous year (or Start amount) to generate the Protection VAMI amount. The Aggressive VAMI calculates yearly returns by multiplying the Start amount by the Aggressive Return % and then adds these two numbers. This calculation assumes compounding, which may or may not be the case. The following year the Aggressive VAMI is calculated by multiplying the previous year amount by the Aggressive Return. Calculations assume holding investment to term of the protection, no redemptive fees assumed.

return, and the compounding method may or may not be the case. The returns throughout this book are not indicative of any individual investment but rather illustrations for the point of understanding the broad concept.

Under this set of circumstances, the $1 million principal-protected program would have a value of over $2.3 million at the end of the 10-year investment term.

Table 8.1 shows a mathematical calculator where the following items are determined by the user: total investment, term of protection, protection allocation, and return percentage.

Change in Returns: Conservative Returns Lower Table 8.2 assumes that the conservative yield used for protection was reduced to 2.75 percent from 5.75 percent, illustrating dramatic results. This reduction in yield could be

TABLE 8.2 Hypothetical Principal Protection Example Calculation: Conservative Return 2.75%; Aggressive Return 15%

Principal-Protection Return Calculator		Year	Protection VAMI	Aggressive VAMI
		Start	$ 850,000	$150,000
Principal Protection Level	**100%**	End Yr 1	$ 873,375	$172,500
		2	$ 896,750	$198,375
Total Investment	$1,000,000	3	$ 920,125	$228,131
Term of Protection	10	4	$ 943,500	$262,351
Protection Allocation %	85%	5	$ 966,875	$301,704
Aggressive Allocation %	15%	6	$ 990,250	$346,959
Conservative Return %	2.75%	7	$1,013,625	$399,003
Aggressive Return %	15.00%	8	$1,037,000	$458,853
Value at End of Term	**$1,690,584**	9	$1,060,375	$527,681
		10	$1,083,750	$606,834

Note: The purpose of this pure mathematical calculator is to educate investors on how different allocations and return allocations impact performance, and does not infer specific investments. This calculator assumes no compounding on the Protection VAMI but does assume compounding on the Aggressive VAMI, which may or may not be based on any actual example. Calculation Logic: The Protection VAMI calculates interest by multiplying the Start amount by the Conservative Return to obtain a potential amount of interest earned on a yearly basis, the interest amount. This interest amount is added to the previous year (or Start amount) to generate the Protection VAMI amount. The Aggressive VAMI calculates yearly returns by multiplying the Start amount by the Aggressive Return % and then adds these two numbers. This calculation assumes compounding, which may or may not be the case. The following year the Aggressive VAMI is calculated by multiplying the previous year amount by the Aggressive Return. Calculations assume holding investment to term of the protection, no redemptive fees assumed.

due to a number of factors, including the interest rate environment, desire for enhanced liquidity, or perhaps the term of the investment was lowered. Note that the total return dropped by almost half, as the amount needed for protection increased to 85 percent from 70 percent in the previous study. This left only 15 percent asset allocation toward the risky asset, hence a significant reduction in return.

In Table 8.3 consider how returns considerably jump in this mathematical study when the level of protection is reduced from 100 percent of the principal to 80 percent, assuming a 5.75 percent 10-year term on the protection allocation. But this proposition becomes even more interesting when we pledge the interest bearing returns generator as collateral for managed futures, changing the defined nature of risk and reward profile as is done in Table 8.4.

TABLE 8.3 Hypothetical Principal Protection Example Calculation: 80% Principal Protection; Conservative Return 5.75%; Aggressive Return 15%

Web Site Principal-Protection Return Calculator		Year	Protection VAMI	Aggressive VAMI
		Start	$550,000	$ 450,000
Principal Protection Level	80%	End Yr 1	$581,625	$ 517,500
		2	$613,250	$ 595,125
Total Investment	$1,000,000	3	$644,875	$ 684,394
Term of Protection	10	4	$676,500	$ 787,053
Protection Allocation %	55%	5	$708,125	$ 905,111
Aggressive Allocation %	45%	6	$739,750	$1,040,877
Conservative Return %	5.75%	7	$771,375	$1,197,009
Aggressive Return %	15.00%	8	$803,000	$1,376,560
Value at End of Term	**$2,686,751**	9	$834,625	$1,583,044
		10	$866,250	$1,820,501

Note: The purpose of this pure mathematical calculator is to educate investors on how different allocations and return allocations impact performance, and does not infer specific investments. This calculator assumes no compounding on the Protection VAMI but does assume compounding on the Aggressive VAMI, which may or may not be based on any actual example. Calculation Logic: The Protection VAMI calculates interest by multiplying the Start amount by the Conservative Return to obtain a potential amount of interest earned on a yearly basis, the interest amount. This interest amount is added to the previous year (or Start amount) to generate the Protection VAMI amount. The Aggressive VAMI calculates yearly returns by multiplying the Start amount by the Aggressive Return % and then adds these two numbers. This calculation assumes compounding, which may or may not be the case. The following year the Aggressive VAMI is calculated by multiplying the previous year amount by the Aggressive Return. Calculations assume holding investment to term of the protection, no redemptive fees assumed.

TABLE 8.4 Hypothetical Principal Protection Example Calculation: Principal Pledged as Margin, No Theoretical Protection When Pledging Assets for Margin. Conservative Return 5.75%; Aggressive Return 15%

Principal-Protection Return Calculator		Year	Protection VAMI	Aggressive VAMI
		Start	$350,000	$ 650,000
Principal Protection Level	NA	End Yr 1	$370,125	$ 747,500
		2	$390,250	$ 859,625
Total Investment	$1,000,000	3	$410,375	$ 988,569
Term of Protection	10	4	$430,500	$1,136,854
Protection Allocation %	35%	5	$450,625	$1,307,382
Aggressive Allocation %	65%	6	$470,750	$1,503,489
Conservative Return %	5.75%	7	$490,875	$1,729,013
Aggressive Return %	15.00%	8	$511,000	$1,988,365
Value at End of Term	**$3,180,863**	9	$531,125	$2,286,620
		10	$551,250	$2,629,613

Note: The purpose of this pure mathematical calculator is to educate investors on how different allocations and return allocations impact performance, and does not infer specific investments. This calculator assumes no compounding on the Protection VAMI but does assume compounding on the Aggressive VAMI, which may or may not be based on any actual example. Calculation Logic: The Protection VAMI calculates interest by multiplying the Start amount by the Conservative Return to obtain a potential amount of interest earned on a yearly basis, the interest amount. This interest amount is added to the previous year (or Start amount) to generate the Protection VAMI amount. The Aggressive VAMI calculates yearly returns by multiplying the Start amount by the Aggressive Return % and then adds these two numbers. This calculation assumes compounding, which may or may not be the case. The following year the Aggressive VAMI is calculated by multiplying the previous year amount by the Aggressive Return. Calculator assumes holding investment to term of the protection, no redemptive fees assumed.

Change in Protection: Source of Protection Used as Margin To obtain true protection, the source of the protection must be free and clear of issues of leverage or margin, such as certain limited liability commodity pool (CPO) account structures, hedge funds, and stock investments. But consider what happens when the source of protection is in fact collateralized and pledged as margin in a leveraged investment such as real estate or certain direct managed futures accounts. This would create a situation where the theoretical risk profile of the investment would compromise the source of protection, but returns would be dramatically impacted. In effect, the $1,000,000 investment could utilize leverage and operate as if it was a $1,700,000 million investment. Investors should clearly understand the theoretical risks of leverage and margin in this investment as 70 percent of the protection amount, or $700,000, is pledged as initial margin. Under a worst-case scenario in a diversified but leveraged real estate portfolio or diversified managed futures portfolio, the investments would essentially require complete failure in order to jeopardize the source of protection. For the academic purpose of understanding the concept, similar return figures have been used, but no specific investment is being inferred.

Readers unsure of the investment methods can visit the book's web site where an interactive principal-protection calculation application helps guide the reader through the decision-making process. Also note: If managed futures is to be considered as the returns driver, it is recommended the investor utilize a diversified portfolio approach and clearly understand how account structure, margin, and leverage impact theoretical risk.[4]

Margin and leverage risk is highlighted in Chapter 11.

On the Book's Web Site

Available to registered book readers:

- Actual examples of principal protection using current performance circumstances.
- Author's video presentation regarding principal protection.

For more information visit www.wiley.com/go/managedfutures.

CHAPTER 9

Use All of It

Overlooked Points of Correlation*

This book makes the argument that managed futures could be the most uncorrelated major asset class in the world today, and perhaps in history. The argument is based in part on historical studies of returns correlation, but is also based on a conceptual knowledge of the strategies and core contract structure of the futures and options contract itself that provides traders very different options for creating uncorrelated strategies.

Managed futures' powerful correlation factor is possible in part due to the different delivery time frames, slight variations on similar contract product types, different obligation structures available between futures and options contracts, and the ability to easily hedge and go long and short in a variety of worldwide markets. These features that drive what can be considered amazing correlation benefits are only available in the futures and options markets.

This chapter has two primary messages:

1. Managed futures might be the world's most uncorrelated asset class due to its unique contract structure.[1]
2. Traditional returns-based correlation logic is not the best method to determine correlation among managed futures programs: Proper correlation analysis should take place among five points, not just returns.

The chapter touches on this concept, with much more detailed study on the book's web site. While the academic argument is clearly interesting,

---

*Past performance is not indicative of future results. This book is significantly based on the author's opinions and these opinions are not appropriate for all investors and should not be construed as individual advice.

this chapter contains practical applications for today's investors, showing how traditional correlation logic is broken and not only can't get up, but shouldn't get up. For traditional investors, the jolting statement that traditional correlation logic may be misleading can be as much of a shock to the system as the argument managed futures is the world's most uncorrelated asset class. It comes as a shock because the traditional returns-based correlation is how core investment decisions are based, those judgments made to determine what assets to integrate with one another. In other words, traditional returns-based correlation is how assessments and many decisions on diversification suitability are made. In an asset class that is all about diversification, correlation analysis is the foundation, the hard earth upon which a diversified investment is based. But there is a problem. The returns-based correlation analysis most common in today's investing is really a foundation built more on sand than sturdy hard earth.

In managed futures simple returns-based correlation can be deceptive due to the complicated nature of the strategies. Yet complicated strategies are a core reason behind the argument that managed futures is the world's most uncorrelated major asset class.

To illustrate how returns only–based correlation analysis is faulty, consider just one example of a short volatility options strategy detailed later in this chapter. On paper the short volatility strategy can look amazingly uncorrelated to the stock market—until a stock market meltdown like the one in fall of 2008 derails the commodity trading advisor (CTA) and its investors. Investors who only considered correlation of this investment to stocks based on a simple returns correlation paid a significant price indeed in September and October of 2008 when they discovered this option-selling strategy was in fact highly correlated to the stock market during times of major stock market dislocation. The fact is, only those who understood the strategic underpinnings of the strategy were those who could have determined that the options strategy was set to get steamrolled in during stock market turbulence.

That's considerable ground to cover in one chapter, so only what's most important is addressed, saving additional intricate details for the book's web site. This chapter pulls apart the fallacy of returns-based correlation and then offers a solution. To end, the chapter tackles the headline of managed futures noncorrelation, something not often (if ever) done from this unique perspective, with the goal to put the managed futures correlation benefits in perspective.

In this chapter readers learn:

- Managed futures generally shows little correlation to stocks, hedge funds, and significantly even the markets in which the CTAs trade.

- Why managed futures is perhaps the most non-correlated asset class.
  - The reason involves more than a simple price-correlation matrix, but with an understanding of the strategies, contract structure, and markets traded.
- Why traditional correlation logic is broken, particularly as it relates to managed futures.
  - Price correlation doesn't tell the whole story, particularly during times of significant market dislocation and with shorter managed futures track records.
- Proper correlation analysis takes place over at least five points:

  1. Traditional returns-based correlation
  2. Strategy correlation
  3. Markets traded correlation
  4. Volatility correlation
  5. Time frame correlation

IS MANAGED FUTURES THE WORLD'S MOST NONCORRELATED ASSET?

How does one determine if an asset class is the most uncorrelated in history? Particularly an asset class that for all practical purposes only recently matured, if one were to judge maturity based on assets under management?

To support the book's theory that managed futures is the world's most uncorrelated asset class, mathematical correlation returns analysis using a traditional correlation matrix is considered as well as managed futures performance during the previous 10 stock market declines.

The next point made is that the real understanding of why managed futures might be the world's most uncorrelated asset class comes when consideration is given to the unique strategies available only through the sophisticated futures and options contract structures.

The core behind the lack of correlation is the ability of managed futures strategies to be designed to be indifferent to economic circumstances at large. It is interesting to consider that most investments are directly correlated to the economy in some way. Real estate investors, for instance, are long in the market and dependent on economic supply and demand, which means the excess capital generated by a robust economy. Real estate, like commodities in general, can rise in price when a strong economy generates both need and capital to spur root demand. Stocks obviously are spurred on by economic strength. But here is the surprise. As readers discover when a correlation matrix is studied, even hedge funds, which were designed to be a hedge against traditional investments, are surprisingly highly correlated to the stock market and economy at large.

Most investments are correlated to the economy and thus by extension to the stock market and certainly the markets in which they invest—except managed futures. In fact, as you will see, managed futures has not been necessarily correlated to the markets in which they invest, including the commodity markets.

BALANCE RISK AND RETURN: MANAGED FUTURES CUSHION DURING STOCK TURBULENCE

Noncorrelation to the stock market is one headline upon which the managed futures asset class hangs its hat. This is because managed futures indexes have performed well when it matters most: during times of stock market turbulence.

Often much can be discovered about a person based on how he or she reacts during times of crisis. The same can be said of an investment. When the chips are down, when the stock market is buckling at the knees, how does managed futures perform? Consider the Chicago Mercantile Exchange (CME) chart in Figure 9.1 that shows during 9 out of the last 10 significant stock market declines managed futures have performed positively. The study was conducted in February of 2008, before the latest stock market meltdown in the fall of 2008. Updating this study from February 2008, when the stock

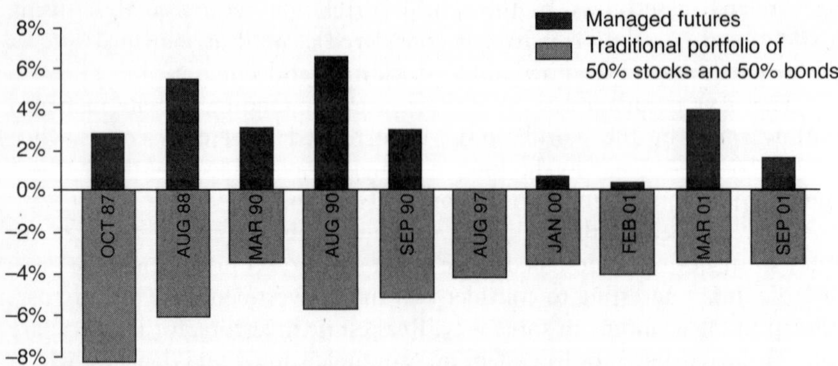

FIGURE 9.1 Managed Futures Correlation Performance during Times of Significant Stock Market Dislocation
Source: Courtesy of CMEGroup.

TABLE 9.1 Correlation Matrix of Stocks, Bonds, and Managed Futures

	Managed Futures	Bonds	U.S. Stocks
Managed Futures	1.00	0.30	−0.23
Bonds	0.30	1.00	−0.29
U.S. Stocks	−0.23	−0.29	1.00

Source: CME Group.
Based on a 10-year period ending December 31, 2007.

market essentially went on another vacation and managed futures babysat its participants again, managed futures has outperformed during 10 of the last 11 stock market meltdowns. This could sound unusual, that an asset class can perform with such past consistency in light of the stock market collapsing around it, but this lack of correlation is its unique attribute.

Significant insight into the investment comes after investors examine the correlation of managed futures to stocks, bonds, commodities, and importantly hedge funds, but it is only the start of this adventure.

In its white paper on managed futures, the CME conducted an interesting study.[2] They considered the correlation of managed futures to stocks and bonds over a 10-year period of time. Managed futures correlated neutrally with both the bond market and the stock market to an impressive extent—more so than other alternatives—as you can see in the correlation matrix shown in Table 9.1.

Investors generally want an investment to perform with indifference to the other asset classes. But that is not all. Managed futures have an interesting noncorrelation to almost everything, including the commodity markets in which they trade. For this reason, managed futures is the single most uncorrelated asset class an investor can choose today.

HOW A CORRELATION MATRIX WORKS

A traditional correlation matrix considers how the returns of various investments move together over a given period of time, averaging each month to determine the correlation.

Table 9.1 contains three investments displayed on a correlation matrix. The assets are listed both horizontally and vertically. In order

(*Continued*)

to determine a correlation between assets, you choose one asset from the top (horizontal) column and match it up with an asset on the left. For instance, comparing U.S. stocks to managed futures in Table 9.1 yields a −0.23 correlation, meaning that the returns of managed futures negatively correlate to stocks 23 percent of the time based on the study parameters used by the CME in their study. Any correlation below −0.70 is considered negatively correlated, meaning the returns or price of an asset move opposite one another, while any correlation above 0.70 is considered positively correlated, meaning the returns move in the same direction. In managed futures, this book considers any correlation beyond 0.50 and −0.50 relatively correlated. A perfect 1.0 means the asset is exactly correlated, the rare level where the returns of one asset exactly mirror the other asset. This generally takes place on the matrix when the same two assets cross.

The goal when building a portfolio is to combine investments that are correlated as close to zero as possible, a rare state of noncorrelation. Correlation values can change depending on the time frame of the study. Correlation matrix work done for this book generally starts from the date of the youngest index or asset. For instance, the correlation study of major indexes in Table 9.2 started in 1997 because this is the date of the youngest index in the study group, the Barclay Hedge Fund index. Also note that for the studies in this book BarclayHedge software was primarily used, but different software and study methodologies can yield different results.

CORRELATION STUDY: MAJOR INDEXES

The CME study was limited to a 10-year period of time and a few asset classes. This book expands that work by adding a significant number of components to the study, and the results amplify what makes this managed futures lack of correlation so interesting.

In Table 9.2 consider how the managed futures asset class (BC CTA) is so noncorrelated to other assets, and even the markets in which the CTAs invest. In this study the correlation to the S&P 500 (SPTR) is −0.16, and we see almost perfect noncorrelation to the Dow Jones Utility Average (Util) at 0.02. This lack of correlation is extended to hedge funds (BC Hdg) at 0.01, near an almost unheard-of zero correlation.

TABLE 9.2 Correlation of Major Indexes

	BC AG	BC CTA	BC FX	BC Disc	BC Div	BC Hdg	BC Sys	CISDM	Indu	Util	MLMI	CRB	RICI	SPTR
BC AG	1.00	0.18	0.01	0.46	0.18	−0.07	0.15	0.20	−0.07	0.03	0.17	0.16	0.16	−0.05
BC CTA	0.18	1.00	0.62	0.51	0.98	0.01	0.99	0.98	−0.17	0.02	0.39	0.22	0.20	−0.16
BC FX	0.01	0.62	1.00	0.23	0.53	0.05	0.61	0.61	0.05	0.11	0.17	−0.01	−0.02	0.02
BC Disc	0.46	0.51	0.23	1.00	0.53	0.03	0.45	0.52	−0.05	−0.02	0.06	0.46	0.39	−0.03
BC Div	0.18	0.98	0.53	0.53	1.00	−0.05	0.98	0.97	−0.24	−0.03	0.44	0.21	0.19	−0.23
BC Hdg	−0.07	0.01	0.05	0.03	−0.05	1.00	−0.03	−0.01	0.67	0.31	−0.21	0.43	0.47	0.76
BC Sys	0.15	0.99	0.61	0.45	0.98	−0.03	1.00	0.98	−0.20	−0.01	0.42	0.16	0.15	−0.20
CISDM	0.20	0.98	0.61	0.52	0.97	−0.01	0.98	1.00	−0.18	0.01	0.41	0.21	0.19	−0.19
Indu	−0.07	−0.17	0.05	−0.05	−0.24	0.67	−0.20	−0.18	1.00	0.38	−0.32	0.20	0.19	0.94
Util	0.03	0.02	0.11	−0.02	−0.03	0.31	−0.01	0.01	0.38	1.00	−0.07	0.24	0.24	0.38
MLMI	0.17	0.39	0.17	0.06	0.44	−0.21	0.42	0.41	−0.32	−0.07	1.00	−0.14	−0.16	−0.33
CRB	0.16	0.22	−0.01	0.46	0.21	0.43	0.16	0.21	0.20	0.24	−0.14	1.00	0.84	0.26
RICI	0.16	0.20	−0.02	0.39	0.19	0.47	0.15	0.19	0.19	0.24	−0.16	0.84	1.00	0.24
SPTR	−0.05	−0.16	0.02	−0.03	−0.23	0.76	−0.20	−0.19	0.94	0.38	−0.33	0.26	0.24	1.00

Source: Barclay MAP Database.

These CTAs have not traded together in this fashion in a regulated CPO structure. These statistics change on a monthly basis and the current month's performance analysis is on the book's web site. Past performance is not indicative of future results. Correlation study methodology was to use an all-period correlation starting from the date of the youngest track record and ending at the point of the oldest track record. This is one of many study methods which may or may not be appropriate. Academic researchers are welcome to download exact study details on the book's web site.

Consider the Barclay hedge fund index (BC Hdg). It is highly correlated with stocks, exhibiting a positive +0.76 correlation to the S&P 500 and an equally troubling +0.67 to the Dow Jones Industrial Average (Indu).

Thus, when the stock market dives lower, hedge funds as an asset class have been likely sharing the ride. This points to an amazing fact:

> *Hedge funds, which were designed to be a hedge against stock market exposure, can be highly correlated to the stock market.*

While the tight correlation of hedge funds to the stock market might come as a surprise to some investors, there is an even bigger surprise to some: the lack of correlation of managed futures to the markets in which it invests.

Consider how uncorrelated managed futures is to the markets in which it invests. Start by looking at the correlation of the Barclay Agricultural Traders index (BC AG) to both the CRB and the Rogers Agricultural index (RICI). The correlation at +0.16 is slight by most standards. The Agricultural index has almost no correlation to the agricultural markets in which it invests. The same is true of the broader Barclay CTA index to the agricultural markets. Consider that the Barclay CTA index is correlated to the Rogers Commodity Index (RICI) by just 0.20 and the Barclay CTA index is correlated to the Barclay Agricultural Traders index (BC AG) by 0.18.

Also interesting to note is that the MLMI index, which is designed to mimic CTA trend following, has little correlation to the Barclay Systematic Traders index (BC Sys) nor to the Barclay CTA index. While this could be a comment on the ineffectiveness of the MLMI index to accurately replicate trend followers in general, it also highlights the amazing low correlation of managed futures. In the author's opinion:

There are literally no major asset classes that have such a low correlation to the markets in which they invest. It is almost unheard of that an investment is uncorrelated to the markets in which it invests, but that is the case with managed futures. As best as can be determined, this is unique in the history of investing.

MANAGED FUTURES NONCORRELATION IS NOT AN ACCIDENT

It is no accident that managed futures indexes are so uncorrelated to the stock market and even the markets in which they invest. This is not a comment on the talent of any individual manager or the markets they trade, although both of these factors are important.

At a high level it is mostly a comment on the strategies available to the managers. As has been outlined throughout this book, futures and options markets enable strategies that can easily go long and short, or spread or option strategies that can easily go both long and short in the same product with different delivery months, or long and short related products, such as soybeans and soybean oil or crude oil and gasoline. And here is one of the most significant yet little-discussed truisms in managed futures: Regardless of the individual CTAs who may come and go, the core contract structure is the primary tool that crafts the product, and that tool is unique because of the contract structure and markets traded.

Consider two brief case studies in correlation that highlight the unique nature of the managed futures asset class.

An Institutional CTA Who Uses Single Stock Futures Instead of Stock

The returns-based correlation of the CTA in Table 9.3 is interesting. A turtle trader in the Richard Dennis–Chicago "school" of trend trading,[3]

TABLE 9.3 Correlation of a CTA That Trades Single Stock Futures to Various Related Indexes

	Lng/Shrt	Hdg Ntrl	CTA 9-1	SPTR	TBILL
Lng/Shrt	1.00	0.48	0.19	0.67	0.21
Hdg Ntrl	0.48	1.00	0.40	0.13	0.30
CTA 9-1	0.19	0.40	1.00	−0.03	0.01
SPTR	0.67	0.13	−0.03	1.00	0.09
TBILL	0.21	0.30	0.01	0.09	1.00

Code	Name
Lng/Shrt	Barclay Equity Long/Short Index
Hdg Ntrl	Barclay Equity Mkt. Neutral Index
CTA 9-1	CTA 9-1
SPTR	S&P 500 Total Return Index (w/Div)
TBILL	Treasury Bills, U.S.

Source: Barclay MAP Database.

These statistics change on a monthly basis and the current month's performance analysis is on the book's web site. Past performance is not indicative of future results. Correlation study methodology was to use an all-period correlation starting from the date of the youngest track record and ending at the point of the oldest track record. This is one of many study methods which may or may not be appropriate. Academic researchers are welcome to download exact study details on the book's web site.

this CTA trades, among other items, futures stock indexes such as the S&P and single stock futures as well as other economically sensitive financial instruments. Having said that, the institutional CTA, founded in 1988 with over $700 million under management and a 13.98 percent compounded annual return with strong risk management, has rather curious correlation statistics.

The CTA exhibits a microscopic −0.03 correlation to the S&P 500 and 0.01 to the Treasury bill, and then a small 0.19 correlation to the Barclay Long/Short Traders index, a measure of hedge funds whose strategy is to go both long and short in various stocks. By contract the Barclay Long/Short Traders index, like other hedge fund indexes, is closely correlated with the stock market at 0.67.

So how can this CTA exhibit such low correlation to the markets in which it trades, and how is the managed futures program different from hedge funds that engage in similar long/short strategies but do not use the futures and options markets?

The point is to identify a managed futures program that trades stocks but is generally uncorrelated to the stock market. Without revealing the individual CTA's strategy, consider on a larger level how CTAs can be so uncorrelated to stocks and other hedge funds who engage in similar tactics.

In part, long/short hedge funds often engage in a strategy of what is known as pairs trading, where both long and short investments are placed in two stocks in a similar category. For instance, a hedge fund might typically go long in Merck and short in Abbott, both pharmaceutical stocks traded on the New York Stock Exchange. Spread trading typically exhibits similar strategies, long one asset and short a related asset.

Managed futures programs have the ability to engage in this strategy but can do so using single stock futures rather than actual shares of stock. This can provide the CTA several benefits, including enhanced capital usage and margin benefits. But perhaps most significant, it provides the CTA additional strategy options. The CTA can trade different delivery months of the same stock, which provides much more diverse opportunities for spread and market-neutral trading than simply trading the actual stock. Here is just one example of how this works:

Hypothetically assume that pharma stock Merck was to have a major product announcement scheduled for the first quarter of 2011.[4] The CTA could go long the March 2011 delivery for the Merck shares but short the September 2011 delivery of the Abbott shares. The core strategic concept of pairs spread trading remains the same, but with future time frames instead of actual stock the spread trader can engage in much more sophisticated and potentially uncorrelated strategies than using stocks alone.

The core contract structure available in futures and options markets, and the different delivery months and leverage usage, often provide enhanced strategy options when compared to the stock market alone.

Because of this, institutional portfolio managers may favor a CTA over another hedge fund because the strategies available to them can be much more sophisticated than a simple long/short hedge fund—and much more transparent and liquid. The managed futures CTA can hedge or spread trade with different delivery months and trade different product nuances, as well as easily short sell options on futures contracts in a capital-efficient environment.

When a decision between hedge funds comes down to one that utilizes futures and options and one that utilizes stocks alone, all else being equal, institutional portfolio managers who understand managed futures might prefer this asset class due to the availability of much more sophisticated and capital-efficient uncorrelated strategies.

Agricultural Traders Don't Necessarily Correlate to Ag Markets

Agricultural CTAs provide another example of how managed futures programs can exhibit very different performance from the underlying markets in which they trade.[5]

In Table 9.4, looking from left to right on the top line, the first two entries, BC Ag and BC CTA, are the Barclay Agricultural Traders index and the Barclay CTA index, followed by two indexes that track the price of commodities, the Reuters Commodity Research Bureau (CRB) and Rogers International Commodity Index (RICI). The next six entries are a sampling of major commodity pool operators (CPOs) or CTAs that trade in the agricultural markets. Note how the agricultural CTAs and even the CTA ag index are uncorrelated to the markets in which they trade and even the general commodity indexes.

Table 9.4's correlation highlights an amazing low correlation characteristic of managed futures. Consider that the Barclay Agricultural Trader's index has a low correlation of 0.29 and 0.23 to the basket of commodities indexes of Reuters Commodity Research Bureau (CRB) and Rogers International Commodity Index (RICI), as do most commodity trading CTAs in this study.

How can it be that an investment is uncorrelated to the markets in which it invests? This book's assertion is this lack of correlation is due primarily to the futures and options strategies available to the CTA, and

TABLE 9.4 Correlation of Major Agricultural CTAs to Commodity Indexes and Agricultural CTA Indexes

	BC Ag	BC CTA	CRB	RICI	CPO 9-2	CTA 9-3	CTA 9-4	CTA 9-5	CTA 9-6	CTA 9-7
BC Ag	1	0.45	0.29	0.23	−0.15	0.2	0.41	0.08	0.38	0.19
BC CTA	0.45	1	0.35	0.28	−0.04	−0.07	0.21	0.05	0.3	0.39
CRB	0.29	0.35	1	0.91	−0.05	−0.07	0.33	0.1	0.13	0.27
RICI	0.23	0.28	0.91	1	0.04	−0.04	0.32	0.11	0.11	0.21
CPO 9-2	−0.15	−0.04	−0.05	0.04	1	0.05	0.17	−0.01	0.08	−0.16
CTA 9-3	0.2	−0.07	−0.07	−0.04	0.05	1	0.17	−0.13	−0.04	−0.27
CTA 9-4	0.41	0.21	0.33	0.32	0.17	0.17	1	0.2	0.11	−0.08
CTA 9-5	0.08	0.05	0.1	0.11	−0.01	−0.13	0.2	1	0.34	0.16
CTA 9-6	0.38	0.3	0.13	0.11	0.08	−0.04	0.11	0.34	1	0.27
CTA 9-7	0.19	0.39	0.27	0.21	−0.16	−0.27	−0.08	0.16	0.27	1

Source: Barclay MAP Database.

These CTAs have not traded together in this fashion in a regulated CPO structure. These statistics change on a monthly basis and the current month's performance analysis is on the book's web site. Past performance is not indicative of future results. Correlation study methodology was to use an all-period correlation starting from the date of the youngest track record and ending at the point of the oldest track record.

the CTA's individual prowess at generating strategies uncorrelated to the markets in which he or she trades. In addition to trading different delivery months, CTAs can also trade the same product type with subtle product differences. Chapter 4 discussed how a CTA can buy feeder cattle and sell live cattle, two similar but slightly different products. Again, these subtle shades of difference allow for unique strategies that might help create a lack of correlation. But it doesn't stop with agricultural CTAs. There are metal-trading CTAs who can buy and sell different delivery months and product types, but also can hedge strategies through long or short trades in gold mining single stock futures. When intelligent CTA strategies and competent, experienced managers are added to the mix, it is this combination with the core markets and contract structures that provide the significant opportunity to create uncorrelated investment opportunity.

Academic papers exist that call managed futures strategies "simple trend following." Simple? Never mind the fact that trend following is but one of the major strategies; the statement is wrong also because of the complicated delivery time frames, subtle product differences, and different short-volatility option structures that are simply not available in traditional stock funds. Anyone who calls managed futures simple doesn't understand the industry and likely won't understand why managed futures, low-correlated to the markets in which they invest, exist. This brings us to an important point: The lack of correlation among assets is important, but the underlying returns logic used to analyze correlation just might be broken, particularly when it comes to systematic market risk, the point where uncorrelated performance could be needed most.

Much like the understanding of why managed futures can be so uncorrelated to practically every market in existence, the logic is dependent on more than a simple returns-based correlation analysis. The true understanding is found deeper and comes from knowledge of the core contract structure, contracts traded, strategy utilized, and markets. This leads to a managed futures truism:

> *Proper correlation planning in managed futures is dependent on much more than simple returns-based analysis.*

True, meaningful correlation analysis occurs when returns-based analysis is accompanied by other correlation logic including strategy, markets traded, volatility, and more. This leads to a conclusion: Traditional returns-based correlation logic, when used in isolation as is typically the case, is faulty.

TRADITIONAL RETURNS-BASED CORRELATION LOGIC IS FAULTY

Intelligent, risk-focused investors might do well to consider a portfolio's true correlation a key point of risk management. In fact, there is an argument to be made that "conservative" portfolios of stocks are actually very risky due to their systemic risk and correlation to the economy, particularly during times of significant market dislocation. The problem is that traditional correlation logic does not accurately identify this risk:

> *A traditional correlation matrix does not accurately convey the systemic market risk during times of significant stress or dislocation, such as during the credit crisis or the 9/11 attacks.*

The problem with this is that it could be argued that a correlation matters most during times of crisis, which on a typical monthly correlation matrix is accounted for only on a fractional basis. In this chapter we highlight a CTA heavily correlated to negative stock market movements who started trading right after the 9/11 tragedy. The CTA's negative performance in the fall of 2008 is not accurately reflective of its overall correlation to the stock market in part because each month is given its own weighting. Thus the two disastrous months in 2008 might be only two of 84 months considered in the overall correlation number. This means that the small fraction of time when systemic market risk is greatest—during times of crisis—the traditional correlation matrix does not place the proper emphasis on this resulting systemic risk.

Traditional correlation logic is broken because it does not tell the whole story. In managed futures the solution is to use the price correlation matrix, but to do so in combination with four other factors. The traditional price correlation matrix does have value by providing a basic indication as to the past correlation of assets to one another. The point is that a traditional correlation matrix only scratches the surface and you cannot judge this book by its cover. The key for investors is to understand the benefits of low correlation and then build managed futures portfolios with the goal to benefit from this low correlation effect.

In order to build those portfolios, it is important to understand the price correlation matrix is but one piece of this puzzle. The best correlation methodology involves at least five primary points:

1. Returns/Price correlation
2. Strategy correlation

3. Market correlation
4. Time frame correlation
5. Volatility correlation

Traditional Returns/Correlation

Price correlation is an interesting and important component of the overall correlation equation. Unfortunately, price correlation is generally the only point of correlation that many portfolio managers utilize. This is a major mistake for several reasons, pointing to the fact that traditional price correlation is important but should be *one consideration* when determining the overall scope of correlation analysis.

The following section explains why.

Modern-Day Issues with Traditional Price Correlation There is one primary issue with traditional returns-based correlation as it relates to managed futures:

> *Price correlation does not consider the CTA strategy or markets traded, which can be critical points of correlation in managed futures that are often not visible in traditional returns correlation.*

This is important particularly during times of financial crisis because in normal market environments many CTAs can seem very uncorrelated to the stock market but might in fact be very correlated when it matters most: during times of crisis. One example discussed here is the S&P Options Strategy, which can seem uncorrelated to the stock market—except during times of crisis.

Assume you were considering an investment in the S&P option premium collection strategy in Table 9.5 before the stock market crashed during the fall of 2008. Table 9.5 shows a price correlation before September of 2008 of two primary CTAs with very low correlation to the stock market, 0.30 and 0.05, before the market meltdown of that year.

If one were to take out the market meltdown, CTA 1a actually looks pretty much uncorrelated to CTA 1b but more importantly to the S&P. A 0.30 correlation to the S&P is reasonably acceptable. But what is most interesting is that CTA 1b's correlation is 0.05 to the S&P 500, looking almost noncorrelated—an amazing state indeed. But this clearly isn't the case with a naked S&P option-selling strategy, as witnessed by Figure 9.2, which shows the CTA's actual reported performance. Essentially at 0.05 CTA 1b looks almost perfectly uncorrelated to the S&P but in fact the strategy was correlated and still is correlated to a catastrophic stock market collapse, a

TABLE 9.5 Correlation of CTAs that Trade Stock Index Options and the Stock Market before Fall of 2008

	CTA 1a	BCXDN	SPTR	CTA 1b
CTA 1a	1	0.01	0.3	0.36
BCXDN	0.01	1	−0.12	0.02
SPTR	0.3	−0.12	1	0.05
CTA 1b	0.36	0.02	0.05	1

Code	Name
CTA 1a	S&P options CTA 1a
BCXDN	Barclay CTA Index
SPTR	S&P 500 Total Return Index (w/Div)
CTA 1b	S&P options CTA 1b

Source: Barclay MAP Database.
These CTAs have not traded together in this fashion in a regulated CPO structure. These statistics change on a monthly basis and the current month's performance analysis is on the book's web site. Past performance is not indicative of future results. Correlation study methodology was to use an all-period correlation starting from the date of the youngest track record and ending at September 2008.

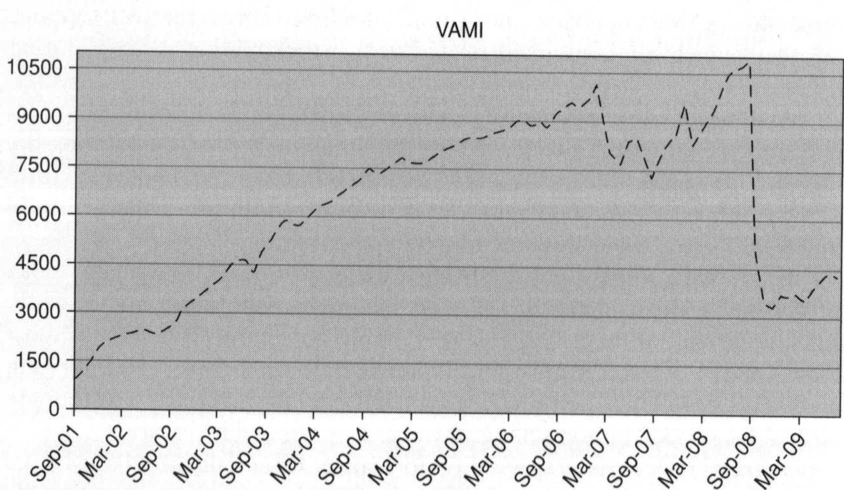

FIGURE 9.2 Actual Reported Performance of CTA 1b

hidden risk that was not evident by considering headline generated from the traditional correlation analysis.

This particular concern is explored further in Chapter 11 when individual manager risk is discussed. For now consider in Figure 9.2 how on a price basis this might have looked uncorrelated to the stock market; however, in 2008 when the stock market tumbled, so did this CTA (Figure 9.2).

When considering price correlation a number of different components should be considered, including price correlation during periods of market dislocation. Ideally the review includes a few periods of market dislocation, but unfortunately in managed futures that often isn't possible due in part to the industry's primary growth spurt over the past 10 years. With short track records, determining a managed futures program's correlation to the stock market could be nothing more than the flip of a coin unless the strategy is understood at a deep level.

For any investor to be on the right side of every market crash is a tall order, if not completely unrealistic. But what investors can attempt to accomplish is to be invested in the right type of markets and right type of strategies to best provide an opportunity to achieve neutral correlation. It is important to be invested where liquidity is deep enough to quickly switch from long to short or short to long, without restriction. The ease with which investors can execute sophisticated long, short, and market-neutral strategies is the case in the futures markets but reasonably rare in other types of investing.

In regards to price correlation, the point is that during a surprise market dislocation, getting it right once is good, but save those "atta-boys" for consistently positive behavior on the right side of a market, which is increasingly difficult.

Strategies Some strategies are more exposed to catastrophic market risk than other strategies, and the problem is, you would never know it from the performance statistics or price correlation unless you understood the strategy.

Consider one example. Remember the CTA grouping from the previous section using a naked option selling strategy exposed to catastrophic stock market risk, as has been previously explained. Conducting a correlation analysis from the start of the strategy, October 2001, to November 2009 is interesting. Table 9.6 considers the correlation of CTA 1a to the S&P 500, the Barclay CTA index, and CTA 1b, another S&P option-selling CTA who also has an interesting story.

First, even after a rough September and October of 2009, CTA 1a is still reasonably uncorrelated to the S&P 500. 0.44 is close to 0.50, but not quite in the high correlation zone. Consider that hedge funds as an asset class are correlated 0.75 to stocks as indicated earlier in the chapter, and it puts the

TABLE 9.6 Correlation of CTAs that Trade Stock Index Options and the Stock Market before Fall of 2008

	CTA 1a	BCXDN	SPTR	CTA 1b
CTA 1a	1	−0.01	0.44	0.41
BCXDN	−0.01	1	−0.18	−0.07
SPTR	0.44	−0.18	1	0.26
CTA 1b	0.41	−0.07	0.26	1

Code	Name
CTA 1a	S&P options CTA 1a
BCXDN	Barclay CTA Index
SPTR	S&P 500 Total Return index (w/Div)
CTA 1b	S&P options CTA 1b

Source: Barclay MAP Database.
These CTAs have not traded together in this fashion in a regulated CPO structure. These statistics change on a monthly basis and the current month's performance analysis is on the book's web site. Past performance is not indicative of future results. Correlation study methodology was to use an all-period correlation starting from the date of the youngest track record and ending at the point of the oldest track record. This is one of many study methods which may or may not be appropriate.

number in perspective. CTA 1a and fellow S&P options trader CTA 1b are correlated to one another at 0.41, near 0.50. But it is interesting that CTA 1b is generally uncorrelated to the stock market at 0.26 on the price correlation matrix, because the strategy actually did not experience monumental losses during both the September 11, 2001 market collapse and the meltdown of 2008. There is another risk point one should consider with correlation during times of major market dislocation: the role of pure luck. Some CTAs can be fortunate to be on the right side of a market during a Black Swan Event and some on the wrong side. Considering past correlation during the statistically limited points of market Black Swan Events calls into question the validity of returns-based correlation only.

But regardless of the past history, it is the strategy that is still exposed to catastrophic market risk, which can only come from an understanding of that strategy, something the correlation matrix doesn't show. The point is that correlation in managed futures can be identified in part by price correlation, but there are other factors, such as strategy and market correlation, that should be considered.

Strategy Correlation

There are a variety of managed futures strategies and it is important to understand which strategies work best in different market environments because this plays into their strategy correlation. For instance, trend traders by their structural design work well when a market starts to move strong in one direction and continues to trend for a significant period of time. On a strategy basis, trend traders are not necessarily correlated to the up or down price movement of any market because they can go long or short. The trend trading strategy, however, is correlated to market environments—something not visible in a correlation matrix and something not often discussed. When markets are indecisive and range bound, trend traders get punished. On the other hand, market-neutral option strategies (short volatility) could benefit during times of indecisive market behavior, the exact opposite market environment that benefits trend traders.

In Table 9.7 it is interesting to note that the Barclay CTA index actually has a very low correlation to various components of the index itself. For instance, the Barclay CTA index correlates just 0.18 to the Barclay Agricultural Traders index, the Discretionary index is correlated 0.51, and the Currency Traders are correlated at 0.62. This relative lack of correlation is not extended to the Barclay Systematic Traders (Trend), illustrating how diversifying within a CTA portfolio can provide benefits. Note that the Barclay Systematic Traders Index, which is essentially compromised of trend followers, the most numerous of all managed futures strategies, is highly correlated to the Barclay CTA index at .99.

The chapter has identified one of many nuances of how strategies correlate to market environments. And that is the point. Each strategy has its own correlation to different types of market events that is not visible from the view of a traditional correlation matrix. In order to properly diversify, the strategies in a portfolio must be uncorrelated and themselves diverse.

The goal when developing portfolios is to create a state of low correlation, and strategy correlation is one important component. This is further demonstrated in the chapter on portfolio building.

For correlation purposes in portfolio building this book recommends categorizing managed futures based on four primary strategies (trend, volatility, spread, and discretionary). The strategies are broken down into these categories because of how they tend to correlate to one another during different market environments.

While strategy correlation is of primary importance, another significant component of diversification involves markets traded.

Markets Traded Correlation

Just as it is not wise to overcorrelate to one strategy, investors are not advised to correlate to one market. The more diversified a managed futures portfolio is relative to markets traded, the better. While tricky market

TABLE 9.7 Correlation of Major CTA and Stock Indexes to One Another

CTA Strategy Correlation

	BC AG	BC CTA	BC Curr	BBC Discr	BC Div	BC Hdg Fd	BC Syst	Dow Indu	Dow Utilit	S&P 500
BC AG	1	0.18	0.01	0.46	0.18	−0.07	0.15	−0.07	0.03	−0.05
BC CTA	0.18	1	0.62	0.51	0.98	0.01	0.99	−0.17	0.02	−0.16
BC Curr	0.01	0.62	1	0.23	0.53	0.05	0.61	0.05	0.11	0.02
BC Discr	0.46	0.51	0.23	1	0.53	0.03	0.45	−0.05	−0.02	−0.03
BC Div	0.18	0.98	0.53	0.53	1	−0.05	0.98	−0.23	−0.03	−0.22
BC Hdge Fnd	−0.07	0.01	0.05	0.03	−0.05	1	−0.03	0.67	0.31	0.76
BC Syst	0.15	0.99	0.61	0.45	0.98	−0.03	1	−0.2	−0.01	−0.2
Dow Indu	−0.07	−0.17	0.05	−0.05	−0.23	0.67	−0.2	1	0.38	0.94
Dow Utilit	0.03	0.02	0.11	−0.02	−0.03	0.31	−0.01	0.38	1	0.38
S&P 500	−0.05	−0.16	0.02	−0.03	−0.22	0.76	−0.2	0.94	0.38	1

Source: Barclay MAP database. Correlation study conducted from date of the youngest index, the Hedge Fund Index, Jan 1997, using BarclayHedge software and rolling correlation methodology.

conditions can plague a variety of markets at some time, spreading investments among a number of different and potentially uncorrelated markets as well as different strategies provides a more significant level of diversification than concentrating on individual markets.

This is one reason trend traders are so attractive: They are mostly diversified among 20 to 40 or more markets. This is also why the S&P naked option selling strategy in one market is more dangerous than is apparent to the untrained eye.

Volatility Correlation

Most people don't consider diversification among volatility, but it is interesting to utilize what is defined as volatility skewing in a portfolio. This is building a portfolio with diversification among various historical standard deviation levels. Consider CTA portfolios that include "conservative, moderate, and aggressive" managed futures programs. Properly skewing a portfolio based on volatility can in fact be an interesting correlation consideration.

Time Frame Correlation

Although it is not as important as strategy and market correlation, trade time frame should also be given a degree of consideration. Some traders may establish positions that last for months and even years while others last just days or weeks. There are many trading legends in the industry known to hold trades for very long periods of time—holding even losers for considerable periods. Integrating such a long-term trader with a shorter–time frame trader can produce a smoother mix of performance and volatility and is a secondary consideration in portfolio building.

NONCORRELATION WITH STOCKS COULD BE THE INVESTOR'S BEST FRIEND

The stock market and the businesses that comprise its core are central to the economic life of any free enterprise system. So when an investment methodology questions the dominance of stocks in investment portfolios it should be done in a careful, balanced manner. But for the purpose of this chapter, understand one important concept: Low correlation to the stock market could in fact be one of the more powerful drivers of investing success on a number of levels, particularly during difficult economic times.

The Amazing Safe Harbor Effect

If the benefit of managed futures providing a potential safe harbor during times of stock market collapse is realized, it is significant in its own right. Any investment that has provided investors a potential hedge against turbulent stock market times merits attention. But here is an important point: The managed futures index has delivered significant returns in both up and down stock markets. The noncorollary benefit of managed futures is perhaps the most significant aspect of managed futures, and it is based on the very structure of the futures market and the unique contract types and strategies resulting from this structure.

The raw returns and lack of correlation speak for themselves. But as readers gaze upon the amazing managed futures index past performance, understand there is no magic investment wand. Before investors get too enamored with powerful past performance, realize that the past is not always indicative of the future. Further, when considering managed futures index returns, recognize that the index performance can be very different from individual manager performance. Further, investing in a managed futures index can be difficult if not impossible at this point in time because there are few if any widely available managed futures index funds. And while the uncorrelation paints an interesting risk picture, be aware that the risks in managed futures are different from those in stocks. There are unique factors and attributes, such as individual manager risk, that any managed futures investor should consider before swimming in these fast-paced waters. These issues and how to manage them are explored throughout the book and on the book's web site.

On the Book's Web Site

Available to registered book readers:

- Additional correlation studies.
- Rolling analysis of managed futures correlation points.
- Download: Correlation analysis guide.
- Download: Tools to assist in correlation planning.
- Author's video presentation regarding correlation.

For more information visit www.wiley.com/go/managedfutures.

CHAPTER 10

Build It

CTA Evaluation and Portfolio Construction*

Discovering a proper solution for portfolio building sometimes requires thinking outside the box to look for an innovative solution; applying rigorous process and thoughtful analysis. While time consuming, the results are more often than not worth the extra effort.

On the surface, investors too often judge commodity trading advisors (CTAs) based on headline performance: compounded annual return, worst drawdown, Sharpe ratio. But does this common method of analysis tell the whole story? In most cases these measures might not be the best method upon which to evaluate past performance, particularly in managed futures.

In managed futures this is true because what lies beneath the surface can matter most. This is due to the importance of the strategy, the trader, and his or her risk-management techniques and business operations—performance-influencing factors not always visible in the headlines.

The author was a researcher in perhaps the most extensive look to date into CTA performance and sustainability with emphasis on survivorship bias. The "CTA Sustainability Study," published August, 2010, considered the difference between successful, surviving CTAs and those that failed. As a result, here are the five key conclusions, part of the book's guidelines for building successful managed futures portfolios:

1. Evaluating CTAs based on a single headline compounded annual return number is perhaps one of the most unreliable indicators of success.

---

*Past performance is not indicative of future results. This book is significantly based on the author's opinions and these opinions are not appropriate for all investors and should not be construed as individual advice.

2. Standard risk measures do not universally work the same throughout managed futures. Certain measures work better than others depending on the trading strategy.
3. Properly selecting uncorrelated strategies and diversifying among risk-appropriate CTAs in a portfolio can shine the most significant light on long-term portfolio performance.
4. Portfolios are best built by focusing on risk and risk management first, letting strong returns follow naturally, and risk management extends into due diligence regarding the CTA's business operations as well as consistency in trading strategy.
5. In managed futures the most important performance measures are those that provide insight into how a CTA manages risk, but the indicators that might best accomplish this task are not the standard, popular measures commonly used in today's portfolio development processes.

These guidelines, combined with proper diversification, might be considered keys to success in managed futures investing. This highlights two essential steps in a due diligence process: individual CTA due diligence and then attentiveness as to how the CTA, its strategy, and markets, traded properly, integrate with other CTAs. The goal is to design a portfolio that includes solid CTAs uncorrelated to each other as well as uncorrelated to the stock market and economy at large.

Managed futures portfolios designed so that solid CTA components are uncorrelated to one another could be one of the more important risk-management techniques.

From one perspective, building a managed futures portfolio could be likened to building an interesting wine cellar with a wide variety of vintages, each suited for a different situation and market environment. A heavy, oak-laden Cabernet could be used for a formal dinner; the firecracker Malbec might be used for situations with a spark, igniting a passion; the breezy Santa Barbara Chardonnay could be used for informal, light settings. Managed futures isn't that different in this odd but interesting regard: Different CTAs work best under certain market environments and conditions. The goal is to design a successful managed futures portfolio, like a diverse wine cellar, that includes components that perform in a variety of market environments. When markets are choppy and trend strategies might falter, a short-volatility strategy in the portfolio might perform. Likewise, a spread-trading strategy might find opportunity during times of fundamental price dislocation, a market environment where a volatility strategy might run into difficulty. The point is to design portfolios with the goal to include diverse strategy components that have the best potential to work well under a wide variety of circumstances, which is a concept behind diversification. There is a statistical logic behind this approach.

In managed futures portfolio building the diversity—the lack of correlation of very different and volatile components—can potentially create a harmonious situation. It is rather a lock and key effect, similar to a good fit with a business partner where one is conceptual and viewing problems from 50,000 feet while the other is practical, detail- and process-oriented, handling day-to-day operations.

This chapter reveals a method for developing the dynamically balanced portfolio that powers high-performance managed futures:

- Highlights of the "CTA Sustainability Study"
- Managed futures portfolio volatility skewing
- Portfolio building using elimination filters
  - Establishing portfolio structure
  - Universal filter criteria
  - Risk, probability, and returns filter criteria
  - Establishment of benchmarks
  - Detailed due diligence

These are the steps in a dynamic process, the results of which are revealed in this chapter, a multistep process to building a portfolio. To begin this journey, the appropriate place to start is with investor goals and risk tolerances.

TRANSLATING INVESTOR GOALS INTO PORTFOLIO DESIGN STRATEGY

Portfolio building starts by identifying several basic components based on investor goals, then establishes appropriate objectives and parameters for a selection process. As identified in this book, particularly in Chapter 3 and in Appendix B, investors should possess a clear indication of the following basic information in order to start building a managed futures portfolio:

Portfolio Stated Objectives

1. Asset allocation: available investment capital
2. Investor risk/reward profile: conservative, moderate, aggressive
3. Tolerance for drawdowns, drawdown recovery time, volatility
4. Investment time frame, access to capital, regulation
5. Specific objectives/correlation needs to other investments

Establishing Portfolio Goals: Portfolio Stated Objectives Document

It is advisable to write down portfolio goals and share these goals with all involved in the portfolio-building process. Following is an abbreviated version of the report used for this chapter's portfolio building exercise.

1. *Asset Allocation*: This exercise targets building an ideal $2.5 million managed futures portfolio using, all risk capital. The allocation to managed futures is 20 percent of the investor's overall investment portfolio.
2. *Risk/Reward Profile*: The portfolios built in this chapter will target a moderate risk profile, as defined in Chapters 2 and 3. The portfolio will be built targeting risk first, with drawdown recovery time as low as possible while past compounded returns fall into the 15 to 30 percent range.
3. *Risk Tolerances*: In this exercise the investor is not as sensitive to individual manager volatility, so long as the overall portfolio generates appropriate performance. The investor is accepting of a design that has larger-than-average volatility (standard deviation) and so long as past drawdown recovery time is reasonably quick, with average past drawdowns in the 5 to 20 percent range and drawdown recovery time three to eight months. The desire is to generate the highest risk/reward profile possible given the moderate risk tolerance. This will allow the managed futures portfolio to be built using a wide variety of CTAs so long as those CTAs are designed to be uncorrelated to one another and generate returns independent of one another.
4. *Time Frame/Access to Capital*: This study assumes a five-year investment time frame for the overall investment but the investor would like the ability to easily access the investment capital. Any long lockup period over one month will be negatively considered in the selection process. This desire for flexible access to capital and transparency will mean the portfolio will be built primarily utilizing audited direct CTA accounts.
5. *Specific Objectives/Correlation Needs Relative to Other Investments*: The hypothetical investor's overall portfolio is highly correlated to the stock market and economy at large. It includes a 60 percent overall investment in the stock market and a 15 percent investment allocation in real estate, with the balance in bonds and other "conservative" interest-bearing assets.

This abbreviated stated objective document is utilized to design a managed futures portfolio in this chapter and use as a benchmark. It is also interesting to note that when benchmarks are set, it is recommended that risk benchmarks are set higher than the actual past performance, highlighting past performance does not indicate future results.

In this chapter we reveal a degree of the logic used to arrive at these decisions. On the book's web site readers can track the performance of this "ideal" portfolio and the real-time decisions, along with the exact methodology used to build the portfolio, the names of all CTAs, screen shots of the software used when developing the actual portfolio, and even the resulting Excel spreadsheets with all CTA data

WHAT IS THE BEST METHOD TO IDENTIFY SUCCESSFUL CTAs?

The common answer might be returns: CTAs with the highest compounded annual return statistic are the most successful. While this may sound logical to some, this simple answer belies the complexity of the managed futures investment. In fact, a single compounded annual return statistic may be among the least reliable methods of identifying successful, sustainable CTA investments. High-flying triple-digit compounded annual return performance so attractive on the surface could really be a sign the CTA is unsustainable and is likely to take a fall. There are methods to analyze past returns and performance that go beyond the headlines that might prove more effective than considering only a simple return number.

Highlights of the "CTA Sustainability Study"

Does the Sharpe ratio provide the best view of risk and reward in managed futures? Is worst drawdown the best risk measure to consider? What makes a sustainable, long-lasting CTA versus a potential one-hit wonder?

The goal of the "CTA Sustainability Study" was to provide insight into what makes a successful CTA, and thus a successful CTA investment. The study started in the first quarter of 2010 and is still being worked on as this book goes to press. The study draws an interesting yet logical conclusion: There is no one "best" risk measure. The insight is that the best performance measures could be dependent on the CTA's strategy.

Investors allocating the same weighting to performance measures common in stock investing could be using the wrong approach in managed futures. For instance, the Sharpe ratio is a common measure used to evaluate the risk and reward of stocks and it bases its measure of risk on standard deviation. As has been outlined, blindly penalizing upside deviation to the same degree as downside deviation might be considered wrong in managed futures, in the author's opinion. Win percentage is another common measure equity investors might consider as a measure of probability. But in managed futures win percentage is a performance measure that is best considered relative to the CTA strategy. For instance, a novice managed futures investor might look at a 70 percent win percentage of a short-volatility strategy and conclude it is a higher probability investment than a trend trader with a 55 percent win percentage. But over the long term this might not be the case.

What Matters When Analyzing Trend Programs In trend trading, win percentage is a statistic that can be relative to the size of win/loss differential as well as upside/downside deviation levels. In the benchmark study in Appendix A, trend trading and spread/arb trading have similar win/loss size differentials as well as similar up/down dev differentials. These two statistics might be among the more important measures for a trend trader. The reason for this again points to risk management. Trend traders with well-conceived risk management programs know how to cut losers short and let winners ride, which would lead to strong win/loss size differential and positive up/down dev numbers. Related to this is win percentage. In the benchmark study, trend traders had the lowest win percentage, at 57.89 percent, highlighting the fact that with trend traders size of win does matter. Another interesting component to consider is how the trend trader handles market environment. For instance, during times of market consolidation that lack price persistence, trend traders can falter—sometimes to significant degrees. The problem occurs when many trend traders utilize the same level of margin and leverage regardless of the market environment. Some trend traders attempt to recognize market environments that lack price persistence and reduce leverage or limit trades during times when market environment might not favor the trend strategy. Some trend traders have an algorithmic scoring model where their computerized system not only gives them a simple buy or sell signal, but provides a scoring for the perceived probability for success of a trade based on a number of factors, including market environment. Thus, trades perceived as highly successful may receive an enhanced leverage allocation while trades perceived as unsuccessful may receive less leverage allocation. To identify these traders, investors should consider an analysis of individual CTA performance compared to the strategy benchmark during times of difficult market environments. For instance, analysis of the 2009 year yields interesting results when considering trend traders who experienced significant losses versus other trend traders who did not. Something to watch out for with trend traders not often considered is the fact that when different commodity and financial markets are highly correlated to one another, even market diversified trend traders can experience de facto position concentration, a risk not easily identifiable. An actively managed portfolio should attempt to consider markets' correlation when managing margin-to-equity ratios so as to expose investors to minimum loss potential. It is interesting to note that trend trading is a different animal entirely than short volatility trading—almost its exact opposite.

What Matters When Analyzing Short Volatility Programs Trend traders can capture profits when identifiable price persistence and volatility breakouts occur. Short volatility strategies, on the other hand, benefit from price indecision, listless markets, and range-bound, countertrend volatility trading, which can occur a large percentage of the time. As such, the volatility strategy has the highest win percentage of all strategies at 74.25 percent, which is a characteristic of the "out-of-the-money, short-volatility" strategy that generally collects smaller-sized wins over many months but is exposed to significant loss during extreme market events. Thus high win percentage is an assumed feature of this strategy. What can matter in a short-volatility strategy is the differential between the worst drawdown and the average drawdown, as well as considering its upside and downside volatility measures. The strategy benchmark is a worst drawdown to average drawdown differential of 24.17 percent, the highest among the major strategies. The drawdown differential with trend trading, for instance, is 15.58 percent. The up/down dev strategy benchmark is 1.41. The short volatility strategy will tend to have low upside deviation numbers based on the fact that option premium time decay is a factor that can move rather slowly, particularly when options are out of the money. It is ideal that short volatility strategies have low downside deviation, which could indicate strong risk management during times when the market moves against them. This is important because it shines light on the CTA's risk management during those statistically rare moments of crisis when the markets inevitably turn against a short-volatility strategy—and far out-of-the-money options are now in the money and behaving with the force of a futures contract. Strong managers using the short-volatility strategy could be said to utilize an equally level-headed risk management program during times of crisis, exiting trades or just sitting on the sidelines during times of outlier events when standard deviation and statistical probability come back to bite the short-vol strategy. When due diligence is conducted on short volatility systems, one focus is generally on how the CTA will handle those rare moments of significant price dislocation: how they potentially roll their options to the forward month or different strike prices or potentially hedge the delta of a short option position with a corresponding future.

The book's web site contains a much more detailed education about each of the primary managed futures strategies and risk factors investors should consider. But one message is clear:

A simple compounded annual return statistic alone does not tell the whole story, a message pounded home throughout this chapter.

If an investor must consider simple compounded annual return, the study points to the fact that combining this analysis with returns distribution analysis using skewness and kurtosis tools and looking for the shape of returns distribution, watching to avoid "fat tail" that could indicate a skew in returns distribution, could be a more effective measure of performance. The study also seeks to address the hot topic of what are the characteristics of CTAs on a road to failure, and some interesting opinions regarding asset growth and volatility are drawn.

This touches the surface of a fascinating study of the best managed futures performance measures, revealing insight into survivorship bias and performance characteristics of surviving CTAs that is utilized in this chapter.

PORTFOLIO BUILDING WITH VOLATILITY SKEWING

Volatility skewing describes a method of balancing of volatility in a portfolio with the goal to reduce overall past portfolio volatility. Individually, CTAs might be volatile but when properly integrated into a portfolio the resulting overall investment exhibits lower combined volatility. For example, of the 13 CTAs included in this chapter's $2.5 million portfolio recommendation, certain CTAs have what the book considers low volatility, moderate volatility, and high volatility, based on standard deviation. Combining this mix of volatility with the goal of reducing overall portfolio volatility is the goal. The consideration for combining different volatility levels into a portfolio is considered volatility skewing in this book.

The unvarnished truth is volatility in managed futures, as in most high-performance investing, cannot be avoided. Attempts to diminish the volatility component of managed futures could be construed as diminishing the potential risk in the investment. While most people fear volatility, a portion of the moderate portfolio's risk capital can often be devoted to uncorrelated high-volatility CTAs while preserving the past moderate portfolio risk profile.

Portfolio Building: Elimination Filtering Process Using Intelligent Diversification

When developing a portfolio it is important to establish a methodical order that is determined by the prioritized goals below. Oftentimes building a portfolio comes down to making choices, setting priorities, and then using these priorities as a template to make decisions and eliminate potential CTAs from consideration.

The decision tree filtering process reduces large pools of potential CTAs by initially using criteria to narrow the list of potentials. The order in which the filters are applied is an important strategic consideration because filters set early in the process can hold a greater degree of influence over the process. Thus, the order in which the list is filtered should be strategically considered. For instance, this exercise considers a risk measure as the first filter, making risk the most important decision criterion. This list of potential CTAs, now limited based on a specific risk criterion, is limited further when a probability filter is applied.

The five-step process in this instance includes:

Step 1: Determine Portfolio Structure: The first step in the process is determining the approximate structure of the portfolio based on strategy diversification. Other correlation considerations will be applied in the detailed due diligence process in Step 5.

Step 2: Universal Filter Criteria: The process filter starts with perhaps two of the more universal criteria, length of track record and assets under management.

Step 3: Risk, Probability, Returns Filtering: These initial filtering steps are based on average drawdown, upside and downside deviation, and compounded returns to narrow the list of potential CTAs.

Step 4: One Difficult Benchmark for Success—Accountability: With the list of potential CTAs filtered based on two universal measures and three primary measures of risk, probability and returns, it is time to establish a benchmark.

Step 5: Detailed Due Diligence and Advanced Analysis: Now that several filters have been applied and benchmark established it is time to really roll up the sleeves and conduct much more detailed due diligence across a number of spectrums and from different perspectives.

Flexible Portfolio-Building System

This portfolio building is flexible, as different search criteria can be substituted depending on client preferences.

While it is advised the basic structure of the portfolio-building process remain intact, investors can change the priorities used in the process at any point. For instance, the basic structure of the process is to start with wide filtering based on search criteria to narrow a list to a manageable perspective, then conduct individual due diligence. In this example the book has chosen risk, probability, and reward, in this order, upon which to filter and then conduct more significant individual due diligence. However, this can be altered to meet individual investor needs.

And this leads us to an important disclosure before we actually reveal how managed futures portfolios are built.

RISK DISCLOSURE

Statistical risk measures are extensively used in this chapter. Statistical risk measures obviously utilize past performance, and past performance is not indicative of future results. There is risk of loss in managed futures investing and only risk capital should be used. The goal of this chapter is to illuminate key principles in portfolio building and not to make individual recommendations. As such, the names of CTAs recommended in the portfolio have been masked so as not to promote any one individual CTA. This chapter combines many subjective and quantitative methods, and it is important to understand several key components. This chapter builds hypothetical portfolios, and it is important to note that the portfolios being built are in fact hypothetical. While the results are from actual results reported by the CTAs, it is hypothetical because the CTAs may not have traded together in a similar fashion in a regulated commodity pool operator (CPO) environment, the book had the benefit of hindsight, see the hypothetical risk disclosure and the Commodity Futures Trading Commission (CFTC) risk disclosure in note 7 for Chapter 3 in the Notes section. What follows are entirely the author's opinions, which are based on his investment perspective and research. These are opinions, subjective in nature and no claim is being made relative to the accuracy, inclusiveness of same.

HIGH-PERFORMANCE MANAGED FUTURES PORTFOLIO-BUILDING EXERCISE

This section reveals, in part, the method for developing managed futures portfolios, which should provide readers a rare glimpse at the foundation of building CTA portfolios.

Step 1: Determine Portfolio Structure

The first step is to determine the ideal portfolio structure based on strategy diversification, and consideration will be given to investing in various CTAs on a drawdown. This is done first because as we run through the elimination filtering process, we will use different performance measures based on each strategy. Further, we may wish to strategically balance the portfolio with heavy weighting to one strategy based on the current market environment and then rebalance the strategy when the market environment is perceived to change. For instance, as of the date of this portfolio building exercise, the trend-following strategy has been in a long drawdown and it might be the appropriate time to invest in the trend-following strategy. Thus, our portfolio will be slightly weighted in favor of trend followers as follows.

Portfolio Strategy Diversification Goals

Trend Following: Approximately 40 percent allocation. Trend trading receives a significantly higher portion of the allocation because it is the author's opinion that the potential exists to invest in this strategy on a drawdown. In 2009 the market did not favor trend following, but this could begin to change, particularly as we enter 2011. Within the trend-following strategy, at least 10 percent of that allocation will be devoted to countertrend traders.

Volatility: Approximately 20 percent allocation

Discretionary: Approximately 20 percent allocation

Spread: Approximately 20 percent allocation

As the market environment changes, we may rebalance the portfolio. The portfolio could also be rebalanced based on statistical asset allocation opportunity based on CTAs in a drawdown.

Investing on a Drawdown In addition to strategically balancing the portfolio based on strategy, we will also strategically invest in very specific CTAs after they have experienced a drawdown, outlined later in this chapter.

Now that a basic structure, a guideline from which to structure the portfolio, has been established, we engage in a process of elimination filtering for all CTAs based on universal measures.

Step 2: Universal Filtering

Universal filtering initially takes place over a large group of managed futures programs and the filters are often common criteria designed to eliminate large numbers of CTAs from consideration. For this education start by looking at all CTAs (indexes excluded) in the BarclayHedge CTA database. The first step is to narrow this extensive list, which is what the first filter will accomplish.

Length of Track Record, Money under Management No measure is perfect to broadly narrow CTA choices because situations are too varied. But the two measures of length of track record and assets under management speak to the universally important measures of core business acumen and trading accomplishment. Interestingly, both of these factors play a role in CTA sustainability to varying degrees. For an individual trader, the road to becoming a successful CTA can be difficult. CTAs are dependent on incentive fees—generating client profit—and this requires a degree of repeatable success. CTAs who make short-term profits but cannot repeat this performance will not experience long-lasting incentive fee income. The dynamic managed futures industry is like a jungle of survival of the fittest; those left standing after three or four years of fast-paced and time-condensing futures trading, a solid track record intact with consistent asset management growth, have in fact passed an important but little-recognized endurance test. Though some deny it, this is true of many CTAs that arrive in managed futures from significant past professional experience. For this reason the minimum track record filter is used as a fundamental component of the filtering process.

Universal Filter: Minimum Track Record 36 Months To start the process, narrow the list of potential CTAs to those with a track record of at least 36 months. Some may say 36 months, encompassing one standard deviation of performance, might not be that long a track record, and under many circumstances they may be correct. The restrictiveness of filtering is often determined by the investment amount and the CTA investment minimums. The goal at the early stages of this filtering process is to keep the potential selection criteria as wide as possible. As the process advances and choices narrow the list of suitable CTAs, the process gets more restrictive based on a number of criteria. Further, if the criteria are narrowed at this point the investor could miss quality programs that may have established strategy offshoots. For instance, a more established CTA with a new risk-management program would not have been included in the final portfolio recommendation, which further reduces selection options.

Once a filter based on at least a 36-month track record is used, then the CTA choices are reduced to 689 possibilities. In Figure 10.1, from left to right: the CTA name, compounded annual return (CpdAnr), upon which the CTAs are ranked (not average return), average drawdown (AvgDD) in months (not worst drawdown), volatility as measured by standard deviation (sdROR), assets under management (MUM), minimum account

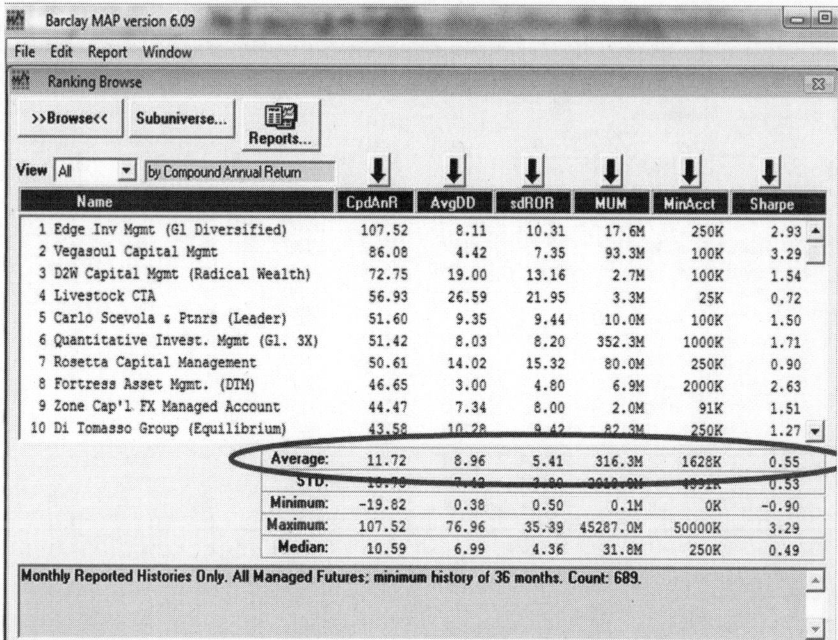

Name	CpdAnR	AvgDD	sdROR	MUM	MinAcct	Sharpe
1 Edge Inv Mgmt (Gl Diversified)	107.52	8.11	10.31	17.6M	250K	2.93
2 Vegasoul Capital Mgmt	86.08	4.42	7.35	93.3M	100K	3.29
3 D2W Capital Mgmt (Radical Wealth)	72.75	19.00	13.16	2.7M	100K	1.54
4 Livestock CTA	56.93	26.59	21.95	3.3M	25K	0.72
5 Carlo Scevola & Ptnrs (Leader)	51.60	9.35	9.44	10.0M	100K	1.50
6 Quantitative Invest. Mgmt (Gl. 3X)	51.42	8.03	8.20	352.3M	1000K	1.71
7 Rosetta Capital Management	50.61	14.02	15.32	80.0M	250K	0.90
8 Fortress Asset Mgmt. (DTM)	46.65	3.00	4.80	6.9M	2000K	2.63
9 Zone Cap'l FX Managed Account	44.47	7.34	8.00	2.0M	91K	1.51
10 Di Tomasso Group (Equilibrium)	43.58	10.28	9.42	82.3M	250K	1.27
Average:	11.72	8.96	5.41	316.3M	1628K	0.55
STD:	[illegible]	[illegible]	[illegible]	[illegible]	[illegible]	0.53
Minimum:	-19.82	0.38	0.50	0.1M	0K	-0.90
Maximum:	107.52	76.96	35.39	45287.0M	50000K	3.29
Median:	10.59	6.99	4.36	31.8M	250K	0.49

Monthly Reported Histories Only. All Managed Futures; minimum history of 36 months. Count: 689.

FIGURE 10.1 Screen Shot of Barclay MAP Software Showing Results of Minimum Track Record Filter
Source: Barclay MAP Database.
These statistics change on a monthly basis and the current month's performance analysis is on the book's web site. Past performance is not indicative of future results. This is one of many study methods which may or may not be appropriate in light of differing individual circumstances.

size (MinAcct) and Sharpe ratio (Sharpe). As we move through this process, note how the average performance statistics, listed at the bottom and circled in Figure 10.1, are going to change once due diligence filters are added throughout this exercise.

Universal Filter: Money under Management Filter Next we filter CTAs based on their assets under management, as evidenced in Figure 10.2. We will set the bar relatively low at $2 million at this point, but might increase this filter as we get further down the process. If a CTA has been in business for three years and has been unable to raise at least $2 million, that would be cause for additional investigation. The CTA sustainability study drew interesting conclusions regarding assets under management—and the trend of assets movement—that points to the fact that stability in assets under management could be an indicator of CTA sustainability. This is not to say

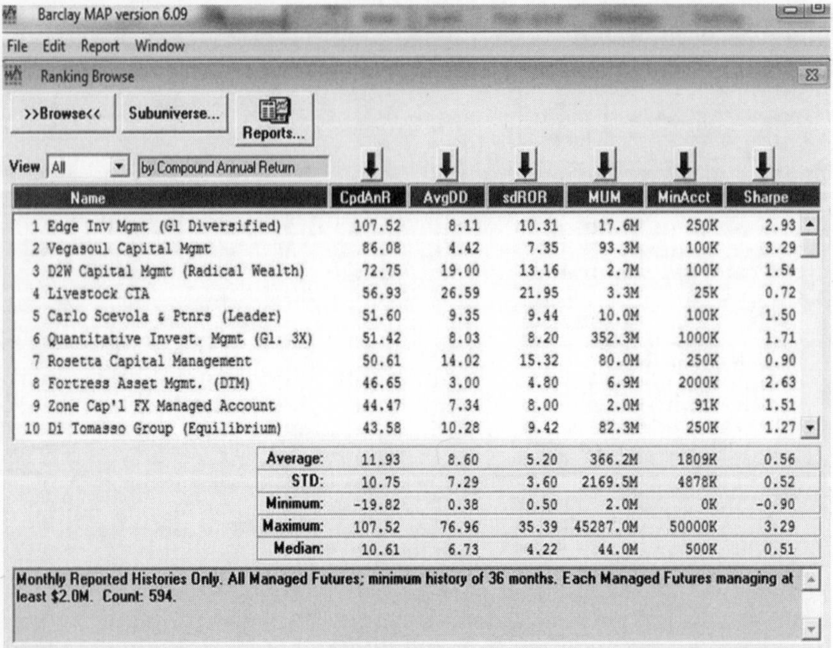

Barclay MAP version 6.09

File Edit Report Window

Ranking Browse

>>Browse<< Subuniverse... Reports...

View All by Compound Annual Return

Name	CpdAnR	AvgDD	sdROR	MUM	MinAcct	Sharpe
1 Edge Inv Mgmt (Gl Diversified)	107.52	8.11	10.31	17.6M	250K	2.93
2 Vegasoul Capital Mgmt	86.08	4.42	7.35	93.3M	100K	3.29
3 D2W Capital Mgmt (Radical Wealth)	72.75	19.00	13.16	2.7M	100K	1.54
4 Livestock CTA	56.93	26.59	21.95	3.3M	25K	0.72
5 Carlo Scevola & Ptnrs (Leader)	51.60	9.35	9.44	10.0M	100K	1.50
6 Quantitative Invest. Mgmt (Gl. 3X)	51.42	8.03	8.20	352.3M	1000K	1.71
7 Rosetta Capital Management	50.61	14.02	15.32	80.0M	250K	0.90
8 Fortress Asset Mgmt. (DTM)	46.65	3.00	4.80	6.9M	2000K	2.63
9 Zone Cap'l FX Managed Account	44.47	7.34	8.00	2.0M	91K	1.51
10 Di Tomasso Group (Equilibrium)	43.58	10.28	9.42	82.3M	250K	1.27
Average:	11.93	8.60	5.20	366.2M	1809K	0.56
STD:	10.75	7.29	3.60	2169.5M	4878K	0.52
Minimum:	-19.82	0.38	0.50	2.0M	0K	-0.90
Maximum:	107.52	76.96	35.39	45287.0M	50000K	3.29
Median:	10.61	6.73	4.22	44.0M	500K	0.51

Monthly Reported Histories Only. All Managed Futures; minimum history of 36 months. Each Managed Futures managing at least $2.0M. Count: 594.

FIGURE 10.2 Screen Shot of Barclay MAP Software Showing Results of Money under Management Filter
Source: Barclay MAP Database.
These statistics change on a monthly basis and the current month's performance analysis is on the book's web site. Past performance is not indicative of future results. This is one of many study methods which may or may not be appropriate in light of differing individual circumstances.

that there are not acceptable CTA choices with under a 36-month track record or $2 million under management, but this filter reflects the level of selectivity one can achieve with higher investment minimums. If this direct CTA portfolio were being built for a $100,000 portfolio, for instance, significant give-and-take sacrifices in past track record and other features would be likely; likewise a $50 million portfolio would further widen selection with high minimum investment CTAs and the criteria could become more selective.

At times when a money under management filter is added it reduces the compounded annual return. In part this could be due to young CTAs reporting high performance, sometimes unsustainable, without significant assets under management. CTAs posting significant performance numbers with a limited number of accounts, short track record, slight assets under management, and importantly before they have received a National Futures

Association (NFA) performance audit, is generally performance that should be treated with an asterisk, interesting but worthy of detailed examination.

Now that we have established the basic filters, it's time to move to more advanced steps.

Step 2: Filtering Based on Risk, Probability, and Returns

To start filtering based on performance measures, we do so independently for each strategy. First we run through the entire process to establish a benchmark, but then we circle back and apply this same filtering process for each strategy. In this example we only run through the process once to establish the benchmark.

In this example a filter function in the search is used to reduce the list of potential CTAs by first focusing on risk, in this case using drawdown recovery time, a generally overlooked measure. After this, a probability measure is used to further filter the list after which returns are considered, applying a very light touch in screening CTAs based on return.

Drawdown Recovery Time Filter In this example, shown in Figure 10.3, the chosen first search criterion is average drawdown recovery time; some may consider this a curious choice. They might prefer to search based on common risk/reward measures such as the popular Sharpe ratio. Drawdown recovery time is an interesting risk measure that can point to potential sustainability. While considering a risk and reward ratio initially might result in a sound selection process, this highlights a key in how intelligent diversification works:

Sharpe ratio considers rewards and is not a true risk-only measure because in its formula the Sharpe ratio considers returns relative to standard deviation. (Additional details on risk measures used in managed futures and their formulas are available on the book's web site.) In this critical initial selection process no measure that considers rewards should be used. The availability of managers that post strong performance numbers isn't the issue; there is plenty of performance, both positive and negative, from which to choose. The issue, and the primary goal, is risk management first in an attempt to identify solid strategies executed by adept and experienced managers and companies.

Average drawdown recovery time is one of the underutilized risk measures. How quickly a CTA can emerge from a drawdown is an important consideration from the standpoint of how intelligent diversification works to reduce overall portfolio volatility. This is not the case with all CTAs, and there are always exceptions to the rule in managed futures. CTAs with quick recovery times may also feature higher standard deviation levels. However,

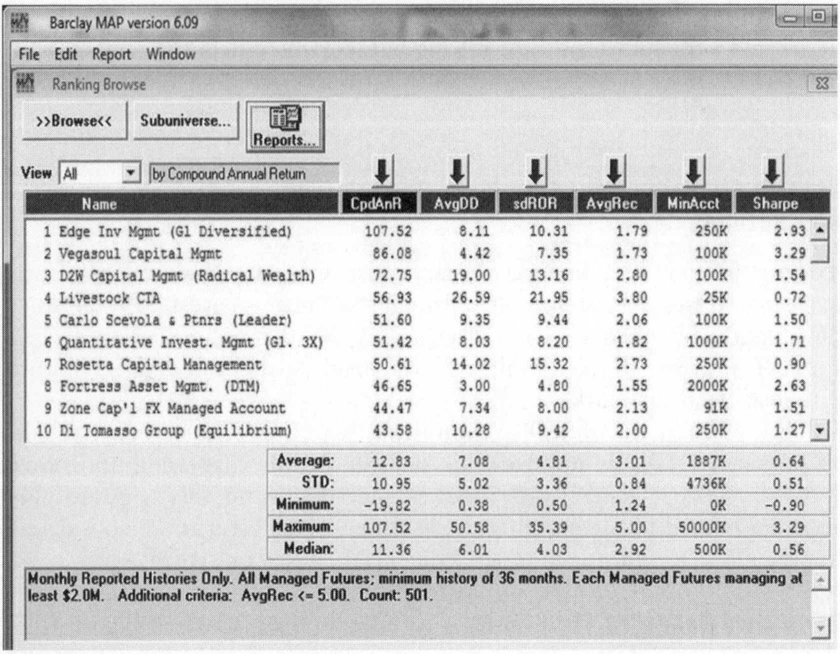

Barclay MAP version 6.09

File Edit Report Window

Ranking Browse

>>Browse<< Subuniverse... Reports...

View All by Compound Annual Return

Name	CpdAnR	AvgDD	sdROR	AvgRec	MinAcct	Sharpe
1 Edge Inv Mgmt (Gl Diversified)	107.52	8.11	10.31	1.79	250K	2.93
2 Vegasoul Capital Mgmt	86.08	4.42	7.35	1.73	100K	3.29
3 D2W Capital Mgmt (Radical Wealth)	72.75	19.00	13.16	2.80	100K	1.54
4 Livestock CTA	56.93	26.59	21.95	3.80	25K	0.72
5 Carlo Scevola & Ptnrs (Leader)	51.60	9.35	9.44	2.06	100K	1.50
6 Quantitative Invest. Mgmt (Gl. 3X)	51.42	8.03	8.20	1.82	1000K	1.71
7 Rosetta Capital Management	50.61	14.02	15.32	2.73	250K	0.90
8 Fortress Asset Mgmt. (DTM)	46.65	3.00	4.80	1.55	2000K	2.63
9 Zone Cap'l FX Managed Account	44.47	7.34	8.00	2.13	91K	1.51
10 Di Tomasso Group (Equilibrium)	43.58	10.28	9.42	2.00	250K	1.27
Average:	12.83	7.08	4.81	3.01	1887K	0.64
STD:	10.95	5.02	3.36	0.84	4736K	0.51
Minimum:	-19.82	0.38	0.50	1.24	0K	-0.90
Maximum:	107.52	50.58	35.39	5.00	50000K	3.29
Median:	11.36	6.01	4.03	2.92	500K	0.56

Monthly Reported Histories Only. All Managed Futures; minimum history of 36 months. Each Managed Futures managing at least $2.0M. Additional criteria: AvgRec <= 5.00. Count: 501.

FIGURE 10.3 Screen Shot of Barclay MAP Software Showing Results of Drawdown Recovery Time Filter
Source: Barclay MAP Database.
These statistics change on a monthly basis and the current month's performance analysis is on the book's web site. Past performance is not indicative of future results. This is one of many study methods which may or may not be appropriate in light of differing individual circumstances.

it is the author's opinion CTAs who recover quickly work well in a properly diversified, uncorrelated portfolio from the standpoint of keeping drawdown risk to a minimum. Statistical evidence exists that some CTAs who have recovered quickly from a drawdown correlate to positive past risk reward ratios, such as the Sharpe ratio. Because the portfolio has a moderate risk profile with a tilt toward above-average returns, drawdown recovery time is used but other risk measures could be substituted based on the investor goals. Average drawdown recovery time is discussed in Appendix D as a powerful yet underutilized risk measure. Certain readers might be wondering why the book did not select worst drawdown as a risk statistic. While this decision is clearly subjective, worst drawdown is not considered at this point because it can be categorized as an outlier event not reflective of the average. In managed futures, worst drawdown might be best to consider as

TABLE 10.1 Comparison of Previous Performance Averages versus Average after Recovery Time Filter

CTA Study Category	CpdAnr	AvgDD	AvgRec	sdROR	Sharpe Ratio
Previous Average	11.93	8.6	X	5.2	0.56
AvgRec Filter	12.83	5.02	3.01	4.81	0.64

Source: Barclay MAP Database.
These statistics change on a monthly basis and the current month's performance analysis is on the book's web site. Past performance is not indicative of future results. This is one of many study methods which may or may not be appropriate in light of differing individual circumstances.

it relates to average drawdown on a percentile basis and relative to size of win. Ideally a degree of consistency in drawdowns is interesting because it could point to a strong risk management, and in part this can be measured based on the variance in drawdown depth. Another interesting consideration is looking at the average losing rate of return as it relates to drawdown statistics, comparing consistency and looking for clues pointing to strong risk management (see Figure 10.3).

Compare the average statistics in Table 10.1 both before and after applying the average recovery time filter. Returns improved, which isn't the consideration at this point; risk management is the first consideration. Average drawdown (AvgDD) improved, as did standard deviation (sdROR), and this is reflected in a positive Sharpe ratio.

Past Probability/Positive Performance Variance Filter With a basic filter on risk in place, the sheer number of CTAs from which selections can be made has been reduced to 501 potential CTAs, as seen in Table 10.2. It is

TABLE 10.2 Comparison of Previous Performance Averages versus Win Percentage Filter

CTA Study Category	CpdAnr	AvgDD	AvgRec	sdROR	Sharpe Ratio
Previous Average	11.93	8.6	X	5.2	0.56
AvgRec Filter	12.83	5.02	3.01	4.81	0.64
Win % Filter	13.11	7.04	3	4.83	0.66

Source: Barclay MAP Database.
These statistics change on a monthly basis and the current month's performance analysis is on the book's web site. Past performance is not indicative of future results. This is one of many study methods which may or may not be appropriate in light of differing individual circumstances.

TABLE 10.3 Comparison of Previous Performance Averages and Up/Down Deviation Filter

CTA Study Category	CpdAnr	AvgDD	AvgRec	SdROR	Sharpe Ratio
Previous Average	11.93	8.6	X	5.2	0.56
AvgRec Filter	12.83	5.02	3.01	4.81	0.64
Win % Filter	13.11	7.04	3	4.83	0.66
Up/Down Dev	14.33	6.8	2.97	4.79	0.72

Source: Barclay MAP Database.
These statistics change on a monthly basis and the current month's performance analysis is on the book's web site. Past performance is not indicative of future results. This is one of many study methods which may or may not be appropriate in light of differing individual circumstances.

time to consider the probability of past success, something that again isn't considered in some standard portfolio-building processes. An important disclosure note: Probability in this book assumes past probability of success, and the past is not necessarily indicative of future results.

In this early-stage filter, several probability measures could be used, such as the less common yet effective force of probability or the more common search filter using win percentage. In Table 10.2 we start by considering the common method of looking at past probability through win percentage, and then we will demonstrate a more effective measure. While win percentage might be considered a statistic that reduces risk, note what happened when this filter was deployed. In Table 10.2 returns improved slightly, but average drawdown jumped to 7.04 percent and volatility actually increased while returns jumped only slightly. Win percentage is a filter that is best used relative to strategy and in combination with other indicators, in the author's opinion.

In Table 10.3 we replace win percentage with upside/downside deviation and notice the difference in performance. Returns jumped significantly, a common feature of this indicator in managed futures, while average drawdown, recovery time, and Sharpe ratio all improved when compared to the win percentage filter. While win percentage may be the common approach, readers should consider what might be an innovative substitute. In managed futures, two significant measures of past probability could be the variance between winning and losing rate of return as well as the variance between upside and downside deviation. Another innovative substitute could be the reward-adjusted deviation (RAD) measure, which considers both upside and downside deviation as it relates to win percentage. As outlined in Chapter 7, the RAD measure is chosen because it considers upside deviation less risky than downside deviation to the extent of win percentage. The Barclay software does not currently have a setting for the RAD indicator, so this calculation is done manually in Excel.

If investors desire a more aggressive portfolio, upside/downside deviation ratio could have been chosen to set a narrow filter, which would have yielded interesting results. The wider the filter the less significance that is placed on that measure as it narrows fewer candidates.

After Risk and Probability, Now Consider Returns Filter After both risk and probability have been considered, it is time to consider returns. For the purpose of this demonstration, a simple filter based on returns is conducted, but on the book's web site are more interesting examples using different filters that don't directly consider returns. While not directly considering compounded annual return in CTA selection may be somewhat controversial, it can yield very interesting results in managed futures. In the initial returns analysis put a basic compounded annual return measure with a low 7 percent minimum hurdle, which might not be the best returns measure but is satisfactory for this basic search filter. In fact, when more detailed due diligence is conducted, consider rolling returns as opposed to compounded returns because here is a key consideration:

> *Returns distribution can be as important as the headline return numbers under certain circumstances.*

In this exercise use a moderate profile target returns of 10 percent to determine the filter. Again, depending on a number of factors, including investment minimum, this filter can be moved up or down. In this case, because the target is moderate risk with higher performance, this level could be considered, but there are issues in this filter eliminating strong programs. For the point of illustration this filter is used, but another interesting filter to use is a ratio of win percentage to average size of win.

This filter does a number of things. First, it dramatically reduces the list of potential CTAs to a more manageable list of potential CTA choices. But perhaps more significantly, a strong rise in compounded annual return that will be a high hurdle, a tough benchmark, as evidenced in Table 10.4. While this might in fact make a good portfolio, it is a party pooper, a dose of reality: In this portfolio the average account minimum is $1.4 million.

TABLE 10.4 Benchmark Performance

	CpdAnr	avgDD%	AvgRec	sdROR	Sharpe Ratio
Benchmark	17.17	7.48	2.88	5.56	0.83

Source: Barclay MAP Database.

These statistics change on a monthly basis and the current month's performance analysis is on the book's web site. Past performance is not indicative of future results. This is one of many study methods which may or may not be appropriate in light of differing individual circumstances.

This highlights a point of detailed due diligence, filtering based on account minimum, which is discussed shortly.

This is interesting. Adding a returns filter does in fact improve returns, but risk statistics worsen. This is one reason this filter was chosen for this chapter, to spotlight the point that filtering based on simple returns does not often generate the best results, and to highlight the risk truism in managed futures: As returns improve, risk rises as well. Because this portfolio is targeting the highest risk/reward ratio in the moderate risk category, this is an acceptable sacrifice. Note a slight worsening of average drawdown to achieve higher returns, which is reflected in the improved Sharpe ratio of 1.07. Again, this filter can be changed to suit individual investor needs.

Step 3: Set a Benchmark

A benchmark is something to which success of an endeavor is compared and is frequently used in financial services. Benchmarks can be critical for some individuals because beating a benchmark in certain industry sectors defines success. In the equity world, for instance, fund managers are always judged based on their success relative to a benchmark, normally the S&P 500, a measure many fund managers find difficult to beat.

In managed futures, one subtle test of intelligent portfolio diversification is that, if correctly executed, the resulting performance statistics should improve with each filter—particularly the risk-performance measures, highlighting the fact not all performance measures are positive. In fact, an interesting clue to the inner workings of any portfolio-building system is how different performance measures are designed to work in building portfolios and the resulting impact on performance statistics.

For the point of this portfolio building exercise use the benchmark shown in Table 10.4.

Now that the CTA list is filtered to what could be considered a relatively select group of CTAs, it is time to set a benchmark, the standard upon which the impact of intelligent diversification will be measured. To set the benchmark, take the average of the remaining CTAs based on five filter components.

THE NEW INDUSTRY BENCHMARK: THE HIGH-PERFORMANCE MANAGED FUTURES (HPMF) INDEX

Why does the managed futures industry need a new index?

This industry requires a benchmark index built based on sustainability that does not rely entirely on voluntary reporting, is reasonably investible, and is a true reflection of the strategy diversification offered in managed futures.

HPMF Index Composition: Managed futures CTAs who are NFA members in good standing are most credible. Thus, the HPMF index will only include CTAs who are members in good standing with the NFA and have undergone a complete NFA performance audit. The index will also be strategy diverse, with no one strategy or trading methodology dominating. Several other filters make this managed futures index unique, including the length of track record, assets under management, availability of investment, investment minimum, as well as specific performance and risk-management requirements. Further, it is confusing for an industry to quote a benchmark index in which investors cannot practically invest. No current managed futures benchmark has these high standards, but in fact these are the minimum standards upon which the industry should be measured. The rules and formula are outlined on the book's web site, as are the reporting methodologies for the major CTA database web sites.

Step 4: Detailed Due Diligence

It is time to engage in more detailed due diligence—that time-consuming and laborious process that will allow us to condense a list of high performers to a list of what are believed to be reasonably appropriate programs. In previous sections absolute filtering was conducted, eliminating from consideration any CTA that did not meet the specific search criterion. Now change the process so the filter criteria become relative, with different values, so the process scores the CTAs rather than eliminates any CTA from consideration. To start, we establish strategy categories and then conduct much more detailed filtering and due diligence. The process will fill each of these categories with the best performing CTAs based on their risk management, letting returns fall where they may. Under ideal circumstances each of these categories has different layers of CTAs with different volatility levels. This is our goal as we consider detailed due diligence.

Past Risk Measures: There are several considerations in this regard, but some of the more innovative are listed here. Several obvious risk considerations are not listed due to space limitations, but a more complete list is available on the web site. For instance, standard deviation is considered, but only to varying degrees based on returns and distribution of the deviation. In managed futures, upside deviation is viewed with a more forgiving light than downside deviation, all based on the strategy, and the upside/downside deviation number is interesting to consider based on sustainability. It is important to look at risk from several standpoints, but perhaps most insightful from the standpoint of strategy risk. Does the strategy have "sleeper" risk that cannot be identified by looking at the performance numbers (much like an S&P options selling strategy)? Returns distribution is considered from the perspective of risk, which isn't something often done. But one of the key points in the CTA sustainability study highlights the importance of returns distribution. This important topic is touched on by providing an example later in this chapter. This due diligence ends by considering several additional risk factors, including providing a rating on the potential for individual manager risk, his or her business and trade execution plan, including risk management plan, and detailed individual manager diligence.

Correlation: After the risk study is conducted in detail, the process tackles a topic that could be categorized in risk as much as it could be in probability: correlation. Perhaps one of the most significant factors in the portfolio-building process is correlation. In fact, it is so important that an entire chapter is devoted to the topic. This study considers CTAs based on a five-point measure of correlation, which was described in detail in Chapter 9 but the critical topic is mentioned here.

Probability: For additional probability due diligence we might consider win size versus loss size, which can be particularly significant in trend following programs. Another consideration is perhaps the controversial method: to consider upside/downside deviation at a much closer level, including relative to percentage of overall wins and the strategy. Consider the force of probability measure outlined in a white paper on managed futures risk measures on the book's web site comparing probability measures relative to the strategy. Then conduct analysis of the strategy probability of success, comparing the individual performance of a CTA to the benchmark in the trading category, considering how the CTA compares to the benchmark based on items including deviation and win percentage, among others.

Returns: After risk and probability heavy lifting is complete, then consider returns. The best method to conduct returns analysis is done through consideration of returns as a function of risk management. One interesting method is to consider returns distribution and, depending on the strategy, the ratio of winning rate of return versus losing rate of return. Alternative methods to consider returns might be consideration of upside deviation as it relates to other risk statistics. However, if the investor must consider simple compounded returns note that this is again the last consideration. Finding high returns in managed futures is not the issue; there is plenty of high performance. The issue isn't high returns, but repeatable performance. Score CTAs based on their performance, but inevitably they might also be scored based on subjective and individual opinion of the individual building the portfolio of the reasonable chance that a CTA and his or her strategy could experience repeatable results. In other words, investors need to determine if the CTA was a "one-trick pony" or has the knowledge, discipline, and skill to develop the appropriate strategy and then execute that strategy in the appropriate markets and at the appropriate times. This is obviously a highly subjective area, but aren't all investment decisions?

At the end of the day all investing decisions are based on opinion that an investment has the appropriate chance for success. Opinions are by nature subjective and can be both right and wrong.

WHY INVESTORS MUST LOOK PAST SIMPLE AVERAGE RETURN HEADLINES

Table 10.5 shows one example of the need to look past headline returns and why many of the CTAs in the list of top performers might not be suitable for the recommended portfolio. The CTA at the top of the list based on reported returns had 108.59 percent compounded annual return, indicating that investors who invested in the CTA received 108.59 percent every year from the start of the offshore trading manager's existence in August of 2005 to October of 2009, the date of this study. On the surface, this CTA appears like Superman: a Sharpe ratio of 2.93 and 108.59 percent compounded annual return and stunning headline performance numbers.

This looks amazing; a Superman CTA that would make any portfolio look like a winner—but it is NOT included in the recommended CTA portfolio below. The most serious issue in this case is the fact the CTA might not be registered with the NFA and may not be subject to the same regulatory environment and auditing protection. While this may not necessarily preclude an investment from consideration, it would require a significant amount of independent due diligence to even consider the CTA, in the author's opinion. But this is not all.

TABLE 10.5 Reported Performance of CTA

Start Date:			5-Aug
Total Return Since Start Date:			2175.16%
Compounded Average Annual ROR:			108.59%
Average Monthly ROR:			6.81%
Standard Deviation of Monthly ROR:			10.41%
Winning Months:	40	**Average Gain:**	10.20%
Losing Months:	11	**Average Loss:**	−5.52%

	2005	2006	2007	2008	2009 YTD
Advisor	7.13%	171.57%	257.12%	132.18%	−5.69%
Barclay CTA Index	3.53%	3.54%	7.64%	14.09%	−0.58%
Funds Managed ($M)	0.1	0.2	1.8	23.3	18.8

Source: Barclay MAP Database.
Past performance is not indicative of future results. This is one of many study methods which may or may not be appropriate in light of differing individual circumstances.

On a practical note, it is the author's Midwestern wisdom that the price of significant reward is equally significant risk. Investors in this CTA have already experienced reward, and they will likely experience risk at some point and when that happens investors may discover that high-flying CTAs can quickly fly in both directions, both up and down. Further, as of this writing the CTA is closed to new investors, who piled into the CTA in 2008 in what looks to an outsider like a case of playing the hot hand. Betting on the hot hand can go cold, as investors in this CTA discovered in 2009. This particular CTA moved from $200,000 in assets under management (AUM) to $23,300,000 in AUM in a rather short period of time. The flow of assets under management is an interesting consideration in CTA sustainability. Such a quick jump in AUM will put to test CTAs and all their skills. It will stress test the strategy, the execution of that strategy, and what is sometimes a "trader's Achilles heel," their business processes. Investors experiencing such a stress test are entertaining a degree of unnecessary risk. Further, there is a potential significant risk in that the CTA is offshore without NFA registration.

This is just one of eight CTAs that were eliminated from the list of top statistical performers, as many top performers in terms of returns are not going to make the due diligence cut due to factors of risk management, probability, and account minimum requirements. This is quite a handicap from the standpoint of trying to create a portfolio that beats the benchmark, but *sacrificing what can appear as attractive returns is sometimes the best risk management strategy.*

THE HIDDEN RISK IN UNEVEN RETURNS DISTRIBUTION

Probability of past success depends on many factors. Many investors consider headline returns numbers without considering the hidden risk behind headline performance and how it can potentially deceive investors, as mentioned earlier in the chapter.

For example, look at headline compounded annual return numbers below and consider how appealing this investment may look.

Compounded Annual Return:	41.35 percent
Sharpe Ratio:	1.43
Average Recovery Time:	2 months
Average Drawdown:	7.50 percent

While these numbers look good on the surface, consider how the returns are actually distributed, per Table 10.6.

For the most part, investors were rewarded with a strong 2004 performance of 47.30 percent, followed by what might seem like compelling 244.46 percent returns in 2005 and more reasonable 29.49 percent returns in 2006. But here is the key: Investors who invested in this CTA after 2006 didn't experience anything near the advertised 41.35 percent annual return. This is an example of a headline compounded annual return number and Sharpe ratio telling a very different story than investors from 2007 forward experienced, when one examines this CTA in more detail from an experienced managed futures perspective. As has been mentioned, returns early in a CTA's life, particularly if that performance has not been audited by the National Futures Association (NFA) or was accomplished with slight assets under management, is performance that should be treated with an

TABLE 10.6 Reported Performance of CTA

2004	2005	2006	2007	2008	2009	2010 (YTD)
47.30%	244.46%	29.49%	14.18%	16.97%	−0.37%	−0.51%

Source: Barclay MAP Database.

Past performance is not indicative of future results. This is one of many study methods which may or may not be appropriate in light of differing individual circumstances.

asterisk—interesting but worthy of further investigation. Further, returns distribution is obviously not even a significant concern in managed futures investing. A somewhat consistent pattern of returns performance can speak to the validity of a trading system and the discipline of its manager. This all highlights the fact that a single compounded annual return number can result in a misleading look at performance.

DON'T JUDGE BY LOOKS ALONE

At the end of the day, investment decisions should be made without any pressure and based on the potential to achieve profitability, and this sometimes means looking past the surface attraction of a strong "looking" portfolio.

Compare the benchmark (Table 10.4) to the recommended portfolio (Table 10.7) and investors will notice some interesting factors. The recommended portfolio has improved performance statistics in every category, most significantly the risk benchmarks. Standard deviation moved to 4.07, and the recommended portfolio had a worst drawdown less than the benchmark's average drawdown. Not pictured is a portfolio drawdown recovery time of 1.75 months compared against a benchmark of 2.88. It is also interesting to consider returns for the year 2010, down −5.97 percent year to date, which might not "look" as good as one would prefer. Conversely, a trained managed futures eye might not like the returns distribution of the abnormally high 2008 performance of 39.43 percent. The negative 2010 YTD performance is due in part to investing in a strategy (trend following) and several CTAs while they are on drawdowns, and the high 2008 performance is due in large part to strong trend trader performance during the year. Here is an important point: Oftentimes it is possible to create a portfolio that looks good by selecting CTAs and strategies that have performed well in the recent past. As has been mentioned, sometimes it is a mistake to follow the hot dot and invest in strategies and managers that currently have the hot hand. The key is selecting a portfolio that might best perform in the future. This can mean selecting a portfolio with slightly lower headline performance statistics. It is also the hidden risk-management factors in the portfolio with lower returns that make the difference in this portfolio. For instance, in this portfolio (Table 10.7), significant diversification exists in layering which can actually reduce past performance statistics. For each diversification category several CTAs were utilized, providing additional but important diversification. It is this ability to layer various diversification components with a variety of CTAs that is one of the book's risk-management techniques. The results of this work can be seen in lower average losing rate of return and lower standard deviation in those losses, hidden risk-management factors

TABLE 10.7 Hypothetical Results of $2.5 Million Diversified Portfolio

Total Return:	57.71%	Avg. Monthly Returns	1.63%
Cmpnd. An. Rtn.:	20.75%	STD Monthly Deviation	2.94%
Last 12 Mo:	5.10%	Sharpe:	1.95
Last 6 Mo:	−0.46%	Sterling:	0.90*
Last 3 Mo:	−2.22%	Barclay:	2.79
Last Month:	−0.86%	Efficiency:	2.04
Winning Mo:	20	Losing Mo:	9
Avg. Win:	3.03%	Avg. Loss:	−1.48%
STD Win:	3.24%	STD Loss:	0.90%
% Winning Mo:	68.97%	% Losing Mo:	31.03%
Worst Drawdown:	4.81%		
Year	**Return**		
2010 (YTD)	−2.22%		
2009	13.98%		
2008	31.59%		
2007 (Partial)	7.54%		

*Calculated values are for the period 11/01/2007 to 03/31/2010.
Source: Barclay MAP Database.
While the results are based on actual returns reported by the individual CTAs, these results are hypothetical because these CTAs have not traded together in a regulated CPO environment and the portfolio was built with the benefit of hindsight. See the hypothetical risk disclosure in note 7 in Chapter 3. Past performance is not indicative of future results.

that point to a potential sustainable investment. But proving the point isn't based on the past; it will be proven right or wrong when you are reading this book several months after the portfolio performance date and can check the updated performance online where much more detailed analysis of this portfolio logic is available.

Timing the Entry of a CTA Investment: Buying on a Drawdown

Is there an appropriate method to allocate to certain CTAs after they have experienced a drawdown or lower allocation after they have experienced a profit surge? There is a handful of studies that discuss the notion of investing in solid programs on a drawdown, including studies in the book *Managed Trading: Myths and Truths.*[1]

Investing on a drawdown requires consideration of a number of factors, including opinions on mean reversion and the cyclical nature of market environments, appropriate strategies, and certain CTA performance. In the author's opinion, selecting appropriate CTAs for investing on a drawdown can include consideration of the CTA strategy and market timing, the ratio of the CTA average drawdown, worst drawdown, up/down deviation levels and recovery time; returns distribution as it relates to market environment timing is also a key consideration. Oftentimes the success in investing in a CTA on a drawdown are based on the CTA's future sustainability and performance persistence, which is never guaranteed.

If CTAs can be identified that have potential to experience cyclical performance behavior and follow mean reversion principals on a somewhat statistical random walk basis, then the opinion might be drawn that investing in sustainable, appropriate CTAs after a drawdown might be preferred to investing after a CTA has captured significant profits outside their statistical norm. Statistical probability drives many managed futures strategies, particularly spread/arbitrage trading, trend following, and to a lesser extent short volatility strategies. These strategies are based on mean reversion and the boundaries of standard deviation of price performance to various extents. If an investor is of the opinion that markets and solid CTAs can be cyclical in nature, then the strategy of investing in traders who are believed to have a strong strategy and risk management after a period of losses in a strategy might make sense. Managed futures is different from stocks where a fundamental change in the company or product can create momentum and emotion and drive prices higher or lower for a sustained period of time. Statistically driven systems attempt to identify patterns and there are market environments where different types of patterns drive market behavior, and their success can come and go. It is important to note that there is a high degree of subjectivity involving the portfolio manager's opinions during the selection and management process. There are no guarantees. Past performance is not indicative of future results.

For this portfolio we have included a wide range of CTA volatilities to illustrate the point that in some cases the selection of investing in a CTA on a drawdown overrode aspects of the filtering process. There are very different risk tolerances and selection considerations when investing in CTAs on a drawdown. Investors should clearly understand the risks and their individual situation in light of this speculative strategy, and CTA recommendations can vary depending on the investor's risk tolerance and individual situation. As of this writing, the wide range of the following CTAs are included in the portfolio as a recommendation to invest on a drawdown. It is not expected that all will be winners, but the goal is that more winners than losers are selected. In this chapter, a method to enter CTA investments

TABLE 10.8 CTAs Invested on a Drawdown Based on Author's Opinions

	CPD An ROR	YTD ROR	2009 ROR	Worst DD	Av DD	Av Rec	STD	Up/ Dwn
CTA 9-1	17.24%	−13.94%	22.02%	−23.16%	−8.97%	2.64	7.04	1.86
CTA 9-2	24.52%	−6.68%	−29.77%	−35.18%	−12.98%	2.45	11.97	2.39
CTA 9-3	43.28%	3.78%	−15.31%	−44.33%	−15%	1.71	13.82	1.67
CTA 9-4	13.61%	−19.31%	−11.01%	−41.09%	−16.66%	2.8	11.68	1.52
CTA 9-5	25.37%	−7.35%	26.75%	−20.41%	−8.09%	3.85	6.5	2.06

Source: Barclay MAP Database.
Performance as of March 2010 reporting cycle. Past performance is not indicative of future results. Investing on a drawdown is a speculative investment and this is one of many study methods which may or may not be appropriate in light of differing individual circumstances. Only risk capital should be used when investing in managed futures.

after a drawdown is not outlined (Table 10.8). The results of "allocating toward a CTA on a drawdown" and the resulting studies are detailed on the book's web site.

Managing Portfolio Manager Bias

It is possible for a portfolio manager to have a bias toward various managers they recommend, which at times may or may not benefit the investor.

A valuable role of a skilled portfolio manager is that, when the portfolio is actively managed, the manager monitors each CTA trading strategy, margin-to-equity ratios, and overall market exposure of CTAs they recommend and thus becomes intimately familiar with the CTA's trade and risk management techniques. This type of knowledge can be beneficial to varying degrees and can result in a certain bias to recommend CTAs with which they are familiar. Thus, bias can be a natural occurrence, as witnessing a CTA's actual daily performance, both positive and negative, can be a powerful confidence builder. A portfolio manager's individual experience could be considered an interesting due diligence point and degree of validity, or it may be construed as individual bias. But here is the real problem: If that bias is based on financial incentive, it can be problematic. Ideally, at the end of the day, everything should be disclosed in writing to the investor. It is advised that investors receive written logic for the recommendations a portfolio manager makes along with a complete disclosure of any potential conflicts of interest. On the book's web site readers can download a disclosure form designed to encourage transparency among CTAs and portfolio managers, as well as analysis of various CTA programs and their projected commission to equity ratios. These are the first known public applications of their kind designed to promote transparency of information not always easily discerned by the investors.

On the Book's Web Site

Available to registered book readers:

- Interactive portfolio-development tool with decision calculator.
- Download: Eight most common portfolio development mistakes.
- Download: White paper and additional studies on allocating to CTAs on a drawdown.
- Download: White paper on investing in emerging managers and a representative portfolio.
- Download: Conflict of interest disclosure form and CTA fees and commissions.
- Download: Various hypothetical portfolio examples and additional studies, ranging from $50,000 to $50 million.
- Professional Download: "CTA Sustainability Study" and how it impacts investors.
- Professional Download: "How to Use Hidden Statistical Measures in Managed Futures to Build Diversified Portfolios."

For more information visit www.wiley.com/go/managedfutures.

CHAPTER 11

Understand It

The Naked Truth Behind Managed Futures Risk*

By most accounts, managed futures' asset class performance and noncorrelation can *appear* amazing. Correlation, drawdown, worst drawdown, and returns tell a compelling story of risk and reward. The positive index performance statistics are hard not to gaze at with awe, but here is a critical insight:

> *The key to success in managed futures is to focus on risk and risk management before returns.*

Don't be blinded by the flashy glitter of returns alone; returns are only one component of a formula. In fact, studies conducted for this book indicate that compounded annual return is the least effective indicator of future success in managed futures. As has been mentioned numerous times throughout this book, investors must understand there is more to the story than attractive returns. Like timeshare programs pitched on exotic vacations, make sure to understand the details and how to manage what can be a different investment.

When the term *managed futures* is discussed, a four-letter word generally comes to mind: risk. While this may be the general impression, the more important question to understand is, "What really makes managed futures a risky investment?" And equally important: "How can investors identify and manage the risk?"

*Past performance is not indicative of future results. This book is significantly based on the author's opinions and these opinions are not appropriate for all investors and should not be construed as individual advice.

It could be said only those with specialized knowledge in financial services understand managed futures and how to manage its related risk. This is in part because some of the investing risks are not always immediately evident. This is true in stocks, hedge funds, managed futures, and even government bonds. While bonds are considered a conservative, rock-solid investment, there is in fact default risk that is generally glossed over because some don't consider the worst-case scenario. The fact is, with mounting government and corporate debt loads, default risk is something "safe" bond investors should consider, much like managed futures investors should understand how to use leverage to dial down potential risk. Once the primary risks are disclosed, it brings the investment's true value into clearest focus.

In this chapter readers discover three primary managed futures risk choke points:

1. Fraud risk
   - The manipulation of investor capital
2. Margin and leverage risk
   - Leverage is a concept homeowners should understand —as should the bankers who were so burned by it.
   - Leverage magnifies gains as well as losses.
   - In managed futures, investors can attempt to manage leverage by dialing it up or down.
   - Margin is a deposit pledged against future potential losses.
   - Margin-to-equity ratios are a key method to identify and manage risk.
3. Individual manager risk: a hidden yet important managed futures risk.
   - Individual manager risk covers all decisions made by the trading manager, which is all-inclusive.
     - Trading strategies utilized
     - Trade time frame and execution
     - Markets in which to invest
     - Risk management
     - Business operations

This chapter attempts to un-complicate a complicated topic and explains in simple terms risk and risk-management techniques. A more detailed and technical description is on the book's web site. This chapter does not purport to have all the answers and is not being represented as a complete look at the complex and elastic topic of risk. In fact, entire books could be written on managed futures risk management. The point is to provide a reasonably significant look at managed futures risk in an easy-to-digest format.

THE SIMPLE WAY TO LOOK AT RISK MANAGEMENT: CHOKE POINTS

Considering all the different risk points of any investment could be a daunting task due to the wide, endless range of possibilities. In stock investing a company could lose a lawsuit that ruins the firm; workers could unexpectedly strike causing major dislocation; new competition or paradigm shifts could render a company obsolete; a hurricane could wipe out a company's production facilities. Looking at the past risk statistics might not always provide a clear picture of risk, particularly in managed futures. This is because each managed futures strategy can have very different risks, and blindly using the same risk measurement across all strategies can be deceiving. If one considers win/loss percentage as a performance measure, short volatility strategies could emerge as the best investment. However, when investors dig deeper, they may consider margin-to-equity usage as a key measure of risk measure and find that these short volatility strategies utilize a high degree of margin, which can represent a significant degree of risk for the strategy, particularly during times of a significant market dislocation. What complicates risk management further is the relatively short track records of some commodity trading advisors (CTAs). For instance, that S&P option strategy can *look* amazing, but if it has not been tested during rare moments of significant stock market dislocation the performance measures can be misleading. Understanding risk management requires an understanding of the CTA's strategy, the markets they trade, and their related margin-to-equity usage.

There are a variety of additional risks the investor can be exposed to; some are outlier risks and some are more common. To name a few: There is market risk, investors getting caught on the wrong side of a fast-moving market, which can happen in any investment; there is related liquidity risk, where the hedge fund manager or a CTA overlooked the deep liquidity in most futures markets and unwisely invested in a thinly traded market where exiting a position was particularly difficult in a fashion close to investments in "penny" stocks; there is strategy risk, where an otherwise intelligent trading system implemented the wrong strategy at the wrong time, similar to a mutual fund manager making the wrong decisions; there is execution risk, where the trade strategy was correct but the execution was improper, which can happen in any investment; there is margin and leverage risk, the primary risk source in a managed futures investment but also an issue with stocks—although the extent of the leverage and the margin structure is somewhat unique in managed futures; there is fraud risk, which, regardless of the best regulation and system, can happen in any investment; there is risk that the CTA's business operations might fail—nothing to do with the trading itself, but interestingly one of the more common reasons for failure of hedge funds. The list of potential risks could go on and on.

Risk management in managed futures can seem elastic, difficult to comprehend considering the sheer scope of the risk to be managed. As such, this book uses a method with the goal of allowing investors to "get their arms around" managed futures by categorizing risk into managed futures risk choke points.

It could be considered that managed futures risk is essentially centered on three categories, or choke points:

- ***Unmonitored Margin and Leverage Risk:*** Margin and leverage are primary measures of day-to-day market exposure used in the next chapter as a method to manage and potentially liquidate CTA investments.
- ***Unsupervised Individual Manager Risk:*** This is the catchall bucket of the wide-ranging, all-encompassing risk of all the CTA manager's decisions, including strategy, markets traded, leverage usage, and business operations. Every action the CTA engages in, and thus all risk, can be linked to the CTA's decisions.
- ***Regulation and Fraud Risk:*** This centers on "Bernie Madoff–type" Ponzi schemes, scams, and other acts of outrageous, unregulated dishonesty.

Of these three topics, it is the author's opinion that the most common in managed futures is margin and leverage risk, an issue investors are exposed to every day; the most significant is individual manager risk because while incidents are few and far between, this risk can represent significant loss; and the most easily preventable is fraud risk, due to strong industry regulation and account segregation.

The chapter will touch on each of these topics and outline methods to manage risk, providing an understanding the source and scope of the risk. Once risk is understood, investors should consider probability and then take steps to actively manage the risk potential.

While reading this chapter, note not only the risk but also pay attention to the important methods to manage this risk, which is further outlined in the next chapter.

Perhaps the most common source of risk, and the most prevalent risk in managed futures, is derived from margin and leverage risk. First understand it from a basic perspective and then consider methods used to manage it.

LEVERAGE CAN MAGNIFY WINS AS WELL AS LOSSES; JUST ASK A BANKER

Leverage is a common principle used in futures investing. It is the notion that the investor puts down a small deposit to control something of a much larger value.

Most investors have purchased a house and likely at one point used leverage. A home buyer who invests 20 percent in a down payment toward the purchase of a $500,000 home is using a $100,000 cash deposit and is using leverage to control the other $400,000 that will be invested in the property. To put it in simple terms:

> *In this case the homeowner used a $100,000 cash value to control an investment with a $500,000 value. This is leverage.*

Leverage became a messy issue in 2008 when the general public started to understand the leverage used by banks in making mortgages. Not only were homeowners highly leveraged to get a mortgage, but the banks were leveraged on top of their homeowners' leverage. When a $1,000 deposit was made in a bank that deposit may actually have been loaned out by the bank as many as 15 times; some investment banks actually used 30 or 40 to 1 and government entities Freddie and Fannie Mae supposedly may have used upwards of 100 to 1 leverage, a dialing up of leverage.

The point is clearly being made that all leverage can be a dangerous, risky concept if not properly managed, and this concept extends past the futures and options markets into everyday, common investments such as real estate. Importantly, in managed futures there are several key aspects to strategically managing leverage that can reduce investors' exposure.

The Investor Can Attempt to Dial Up and Dial Down Leverage

As has been previously outlined in Chapter 3, beware: Leverage can work both for and against an investor, and when an investor uses what is known as notional funding to increase returns, this can also magnify losses. While it is not often discussed or offered to clients, it is possible for investors to determine the level of leverage they use. Conservative investors, for instance, can dial down the leverage in managed futures as was done in the moderate portfolio in Chapter 3; more aggressive investors can dial up the leverage. Aggressive, qualified investors who understand the risk and are utilizing risk capital might choose to increase the leverage of an account through notional funding. While many CTAs allow investors to increase their leverage through notional funding, investors must sign risk disclosures stating they understand the risk and reward of doing so.

Notional funding significantly magnifies the risk of an already risky investment. The following is an example.

Assume an investor allocated $100,000 in actual cash to invest in a CTA with a $200,000 account minimum. The CTA would allow notional funding to the 50 percent level and the investor would deposit $100,000 and then pledge another $100,000 in notional funding. Based on the nominal account size of $200,000 the CTA used a 35 percent margin-to-equity ratio. However, with notional funding the margin-to-equity ratio actually doubled to 70 percent and the risk in the account, based on margin usage and the potential for a margin call, doubled. If the CTA were to report a 10 percent loss, that loss is reported based on the full, nominal $200,000 investment amount. If the account were notionally funded at $100,000, then the actual loss the client would have received on his or her actual cash investment of $100,000 would have doubled on a percentile basis: The notionally funded account would have experienced a 20 percent loss on the initial cash deposit of $100,000. As you might expect, when notional funding is utilized investors could increase the likelihood of receiving a margin call.

Margin calls are not always considered negative by some investors utilizing appropriate master account structures, but a method of investing to get the most usage out of their risk capital. Qualified investors with appropriate risk capital often utilize master account structures where all capital is placed in one master account and then moved from CTA to CTA as margin needs dictate. These accounts are required to be funded to the appropriate levels, but much of the margin excess can be used where needed. Qualified investors who engage in this activity should have deep pockets of liquid capital on hand just in case it is needed.

Now that margin is mentioned, explore the concept of pledging money against potential loss rather than buying or selling something.

Margin: Buying Without Paying and Selling What You Don't Own

When investing in managed futures, the investor is essentially providing the CTA a margin deposit to trade his account. The CTA is granted power of attorney (POA) by the investor for that CTA to buy or sell various futures and option products on behalf of the investor using the investor's margin deposit as collateral for any potential loses.

Margin is another unique aspect of managed futures investing. When the CTA buys a future on sugar for a given investor account, for instance, they don't actually pay for anything. Further, if they were to initiate a short position, selling sugar, they would essentially be selling something they don't own. This is done through margin.

Margin is essentially a good faith deposit that ensures the investor has the capital available to pay for any potential losses.

Margin is similar in some respects to placing a bet on a blackjack table. When the bet hits the table, the player has not bought or sold anything. The money on the table is a good faith deposit used against his future winning or losing. If he wins, the margin amount stays in place and he collects the profits. If he loses, the margin amount is taken from him to pay for his loss. In this respect you will often hear managed futures professionals discussing a manager's margin-to-equity ratio when considering their true risk. In part they are discussing how much risk the manager is willing to accept.

Margin in managed futures is different from margin in stocks. With stocks, there is a related cost of carry to purchase the stock. Investors borrow money from their brokerage to purchase a stock and pay an often higher interest rate to the brokerage firm (unless the investor utilizes single stock futures for his or her investing). In managed futures, there is no cost associated with the margin because the investor didn't buy or sell anything but just placed a deposit as collateral against future potential loss.

When investing directly in futures, the margin money "placed on the table" is not generally won or lost all at one time. Sometimes the investor can lose a little and sometimes a lot—even more than the specified margin amount. This is where the phrase *theoretical unlimited loss* in futures and options comes into play. If the investor is not careful, this could result in a margin call.

The Margin Call When margin and leverage are combined it can create a risk mixture that must be carefully managed at all times. Because the investor has placed a good faith deposit on potential losses, there are times when losses can exceed the deposit amount; this can result in first a margin call and then the account going debit. A margin call happens when the account value dips below what is known as the "maintenance margin." Maintenance margin, described below, might be considered a warning or cushion before an account goes debit. The account is debit when the account value dips below the initial good faith deposit used as collateral to buy or sell the futures contract. This applies to direct account structures but not to investors in commodity pool operator (CPO) investments and other limited liability account structures; these structures limit investors' liability and eliminate the potential for margin calls, making a CPO investment a defined loss investment. The margin call is perhaps the most feared aspect of the direct account; on a conceptual level it is difficult to understand. In the past the reality of a margin call and the negative perception of this scary term are what many investors don't understand: a disconnect of sorts. When considering commodity investments and margin calls, the thought of an investor being required to invest additional capital can be disconcerting. However, generally speaking, in managed futures a CTA who would allow an account to be placed on cash margin call would be considered a highly risky CTA, one that would likely not receive many recommendations from conservative, risk-conscious future commission merchants (FCMs). While past performance is not indicative of future results, the past reality of managed futures margin calls is interesting to note. For instance, cash margin calls among experienced CTAs have been somewhat rare. A first-of-its-kind study conducted by the author and BarclayHedge, one of the leading providers of managed futures information, yields very interesting results. In the study, 91.5 percent of CTAs that voluntarily responded to the survey had never had a cash margin call on fully funded accounts.[1] While the study is not conclusive and all CTAs did not participate, the findings coincide with the author's individual opinion observing registered CTA performance as a FCM managed futures division director and coincides with other publicly expressed opinions of other credible officials in the futures and options industry.[2] This warrants further academic study and should not be used to draw definitive conclusions.

The margin call process can vary depending on the FCM. Typically, on a day one margin call the trader is given the call and allowed time to adjust the account. In managed futures, this can mean changing or liquidating the positions. If the account is still on call the third day, the FCM is required to notify the National Futures Association (NFA) of the margin call and the margin call negatively reflects on their capital charge. At any point in the margin process the FCM has the right to liquidate positions in the account to satisfy the margin call, which can happen particularly if the trader is nonresponsive, the positions are not being adjusted, or the account becomes debit. Just because the account is on margin call does not mean its value is zero. The margin call can warn investors before an account reaches the zero point—an early warning sign. If the account were to go past a zero balance it would be "debit" and positions could be immediately liquidated at the market or the investor would be required to invest more capital, which is a cash margin call.

Margin levels are set by the exchanges and can change depending on market circumstances. FCMs can increase margin levels if they so choose, but cannot decrease overnight margin requirements. There is a higher initial margin level, which is the absolute minimum required to invest in a futures contract, and there is the lower maintenance margin level, the point at which an investor would receive a margin call. One example follows.

As of this writing, the initial margin required for an investor to buy or sell a heating oil contract is $5,063, a cash value that is the amount the investor would be required to have in their account at the time of a trade. The maintenance margin for heating oil is $3,750. If the account value were to drop from $5,063 to a value of $3,000, for instance, $750 below the maintenance margin, then the investor would receive a margin call and would be required to liquidate the position or provide additional capital to bring the account back to the appropriate margin level. The account would go debit when the value moved from $5,063 past the maintenance level of $3,750 where the margin call was generated to below the zero point. Some people might consider a margin call a cushion, a red flag warning before the account goes debit. As is evidenced from the levels of initial and maintenance margin, exchanges generally set margins at a level based on the volatility and statistical price movement history of a market. The ideal is that the margin is set at a high so that moving from the initial margin to the maintenance level to debit does not typically happen in a short period of time, allowing traders to adjust positions to meet any margin call. However, there are no guarantees regarding future performance. The topic is further investigated on the book's web site with several examples.

While past cash margin calls with NFA-registered CTAs might be considered unusual on a past performance basis, past performance does not indicate future results and margin calls do occur. There are no guarantees margin calls or significant loss won't occur in the future and no attempt is being made to diminish the risk in managed futures investing. Any investor entering a high-performance investment must understand all the risks and be prepared to accept whatever unpredictable consequences occur. This is true in stocks, hedge funds, and managed futures.

Margin-to-Equity Ratio as a Risk-Management Tool To a degree, the best CTAs can be characterized as such based on the specific trading plan or strategy they follow. A critical component of the CTA's strategy should be his or her margin-to-equity ratio management. In fact, margin-to-equity management is an important consideration when selecting CTAs and one useful tool when managing those CTAs and the related risk.

It is often the case that the higher the margin-to-equity ratios, the more risk in an investment. A CTA who uses 70 percent margin to equity might be considered a very high risk trader and a manager who uses 5 percent margin to equity might be considered to be using a conservative level of leverage. As you might guess, margin-to-equity ratios can be used to measure CTA risk to a certain degree. CTAs that utilize a high level of margin and leverage could represent a significant amount more risk than managers who do not utilize as much margin to equity.

It is the author's observation that most solid CTAs use relatively low levels of margin and leverage. Different strategies utilize different margin levels. Short volatility option strategies tend to have the highest margin to equity ratios while spread/arbitrage traders might utilize the lower amounts of margin to equity of the major strategies. (The book's web site has a section that monitors the reported margin-to-equity ratios of many given CTA strategies and provides benchmarks for CTA margin-to-equity usage.)

Understand that margin to equity is just one measure of risk and not a complete view. While there are no guarantees that these levels entirely indicate a degree of risk, investors should give appropriate consideration to margin-to-equity ratios as one good measure of risk.

Here is an example of how margin-to-equity (M/E) ratios can be used to monitor risk on an ongoing basis. A short-volatility CTA diversified across different markets may have higher margin-to-equity ratios included in his risk-management plan. Part of this plan is the management of margin-to-equity ratios. Typically, this CTA will utilize M/E ratios in the 35 percent to 40 percent range—slightly less than the 50 percent the CTA reports on the BarclayHedge database. It is no random coincidence that one of the rare moments the CTA exceeded his margin-to-equity ratios also coincided with the only significant negative month of performance in an otherwise very compelling track record. This highlights an important insight:

> *When a CTA strays from his or her margin-to-equity plan, attention should be paid to this CTA and his or her market exposure. It might indicate problems with the CTA, the strategy, and the markets traded, which could require immediate attention and understanding.*

CTAs can have points in their history when M/E gets a little high, to degrees. This is the reality in a high-performing investment. M/E can increase when a market moves significantly against the CTA's position and the CTA has difficulty executing on his or her risk management and trading plan. These are risk inflection points, intense moments where the alarm bells sound; and how the CTA answers the bell in this heavyweight fight with risk says volumes for the CTA's skill, discipline, and power to execute on his or her trading strategy. It is also a good test of the FCM's portfolio manager and an active risk-management program. It is when the chips are down—when the market is working against the CTA—that often determines long-term success in what can be a fast-paced pressure cooker. Executing on a risk-management plan is an issue with human-based decision models. Many of the computer-based algorithms that drive systematic CTAs don't have such "human" issues, as trades are automatically executed. However, there is no guarantee that a CTA will perform to any degree, regardless of the trade execution methodology, be it discretionary or computer-based. No system is perfect, which is why it is preferable to create and actively manage diversified portfolios that include different trading methodologies, strategies, volatilities and market exposure. It is the author's experience that such intense risk-management issues are few and far between, but just like a fireman who works around the firehouse all day and rarely receives the alarm bell, when risk appears it is time for a professional, calm approach to risk management.

Margin-to-equity ratios can be used as one method to identify when a CTA has lost discipline, as is the key risk consideration of strategy drift, which also indicates a CTA is straying from his or her core strategy to degrees. These are a red and a yellow flag in the active management program, and when combined with other negative issues, may provide a trigger to liquidate a CTA investment, which essentially involves revoking the CTA's POA. This is often done with a fax letter and e-mail or brokerage portfolio manager and CTA. While CTA policies for revoking POA can vary and are described in the CTA Disclosure Document, many CTAs allow for very quick exiting of their programs. The speed and ability for an investor to exit an investment is an important risk management issue that should be clearly outlined and considered up front before the investor makes an investment.

Managing Risk through Margin and Leverage For stock investors, the concept of margin and leverage can seem odd, thus the methods to manage margin and leverage can seem equally unique. But once you understand the basics, the concept of risk management will seem less daunting.

In an actively managed portfolio, the FCM portfolio manager keeps an eye on margin-to-equity ratios, understands what can be complicated strategies, and monitors overall market exposure risk. If the investor set up a hedge account, the portfolio manager could potentially adjust hedge positions in a separate account if the overall market exposure is overly biased in one direction or another, and provides regular reports to clients. This unique account type is described in the next chapter.

It could be argued that margin and leverage risk is technically a subset of individual manager risk, because it is the manager that determines the levels of margin and equity to use. This is correct because from the perspective of this chapter all risk is tied in some respect to individual managers' decisions. However, both fraud risk and margin and leverage risk are significant enough to warrant their own category. Margin and leverage risk and individual manager risk are intertwined at the execution level, which is what is considered next.

EXPLORING INDIVIDUAL MANAGER RISK

Individual manager risk can be derived from too much concentration in a single CTA program or a undiversified portfolio of CTAs. Individual manager risk in managed futures shares similarities to stocks and hedge funds. With a stock investment, for instance, the decisions and actions of individual company executives can have significant impact on the company stock price, both positive and negative. Imagine a company president making the decision to spend significant capital on a new product launch only to have significant unforeseen market forces render the new product obsolete shortly after its launch. While outside factors, such as unforeseen market forces, can impact stock prices, it is the individual manager's decision to enter a particular market that is the root of the risk. From this unique perspective of individual manager risk, all risk in investing can come down to management decisions.

If investors follow this logic, then individual manager risk is perhaps the most all-encompassing source of risk, the most significant risk in managed futures investing, yet it is a risk factor that is generally not visible within a CTA's statistics and rarely discussed or disclosed. In fact, the industry practice has been to promote individual managers rather than diversified portfolios, exposing investors to significant individual manager risk, and this is a major mistake.

Individual manager risk can take many forms. Individual manager risk can occur when one CTA has a significantly bad month, quarter, or time frame where he or she experiences significantly negative performance. The CTA might have been stuck on the wrong side of a limit down market or find the position might not have appropriate liquidity, much like being caught in long stocks in a market meltdown or during a negative news event. This can happen in the stock market as it can in futures and options markets. The CTA might have chosen the wrong market or wrong strategy at the wrong time, the manager could freeze as the market dynamics completely change course against his position, or a debilitating accident could render the CTA's trading manager out of commission. All are situations that could happen to a mutual fund manager the same as a CTA. After a string of bad months the CTA could increase margin-to-equity ratios in an attempt to overcome a drawdown, commonly referred to as revenge trading, something astute portfolio managers are vigilant to detect. These are just a few of the scenarios that must be considered when over exposing a portfolio to a single CTA investment.

Almost all risk can be traced to the individual manager and his or her decisions, to certain degrees. Figure 11.1 is just one example of individual manager risk. The performance of this CTA is associated with one of the more highly marketed S&P options players over the last decade. His performance might have looked stellar from October 2001 until September of 2008. However, the CTA encountered rough stock market conditions in September and October of 2008, wiping out significant gains made over an

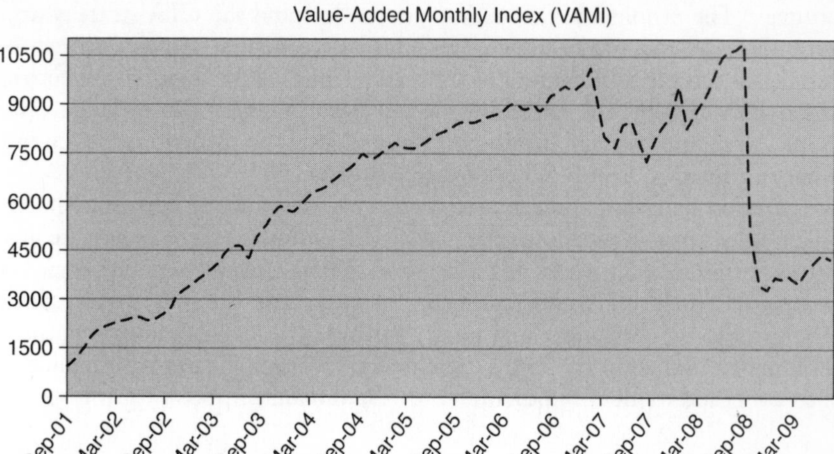

FIGURE 11.1 Reported Performance of CTA
Source: Barclay MAP Database.
Past performance is not indicative of future results. This is one of many study methods which may or may not be appropriate in light of differing individual circumstances.

eight-year period of time. This particular short volatility strategy had large correlation exposure to the negative performance of the S&P 500, although, as outlined in Chapter 9 on correlation, the negative exposure was not evident on a traditional returns-based correlation matrix. This is a red flag in an active portfolio management program and intelligent diversification methodology because of the strategy's hidden exposure to a stock market meltdown. In fact, looking at the drawdown it looks worse than the stock market's decline in 2008.

With this particular short volatility strategy, the difference between managers can often be identified through their risk management. During times of extreme market volatility, certain option CTAs can be adept at rolling their positions to the forward month or appropriately hedging their short option positions with corresponding futures positions; other option CTAs can be caught like a deer in the headlights and fail to execute appropriate risk management. The same is true in other strategies and positions. A key component to understand with a trend-trading strategy is the CTA's stop loss management. Certain trend traders may enter a position and have that position turn against them, but hold that position for a considerable period of time until it turns positive. If the investor is uncomfortable with sustained loses, investing with such managers is not advised. The point is that each CTA's risk management needs to be understood in light of their strategy. The problem is that unless you understand the CTA strategy and how the risk and performance measures relate to that strategy investors might not have a clear picture of true risk. This analysis is often subjective, the quality of which is based on the portfolio manager's knowledge. The book's web site contains frank and pointed analysis of various CTAs and their risk management practices relative to strategy.

After a bad run, some managers simply close shop, knowing that it might take years to overcome the negative drawdown and once again enjoy an incentive fee. However, if the trading manager were to shut down his poor performing CTA and establish a new version, the past performance track record would follow him in any further NFA or Commodity Futures Trading Commission (CFTC)—regulated CTA trading enterprise, which is also a method to identify potential individual manager risk.

FRAUD RISK

Perhaps the key to preventing fraud in managed futures is to understand how the market regulation works in your favor. The top method to prevent fraud is summed up in one sentence: Make sure you are working with a member in good standing of the National Futures Association.

As outlined in this book, CTA members of the NFA are highly regulated, as is the treatment of client investment capital. Ensuring that the investor account and its management fall under these auspices is important but no regulator can guarantee success and there are circumstances when an NFA-regulated entity could commit fraud. Having said that, below are several considerations investors might do well to consider when opening a managed futures account:

- *Segregated Account*: The segregated account structure is unique to the futures and options industry. It is designed to prevent the trading manager from being able to directly manipulate client capital and protector investors from fraud. The segregated account is a regulatory benefit that all alternative investors could benefit from and something that should be examined on a more widespread basis, not just in managed futures. When investing in a direct CTA account, make certain your capital is placed in a segregated account held at a regulated FCM in good standing with the NFA. Further, it is advisable to hold your segregated account with a larger FCM that has managed futures experience and who does not have significant conflicts of interest with the CTAs. While this isn't the answer to all woes, it plays a part in helping make sure you are not going to be a fraud victim.

- *Funds Payable to FCM, Not Trading Manager*: When allocating capital to a direct CTA, the funds should be deposited with the FCM, not the trading manager or the sales agent's introducing broker (IB). If you open a direct account and are asked to deposit money in the name of a CTA or IB, call the NFA immediately and report all violators; this could be fraud.
- *Demand Transparency*: All FCMs should be able to provide daily online transparency into your account. Make sure to receive account statements directly from the FCM and do not exclusively rely on your broker to communicate account balances and activity. While CPO investments generally don't provide transparency into their positions, they should, in the author's opinion. If you invest in a direct CTA account and do not receive transparency, this is a major cause for pause and a sign of potential fraud.
- *Three Separate Entities Watch the Money*: In a direct managed futures account, three independent sets of eyes, the three-headed monster, should have an eye on the money: The FCM/your portfolio manager, the CTA, and the investor—with auditing from the NFA on a semiregular basis. Make sure the FCM and CTA do not share conflicts of interest with one another and ask the FCM/IB to disclose in writing any potential conflicts of interest he or she has regarding a CTA, particularly if the FCM is the clearing agent or receives accounts from the CTA.
- *Audited Results*: Before investing, ensure results have been audited, and if unsure ask to see the NFA's audit report or NFA no comment letter. An often-overlooked aspect is the auditing done by independent third parties. Many CTAs have their monthly performance audited by independent third-party accounting firms well known in the industry, which is an additional benefit to investors.
- *Get It in Writing*: A verbal promise is only as good as the paper it is written on. Remember these words, and when dealing with people in this industry have them put all critical variables in writing. While many FCMs routinely tape phone conversations that take place with clients, it is always a good idea to get all key points in writing.
- *Work with NFA-Registered Members in Good Standing*: On this book's web site and at www.nfa.futures.org there is a list of the top FCMs, CTAs, and CPOs registered and in good standing with the NFA.
- *If It Doesn't Sound Right, Ask the NFA*: A primary role of the NFA is to protect investors. If you have even the slightest suspicion regarding any managed futures investment, call the NFA's information line at 800-621-3570, e-mail information@nfa.futures.org, or visit their web site at www.nfa.futures.org and investigate further.

There will always be individuals who dedicate their lives to figuring out the deception of fraud, and deceptive people will unfortunately always develop fraud schemes that work to assist unsophisticated investors in parting with their capital. While no system can guarantee against fraud loss, basic principles of transparency, account segregation, strong regulation, the trading manager not controlling investment capital, and three separate entities keeping their eyes on the investment is a pretty good foundation from which start.

What Are the Odds? The Statistical Probability of a Worst-Case Scenario

There is perception of risk and then there is the actual probability of that risk occurring; these are often two separate issues.

Surfing in L.A.'s South Bay is a good example. To a nonsurfer, the brutal image of a shark attack, someone's vibrant soul being ripped apart from flesh and body while the mind is still active, is a horrifying risk, enough to scare certain people away from the unknown of that which lies beneath. But the funny reality is that, on a cold statistical basis, there is a greater past probability of serious injury in the L.A. county beach parking lots than any injury inflicted from a shark attack. But never say never. Shark attacks, like investing risk, can surprise.

The point being made is that readers must understand risk and the probability of risk in all investing. And here is a critical point:

> *In all investing, plan how to avoid worst-case risk first, but also plan how to manage that risk if it were to occur.*

This sounds so simple, but in fact it can be difficult in practice. Think about the mortgage meltdown of 2008. The brightest minds in the world failed to consider and plan for the worst-case scenario: The collapse of the housing market and its related impact. In managed futures, investors need to learn from these mistakes and clearly understand the risk, recognizing even the best risk-management plans are not perfect.

Good Luck = Good Planning

There is a saying, "The harder I work, the luckier I get." In managed futures the saying might be "The more I plan to manage risk, the luckier I get."

Investors should first understand risk and the variables of risk management, then find a level at which the investor is comfortable, make sure the portfolio is properly and actively supervised. A risk-appropriate, well-diversified portfolio of solid managers with intelligent, active portfolio management is a most effective method of risk management, in the author's opinion. This means diversification based on more than a traditional correlation matrix—the extent where most managed futures diversification efforts end. Diversification should take place based on price correlation, volatility, and the CTA's strategy diversification and markets traded. This means selecting solid managers based on not just performance statistics, but also taking into consideration the stability of their business operation and background. It means active portfolio management that keeps an eye on the CTA portfolio to consider overall market weighting, considering margin-to-equity ratios and following a risk management plan. These keys to risk management, and all risk management, are designed to mitigate risk, but regardless, understand this key point:

> *No risk-management program is perfect and no investment is devoid of risk. There is no guarantee relative to the future performance (or lack of performance) of any investment program or risk management system.*

On the Book's Web Site

Available to registered book readers:

- List of top FCMs in good standing with the NFA.
- Recent list of managed futures programs that have been involved in NFA/CFTC complaints or actions.
- Full details of the margin call study conducted with BarclayHedge.
- Download: CTA margin-to-equity ratios based on strategy.
- Professional download: "The User's Guide to the Most Important Managed Futures Risk-Management Techniques."
- Professional download: "How to Actively Manage a Managed Futures Portfolio."

For more information visit www.wiley.com/go/managedfutures.

CHAPTER 12

Don't Sit Back

Active Management of Risky Investments*

Buy and hold is dead.

The reason for this is a little insight that hasn't taken center stage just yet:

Perhaps the subtle message behind buy and hold is that investors can "set it and forget it," put investments on cruise control, invest then fall asleep.

This assumption is false for no other reason than the following risk disclosure:

> *Any investment with the potential to provide above-average returns equally has the potential to provide above-average risk.*

Don't mistake the point. This does not mean that investors should not hold quality investments. It means that set it and forget it, which is the easy way out, is obsolete, particularly in a bear market; it means that risk in all investments should be actively considered. Investors can choose to watch the risks themselves or work with many talented firms to help them manage that risk. But regardless of the investment, when the investor achieves higher-than-average performance there is a strong likelihood risk follows suit with return potential. This may sound basic, but the logic isn't evenly applied when considering different risky investments, including stock investments.

Some people accurately characterize hedge funds and managed futures as risk-laden investments with "unthinkable" risk. Here is a key insight:

> *"Unthinkable" risk exists in all investments, including stocks. The issue is how the risk managed.*

---

*Past performance is not indicative of future results. This book is significantly based on the author's opinions and these opinions are not appropriate for all investors and should not be construed as individual advice.

Consider the unimaginable, unidentified risk that took center stage in stock investing, such as a September 11 event or even the fate of fallen stock stars. When considering unimaginable risk, look at the list below of what might have been considered "safe" by staring at these once powerhouse stock investments from years past:

- General Motors
- AIG
- Lehman Brothers
- Bear Stearns
- Wells Fargo
- Freddie Mac and Fannie Mae
- Merrill Lynch
- Tribune Company

The list of "safe" previous blue chip investments that faced what was at one point unimaginable financial peril can go on and on. In fact, that list is a poster child for survivorship bias, as many of the big names were dropped from major stock indexes as their stock performance sank to new lows (or received government bailouts).

Can you identify one commonality, a unique trait that each of these diverse investments shared? They all encountered risks that at one point in their investment history investors considered "unthinkable." Yes, stocks can have unthinkable risks more often than not. They can creep up on investors, striking in some cases without warning.

This chapter reveals what some might consider a potential early warning system in managed futures; an active portfolio-management system that is constantly on guard for risk and risk management, attempting to identify risk-based choke points and systematically designed to take an active role in risk management. Risk management is obviously a complicated topic with guarantees of any type unavailable, but the point is that a strategic, proactive risk-management focus can be considered better than the alternative: ignorance of risk.

This chapter touches on key points of how to actively manage a managed futures portfolio—because this book makes the point that any investment with significant return potential is one that requires active consideration of risk.

The issue is, how can managed futures risk be properly managed? This chapter reveals a structure for a risk-management program at a high level without providing granular details or numeric formulas. This is so for several reasons, the least of which is the proprietary and individual nature of varying risk management programs.

The last chapter outlined primary risk factors, and this chapter highlights the author's preferred method to manage this risk in a risky investment; an attempt to provide some better bulletproofing to a bullet-ridden investment.

In this chapter, readers will discover:

- A graphical reporting system recognizing risk factors:
  - CTA asset allocation
  - Margin-to-equity exposure
  - Market exposure
  - Strategy exposure
- Active management of three risk factors:
  - Margin and leverage risk
  - Individual manager risk
  - Fraud risk
- Portfolio rebalancing
- The future of managed futures
- Book conclusion

Any investment that offers the potential for statistically above-average returns involves risk, and risk cannot be avoided in any investing. This is true in stocks, hedge funds, and managed futures. This is the hard truth that sophisticated investors will understand.

This chapter touches on the complicated and dynamic topic of how to manage risk in managed futures. Intelligent readers have no doubt noted throughout this book the numerous risk disclaimers that are there for a reason that is underscored in this chapter: Investing risk and risk management is a hot potato.

If risk management is viewed from the standpoint of the three choke points outlined in the previous chapter, investors can categorize that risk and attempt to form a strategy for getting their arms around investing risk. To start this process, ask the question: Are the biggest risks those that are unknown?

ARE THE BIGGEST RISKS THOSE THAT ARE UNKNOWN?

It could be argued the biggest risks are those that are unknown. Two of the more significant risks in managed futures are margin and leverage risk, followed by overall market exposure risk—but are these risks really known to the investor? Figure 12.1 shows the standard account statement provided

12/04/09-X		*	4 *	.0 DQ .012 DF AV	.230	CABINET **	.00 *
						(99.760 - UC)	
10/26/09	F1		3 GI	CALL DEC 09 SWISS FRANC	1045	.200 US	
12/04/09-X		*	3 *	.0 DQ .008 DF AV	.200	CABINET **	.00 *
						(99.760 - UC)	
12/01/09	F1		4 GI	CALL JAN 10 SWISS FRANC	1050	.200 US	
1/08/10-X		*	4 *	.3-DQ .085 DF AV	.200	.140 **	.00 *
						(99.830 - UC)	
						NET FUT:	.3-

F1 MONEY TOTALS	145,083.92 ACB	.00 OTE	.00 MV	138,264.83 LV
	82,496.83 M/E	82,496.83 WF	.00 TC	.00 LOV
	.00 LIM	.00 SIM	.00 NIM	62,587.09 FIR
	.00 ULV	.00 USV	145,083.92 TB	.00 EIR
	62,587.09 FXI	25.48-COM	.00 SRL	1.00000000 FCV

	TODAY'S AMOUNT	MONTH-TO-DATE	YEAR-TO-DATE
F1 COMMISSIONS	10.76-	25.48-	658.72-
F1 CLEARING FEES	.80-	2.40-	50.15-
F1 EXCHANGE FEES	2.40-	14.00-	270.45-
F1 NFA FEES	.04-	.12-	2.38-
F1 BROKERAGE FEES	8.00-	24.00-	421.80-
F1 TRANSACTION FEES	18.00-	54.00-	976.50-
F1 OPTION PREMIUM	1,000.00	2,080.00	42,361.99
F1 NET CASH AMOUNT	.00	.00	105,101.93

FIGURE 12.1 Illustration of Daily Client Account Statement
The numeric values and screen shot are for illustrative purposes only and do not reflect actual account values or imply actual performance. These screen shots are used for illustrative purposes only. Screen shots in this book may vary from the actual version.

to most investors by futures commission merchants (FCMs) and the limited software providers. Consider the account statement and let me know if you, the reader, can identify the market exposure and primary risk factors by looking at this common client statement, known as the daily equity run.

If you can understand risk by looking at this common statement you likely possess futures and options investing experience—and you are a reasonably unique investor on a statistical basis. Most investors, including many professionals, are not entirely familiar with a futures account statement, and might not understand how to determine their account balance. In fact, a little insight in this regard is to always consider the liquidation value (LV) or market value (MV) of an account, as this is the account value marked to the market at the end of the day. Some investors might consider the account cash balance (ACB), but in fact this number can be deceptive due to the impact on short and long volatility option position and is not considered as reliable as LV. Further, it should be noted investors might not be able to liquidate at the exact end of the day prices, making the LV a relative benchmark and not an exact determinant of the amount of money the investor might net.

There is nothing to be ashamed of in not understanding a managed futures account statement; this is more a comment on a slowly maturing industry than the intelligence of any investor. Complicated client statements are not often explained to the client in the futures industry, and this is odd:

> *An investor who does not clearly understand risk in real terms is perhaps most at risk. Managed futures statements should help the investor understand his or her current investment and associated risk.*

Many managed futures client statements are somewhat prehistoric in their display of information when compared to the statements provided in the equity world. It is not uncommon for equity account statements to include graphical analysis of asset allocation and market values. Existing futures statements are nowhere close to the graphical standards in the equity world, and this is one area the futures industry should improve upon, specifically as it relates to the most significant risk factors that are not overtly evident or even visible on many statements. Most FCM account statements do not put on display two very significant risk factors: overall market exposure and margin and leverage risk, not to mention strategy exposure.

This chapter shows how account statements could look, as the key components of an active risk management program are outlined.

A GRAPHICAL LOOK AT THE MANAGED FUTURES ACCOUNT

In Figure 12.2, start with a basic understanding of how graphical market statements should look (if your statement doesn't look like this, you can purchase an application on the Internet that provides statements in a graphical display. Further, a complete guide to reading the traditional FCM account statement is online as well).

The first component of a graphical statement should provide investors a basic graphical understanding of their CTA asset allocation, which is reasonably easy to understand, along with a basic profit analysis. This may sound basic to equity investors, but it sometimes takes a technical knowledge to decipher many managed futures statements.

Monthly Statement: November 1, 2009—December 1, 2009

Account: Smith Family Trust

Current Asset Allocation: Asset allocation as of December 1, 2009 (based on LV from client statement)

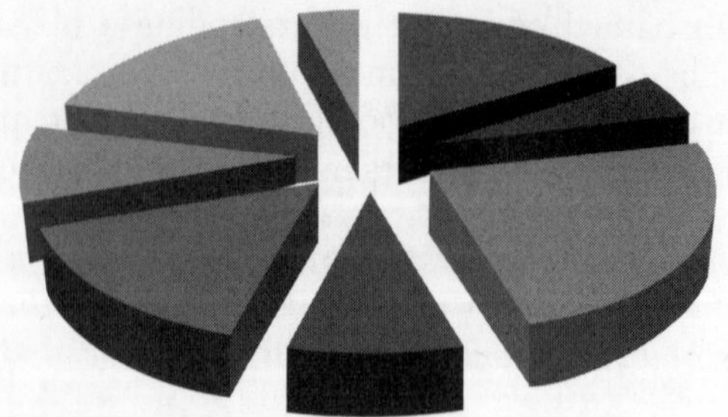

December 1, 2009 Liquidating Values	
CTA 12-1	79,591.73
CTA 12-2	28,927.56
CTA 12-3	136,140.79
CTA 12-4	49,630.40
CTA 12-5	67,083.52
CTA 12-6	50,822.90
CTA 12-7	97,032.96
CTA 12-8	23,030.29
	532,260.15

November 2, 2009 Liquidating Values	
CTA 12-1	94,807.83
CTA 12-2	24,870.91
CTA 12-3	130,166.67
CTA 12-4	49,403.75
CTA 12-5	53,595.21
CTA 12-6	50,597.79
CTA 12-7	94,312.96
CTA 12-8	24,605.74
	522.360.86

FIGURE 12.2 Hypothetical Illustration of Liquidating Values
The numeric values and screen shot are for illustrative purposes only and do not reflect actual account values or imply actual performance. These screen shots are used for illustrative purposes only. Screen shots in this book may vary from the actual version.

Profit Analysis

Each month the investor should know how and why various CTAs performed in the overall portfolio, and this analysis ideally comes with detail/opinions of the CTA's positions, as is on display in Table 12.1.

Share of Profit/Loss

While looking at Table 12.1, note the opinion section of the report. This analysis is something generally provided by the investor's portfolio manager, and the quality of the analysis is important as it will come into play when

TABLE 12.1 Hypothetical Illustration of Profit/Loss of an Account

	Profit/Loss	Opinions, Comments, Observations
CTA 12-1	−15,216.10	CTA long dollar position generates red ink. I've seen this hold strategy before...
CTA 12-2	4,056.65	Trend trader initially had long U.S./short German interest rate spread, then switched position. Like this CTA going forward, buy on a drawdown.
CTA 12-3	5,974.12	Short-volatility trader benefits from trading range markets.
CTA 12-4	226.65	Discretionary trader ends month with sugar put spread and short oil and e-mini spread.
CTA 12-5	13,488.31	CTA starts move, watch heavy metals exposure.
CTA 12-6	225.11	Currently flat. Lean hog spread trade generated small profit.
CTA 12-7	2,720.00	Long S+P pays off heading into seasonal strength.
CTA 12-8	−1,575.45	Short lean hog position lost money.

The numeric values and screen shot are for illustrative purposes only and do not reflect actual account values or imply actual performance. These screen shots are used for illustrative purposes only. Screen shots in this book may vary from the actual version.

more significant applications of active portfolio management are revealed shortly.

Also consider the profit/loss distribution and look at how uneven it is. In active portfolio management it is important to consider the overall profit/loss distribution. In aggressive and certain moderate portfolios this type of significant distribution in one CTA might be more acceptable on a short-term basis, but in conservative portfolios it should be questioned.

Profit/Loss Momentum

When considering account gains and losses, it is important to consider the momentum of those gains and losses. As you will see, this is particularly true when things take a turn for the worst with a CTA, and the portfolio manager considers momentum alongside other factors, such as strategy drift, that may lead to eliminating the CTA from inclusion in the portfolio.

In the active management report, a section should address the profit loss momentum on a six-month and twelve-month basis. The portfolio manager must determine if the CTA made a single bad trade, which is part of the process of managed futures investing, or if he or she has lost focus and discipline and it is time to take action. This judgment call is always difficult, but particularly a concern with CTAs that have a shorter track record.

Strategy Diversification

Strategy diversification is important in managed futures risk management. Investors might want to see consistent diversification of strategy as much as possible, and a graphical statement can illuminate this piece of the puzzle. However, as investors climb the risk/reward ladder they may engage in a little volatility skewing based on the perceived market environment at the time, or we might get opportunistic and invest in what are considered quality CTAs when they incur inevitable drawdowns, a very interesting managed futures investment methodology that is detailed on the book's web site. Such activities should always be considered in light of existing strategy diversification.

Strategy diversification, as illustrated in Table 12.2, is something investors should consider on a regular basis and it can be done on a monthly, quarterly, or yearly basis depending on the level of activity in the portfolio. Aggressive portfolios where more active volatility skewing is utilized might equally require more active rebalancing while conservative portfolios should not experience significant shifts in strategy. In part, strategy diversification

TABLE 12.2 Hypothetical Illustration of Strategy Asset Allocation

CTA	Individual Strategies	LV as of Dec 1	CTA Strategy Compilation	Total Asset Allocated Towards
CTA 12-1	Trend	89,591.73		
CTA 12-2	Trend	28,927.56	Trend	118,519.29
CTA 12-3	Volatility	136,140.79	Counter Trend	97,032.96
CTA 12-4	Discretionary	49,630.40	Discretionary	136,713.92
CTA 12-5	Discretionary	87,083.52	Spread	73,853.19
CTA 12-6	Spread	50,822.90	Volatility	136,140.79
CTA 12-7	Counter Trend	97,032.96		
CTA 12-8	Spread	23,030.29		

The numeric values and screen shot are for illustrative purposes only and do not reflect actual account values or imply actual performance. These screen shots are used for illustrative purposes only. Screen shots in this book may vary from the actual version.

is interesting to watch from the standpoint of providing a yellow or red flag in the active portfolio management system because it could indicate strategy drift.

Strategy drift is a term used frequently by those inside the managed futures portfolio management industry. It refers to a CTA who may be straying from his or her core trading strategy; perhaps venturing into different markets or, more ominously, engaging in a different trading method. Strategy drift can be a significant point of consideration in an active portfolio management program. Strategy drift can generate a critical red flag that would indicate CTA liquidation in an active portfolio management system. This is particularly true when combined with other issues. Like many issues, strategy drift might not be a fatal issue, depending on the CTA and his or her profit/loss circumstance. There are different algorithms, available for purchase on the book's web site, that can help guide sophisticated investors and portfolio managers regarding the active portfolio management process and the yellow flag/red flag system.

Roll Up the Sleeves with Margin-to-Equity Management Active management always needs to consider margin-to-equity ratios. In fact, in the high-performance managed futures (HMPF) active portfolio-management system the algorithm scoring system assigns heavy rating to margin-to-equity usage. In some cases improper margin-to-equity management could result in immediate and fatal red flag execution systems, indicating adjustments in CTA asset allocation are required.

While many people consider margin-to-equity ratio the only point of margin usage under consideration, it is not the only consideration. Margin to equity as it relates to market environment and strategy is also an important consideration, among others. However, since it is the primary margin consideration, start with the simple margin-to-equity ratio.

Margin Usage

Table 12.3 shows the margin-to-equity usage of a CTA portfolio, based on LV value from the client statement. These margin-to-equity ratios need to be carefully considered by a qualified portfolio manager, who assesses the overall CTA portfolio risk on a daily basis.

It might be tempting to end CTA analysis based on simple margin-to-equity exposure, but that would not be complete, particularly since a primary goal of the active portfolio management system is to identify overall market exposure. For this reason, we consider margin-to-market exposure in Table 12.4 as well as margin-to-strategy analysis in Table 12.5.

TABLE 12.3 Hypothetical Illustration of Margin Usage

CTA	LV Dec 1	Margin Excess	Position	Margin Usage	Margin Usage %
CTA 12-1	89,591.73	78,773.73	CTA 12-1	10,818.00	12%
CTA 12-2	28,927.56	24,742.56	CTA 12-2	4,185.00	14%
CTA 12-3	136,140.79	76,927.79	CTA 12-3	59,213.00	43%
CTA 12-4	49,630.40	42,402.40	CTA 12-4	7,228.00	15%
CTA 12-5	87,083.52	54,833.52	CTA 12-5	32,250.00	37%
CTA 12-6	50,822.90	50,822.90	CTA 12-6	0.00	0%
CTA 12-7	97,032.96	74,532.96	CTA 12-7	22,500.00	23%
CTA 12-8	23,030.29	21,612.29	CTA 12-8	1,418.00	6%

The numeric values and screen shot are for illustrative purposes only and do not reflect actual account values or imply actual performance. These screen shots are from an author-developed application and are used for illustrative purposes only. Readers can learn more about this application and download a copy on the book's web site. Screen shots in this book may vary from the actual version.

TABLE 12.4 Hypothetical Illustration of Margin Usage Relative to Market Exposure

Position	Margin to Equity
Long dollar	12%
Long U.S./German rates	14%
Short sugar, long crude, oil	15%
Long metals, long euro	37%
Flat	0%
Long equities	23%
Short lean hogs	6%

The numeric values and screen shot are for illustrative purposes only and do not reflect actual account values or imply actual performance. These screen shots are used for illustrative purposes only. Screen shots in this book may vary from the actual version.

Margin Usage Relative to Market Exposure

Table 12.4 shows the margin usage based on market exposure, based on LV value from the client statement. This margin exposure based on market can become important, particularly if the markets were to significantly move against a CTA and his or her position.

TABLE 12.5 Hypothetical Illustration of Liquidating Values

CTA Strategy	Margin to Equity
Trend	27%
Counter Trend	23%
Discretionary	52%
Spread	6%
Volatility	43%

The numeric values and screen shot are for illustrative purposes only and do not reflect actual account values or imply actual performance. These screen shots are used for illustrative purposes only. Screen shots in this book may vary from the actual version.

Margin Usage Relative to Strategy

Table 12.5 shows the margin usage based on the strategy, based on LV value from the client statement.

This section has only briefly outlined a topic on which an entire book could be written, highlighting key aspects of the program. Readers can visit the book's web site to sign up for a newsletter that demonstrates how active portfolio management works on a daily basis.

INDIVIDUAL MANAGER RISK

Individual manager risk is another important topic that a portfolio manager must be aware of and prepared to manage. In similar fashion to the statistical measures of margin to equity and performance, individual manager risk has a series of categories with different scoring algorithms to identify yellow and red flag execution points. The difference is that individual manager risk may combine elements of statistical analysis with discretionary analysis, which makes risk-management decisions subjective in this regard. Having said that, the algorithms can be adjusted so that weighting can change based on the desires of the user.

The Hedge Account

Even diversified portfolios designed to the last detail can find a situation where they can be overexposed to one market, one strategy or market move. For instance, it is possible for a discretionary strategy to be exposed to the same market risk as a trend-trading strategy. The key is for the investor or portfolio manager to be actively monitoring the account to identify times when the portfolio may be over-exposed to any one market or potential market move. When this happens the investor can either rebalance the portfolio by eliminating certain CTAs or they can utilize a hedge account in an attempt to mitigate what might be temporary over exposure to a given market.

Rebalancing the portfolio presents many logistical challenges as CTAs do not often allow excessive in-and-out rebalancing. In fact, there are successful CTAs that may allow you to leave but not reenter a program. This is one circumstance where the hedge account may be created.

The hedge account is designed to balance a portfolio due to a number of issues, including market or strategy exposure, as well as a method to manage individual manager risk and get in and out of various CTAs by hedging their positions rather than exiting the CTA program. The hedge account is a separate account that would carry positions opposite that of the CTA in an attempt to neutralize the CTA's position. The hedge account can be utilized to hedge market risk, and also at times when certain CTAs have experienced a profit surge. Just like there is justification for entering certain CTA investments after a drawdown, there is also justification for exiting certain CTAs after a profit surge. Because many CTAs will not allow in-and-out behavior, the hedge account can be utilized in an attempt to lock in profits generated by the CTA.

Yellow Flag/Red Flag Active Portfolio Management The HPMF program features a flag system for active portfolio management, based on a number of monitored factors. The exact system and screen shots are outlined in a PDF white paper on the book's web site. The system is briefly highlighted below:

- The *green flag* indicates the CTA is under watch, but not a top active consideration at this point based on the system's scoring algorithm.
- The *blue flag* indicates the CTA may be in a drawdown and indicates an investment opportunity.
- The *yellow flag* indicates that the CTA warrants active risk consideration.
- The *red flag* indicates that immediate risk action might be required, such as liquidating a CTA investment.

In this system each flag has different priorities. Green and blue flags are what we consider subordinate flags to the more powerful yellow and red flags. If the portfolio-management system were to identify a blue flag based on certain performance behavior and at the same time identify a red flag based on a different set of combined criteria, the red flag would take precedence. For instance, the CTA may be in the middle of a significant drawdown which, when combined with average drawdown, deviation analysis, and returns distribution analysis might indicate as a statistical opportunity to invest in a CTA. However, this same drawdown might be used in combination with excessive margin-to-equity ratio usage, strategy drift, and longer-term momentum of returns to indicate a red flag. If this were the case, the red flag would take precedence over the blue flag.

In active portfolio management the flag system can be replaced by a number of indicators and scoring display systems. A numeric 1–10 scoring or an alphanumeric scoring system can provide detailed attention to subtle degrees of difference. The output of the scoring isn't as important as the underlying algorithm driving the system; the display of information can be easily adjusted to accommodate the user.

We have discussed metrics that should be relatively easy for professional investors to manage based on their experience, but we also crossed the line to address the critical issues of margin to equity management that are often the domain of experienced managed futures professionals. This is because margin/equity management is a key component in this active portfolio management system and it is the subtle nuances that often make a difference in what can be both a statistical as well as subjective process.

THE FUTURE OF MANAGED FUTURES CAN BE FOUND IN ITS HISTORY

What is the future of managed futures? In part, we might see the future by looking considering industry developments in the past.

There are legends of longevity, such as John Henry and David Harding, who built significant trend following systems that had the staying power over the long haul, and such long-term CTA sustainability will be critical to the industry's future. The next step in the development of the industry could be offering the benefits of managed futures without requiring a seven figure investment. One of the keys to success of the asset class is integrating traditional equity brokerage firms and financial advisors, making it easy for investors to access and manage the asset class. When the history of managed futures is written, another prominent industry leader in regards to bringing the asset class to the retail investor is Christian Baha. The first to provide retail investors easy access to managed futures in 1996, this fund is one of a handful at ground zero for industry product innovation, having developed and marketed the gold denominated managed futures investment that speaks to the core of the asset class identity of diversification from economic risk. The firm also managed a significant distribution network with financial advisors and possesses a strong marketing prowess. For the asset class to reach its full potential it will require that ability to reach out to new investors, as Charles Merrill did with stocks and Ned Johnston did with mutual funds.

In the future, product innovation might be best targeted towards risk management first. Consider how the short volatility options strategy developed to focus on risk management. The CTA strategy generally began with CTAs focusing on a single market, the primarily the S&P 500. The problem with this strategy is overexposure to risk during events of significant stock market dislocation. The next step innovation was the market diversified, directional short volatility option seller. This strategy was developed as a risk answer to the overexposure to single market stock market risk. Focusing on risk and management innovation is why Ranjan Bhaduri deserves credit. His company developed an innovative platform that provides unique benefits of transparency and risk management and it fits a profile of future innovations that will move the industry forward: key developments will focus on risk management and ease of access to and management of the investment. For managed futures to reach its full potential the industry must make it easy for the traditional equity financial advisor must be included in the process. The distribution network created by many of these funds is sophisticated to the point of providing financial advisors ease of use, a key issue going forward. Managed futures is somewhat difficult for a financial advisor to access. A financial advisor who wishes to offer their customers sophisticated products is required to undertake considerable amount more work on behalf of their investors than with stocks, and this needs to improve. To substantiate sustained growth, managed futures needs an advisor and investor friendly package, because right now the financial advisors that actively integrate the best programs into their clients portfolios are those that made a substantial effort to diversify their client's portfolios. Likewise, investors of all stripes who have sought out the best managed futures programs have likely been required to engage in a considerable amount of work educating themselves, finding appropriate brokers and CTAs and funds with which to work. But establishing the investment is only one part of the story—and unfortunately this is where most of the industry has focused the lion's share of its attention and resources. The cold reality is that after an investment is made, too many managed futures investors are left without any assistance in interrupting what can be very complex strategies and positions. For instance, even some professionals might have difficulty immediately understanding how a covered short option calendar spread can have varying degrees of risk based on the distance between calendar months. There is a clear method to communicate the risk exposure in that position, but it is generally not done. Industry leaders pushing towards this direction include insightful writing from Matthias Knab, Chidem Kurdas, Daniel Collins among other industry communication leaders. The industry needs an interpretative level between the execution of a strategy and the investor, providing a blow by blow account of the total risk picture and focus on the various strategies. There are good industry newsletters, and it is this type of strong educational communication, without sales hype, that will help propel the industry to new heights. In terms of thought leaders, academia has a wide open laboratory to study. Academics such as Thomas Scheeweis have lead the effort of enlightenment but further studies, particularly in the areas of risk, warrant further consideration. Other areas of concern exist. For instance, long only commodity ETFs are somewhat like an invasive species, Asian Carp if you will, upsetting the natural habitat of the futures and options markets and disrupting the contango balance of the supply and demand ecosystem. Long only commodity ETFs that utilize futures (the most efficient method for such financial management) are creating supply and demand imbalances in certain delivery months when they roll from one month to the next. In the Chicago floor trader's tradition of getting in front of the orders of big funds coming into the pit, some spread arb CTAs are clever enough to identify potential the movement of ETF investments and attempt to profit from the imbalance of demand placed on certain contract months. But is it right for a market to have such an unnatural influence on supply and demand? Long only ETFs do not represent true product demand and their growing and significant impact on the market pricing ecosystem should be questioned. This leads to the point of physical delivery versus cash settlement. Rick Santelli is a television commentator who is also respected on the trading floor. He recognizes "physical delivery puts a little religion into traders." Physical delivery is in line with the spirit of the concept behind a futures exchange, as opposed to the cash settlement, which makes the market feel more like a speculative casino, in the author's opinion. The issues with ETFs is that they are easily accessible through traditional financial advisors, as are the small numbers of managed futures mutual funds, which currently provide investors a rather poor example of managed futures returns potential. Popular mutual funds from within the industry with an understanding of managed futures need to emerge, because the initial investor experience with the product can be important and if that experience comes through a financial advisor the industry must make sure it is well represented. In the future, a simple method for investors to access and manage the investment is critical, and that will likely occur from the ranks of the equity-based financial advisor and consultant.

What the Managed Futures Industry Needs

Following is a summary of what the managed futures industry needs.

- *FCM/Portfolio Manager Sophistication:* FCMs and brokerage firms need to actively engage and recruit top money managers in the financial services industry and bring them into the world of managed futures. Ideally, a sophisticated firm could manage both equity and direct managed futures exposure from a single account and through a single portfolio manager.
- *Additional Top Managers:* Talented hedge fund managers need to discover the futures and options markets and understand that their strategies can take on significant sophistication with the benefit derived from

the unique contracts and markets offered in the futures and options industry.

- *Diversification, Diversification, Diversification:* The reality of the situation is that the current structure makes it very difficult for average investors to invest in managed futures to achieve diversification. In fact, it could be argued that unqualified investors with under $20,000 to invest are in fact exposed to the greatest risk: lack of diversification through an individual investment in a single CTA with a generally short track record associated with a low minimum investment level.
- *Industry Voice:* An independent voice promoting the specific needs of managed futures is badly needed. When outrageous claims unfairly stereotype an industry, a voice needs to accurately set the record straight. There have been several casual conversations among industry leaders regarding creating an industry group with the sole purpose of protecting and promoting the industry. This needs to be supported by all the major players, who might have different interests but must understand common industry goals benefit all participants.

Is Government Regulation All Bad? Or Is *Derivative* a Dirty Word?

There is often consternation regarding government regulation in the financial services industry. But is government regulation really all that bad? From one perspective, managed futures owes a large degree of its success and credibility to government regulation and its associated investor protections such as performance auditing and account segregation rules. This industry regulation is an interesting template: a financially self-supporting regulatory body independent of the industry it regulates and reasonably immune to the whims of Congress and their influential lobbyists, promoting transparency and multiple points of accountability for tracking investor capital. And what follows is a critical point.

Transparency and accountability are the key words that industry regulatory bodies appear to embrace, concepts that should be spread to other sectors of government and *any* area, public and private, that significantly impacts the American economy. The regulatory bodies also seem to understand the power and benefit of true asset diversification, echoing the voices of several Nobel Prize winners. But alas, it is unfortunate when such words of wisdom fall on certain deaf Wall Street ears.

In the lexicon of finance, the word *derivative* has become synonymous with words such as *complicated*, *mysterious*, and *dangerous*. But is this generic categorization accurate to the same degree for all derivatives? Consider many of the unregulated mortgage derivatives strategically engineered by Wall Street so that a lack of regulation, transparency, and price discovery were key features. In an ironic turn of events, the financial products that were designed with a lack of governmental oversight were in fact the cause for significant government intervention in cleaning up an unregulated, un-transparent mess. As American taxpayers view with righteous disgust the likes of Wall Street icon AIG as it nurtures off the apparent ample governmental bosom, proving in a free market society certain Wall Street firms are more free than others and can make fatal mistakes and still receive a socialist "do-over," perhaps it's time to recognize that that all derivatives are not the same degree of bad. In fact, if there were a poster child for the phrase "an ounce of prevention is worth a pound of cure," the mortgage-backed security crisis and its unregulated derivatives that almost decapitated the U.S. economy could be it.

It will forever be an interesting irony that it was the Commodity Futures Trading Commission (CFTC) commissioner who, in the late 1990s, warned of the lack of transparency in the mortgage-backed securities that she believed had become too critical a pillar of the economy to be ignored. A determined and dedicated woman, Brooksley Born had a vision that these mortgage-backed securities were a problem. In what has been an underpublicized milestone of the credit crisis, she bucked Wall Street's groupthink wisdom and omnipotent lobby in late 1990s, but discovered her warning regarding nontransparent, unregulated mortgage-backed securities was ignored—well before these assets exploded upon the U.S. economy. Born's reward for standing up to the Fed and Treasury Department and ultimately exposing this danger to a sleeping U.S. Congress was that she was forced out of her position as CFTC chair. The fact that both Wall Street's lobbyists and the highest economic policymakers in Washington worked together to actively silence her warnings about mortgage derivatives is an interesting sidebar, particularly in light of certain Wall Street wizards engineering sophisticated bets against the mortgage market and U.S. economy. This is the missing link in this story, pointing to the fact that perhaps it is time for Wall Street activity to be considered in the light of day and for investors to consider the reality of stock market investing risk.

The Stock Market Has a Very Good PR Agent

The image of the stock market seems so clean compared to the reality, as if a master public relations practitioner was pulling strings behind a squad of equity cheerleaders to prop up the stock market as the only legitimate investment, ignoring anything alternative as too risky—as if the stock market didn't carry significant risk.

If this were high school, the stock market is similar to the kid with the conservative reputation among parents. But once parental backs are turned the "nice" boy turns from Dr. Jekyll to Mr. Hyde rather quickly, just as investors think the stock market is a "safe" investment when it is in fact very risky. Investors consider the stock market safe when judging the book by its cover, but just like the bad kid with the good reputation, what appears good on the outside can be deceptive when the investor becomes aware of hard facts. It's kind of like the stock with the great reputation playing accounting games to juice its returns, and shifting accounting standards for stocks, which are not much of a standard at all and can lead to deceptive earnings reports. There isn't an accounting rule that can change the value of a bushel of corn or an ounce of gold, but accounting rules can dramatically change stock prices without changing the underlying fundamentals of the company. But this glossed over misconception isn't the only deficiency.

Hurdles to True Diversification Being Reduced

The most amazing aspect of this book is that some on traditional Wall Street regularly overlook a major asset class that is arguably the most uncorrelated in existence. The last 10 times the stock market buckled, managed futures indexes have provided a positive safe harbor crutch nine of those times. How can this be ignored? The same people who overlook managed futures generally hold the belief that Markowitz, modern portfolio theory, and asset allocation don't work. But here is the real punch line. These investing concepts are based on one underlying principal so fundamental it is surprising to miss: *true* uncorrelated asset diversification. Generally the same people who criticize asset allocation are the ones who try to diversify portfolios with stocks: They don't include truly uncorrelated assets in their portfolios.

This is not to say all of Wall Street is the same. Innovative firms looking for new, diversified solutions in uncorrelated investing exist, and in fact regulators are helping make this happen. New rules for independent RIAs (registered investment advisors) developed late in 2009 essentially allow objective RIAs to more easily diversify client portfolios using direct managed futures investments. Further, innovative broker–dealers (BDs) are working to offer complete diversification programs using direct managed futures programs that provide their clients a real dose of diversification. Yes, forward-looking people are in all corners of the investment world and they are open to true diversification, transparency, and accountability. On the book's web site readers can find more information relative to this rapidly developing story along with a list of RIAs and BDs that offer true asset diversification using managed futures.

CONCLUSION

The point of this chapter is reflection and understanding; wrapping it up and tying it all together. Readers should reflect on what they learned and consider their individual situation, particularly if they are concerned about future stock market volatility. There are good reasons for investors to seek true asset diversification. With government debt bouncing around historic levels, the U.S. dollar's dominance as the "international currency of choice" being questioned, and the government's previously unlimited ability to simply crank up a dollar printing press to solve its problems, the world could prove a very different and challenging environment for undiversified investors, indeed. Remember this fact: In history it is common for a currency to have its intrinsic value fall to zero at some point. There is no telling if stock market risk from the dollar or the significantly mounting U.S. debt load will be a reason for the stock market to fall again. The reasons can vary, but the point is an unforeseen crisis will likely hit the stock market again and this time investors might have an option not to care. From one perspective, stock investing can be characterized by the amazingly wide variety of unknown risks—the outliers behind the corporate scenes—which come from left field to shock both professional and individual investor. But here is the key point:

> *While future risks are unknown and unpredictable, it can be said with a strong degree of confidence that an investment portfolio built using the principles of true asset diversification may be best at weathering future investing storms.*

Active management of stock market risk is very difficult if one views it from the standpoint of what is hidden, the risks behind closed management doors. There are risks in managed futures, to be sure. But the risks are primarily based on price, which is transparent on an open and regulated exchange. Here is the good news in managed futures. Throughout this book we have made an attempt to identify major managed futures risk factors. It is important for investors to understand how difficult a task this can be in any investment: Getting one's arms around investing risk in any asset class is difficult if not impossible. But the argument could be made that direct managed futures investing can be among the most transparent of investment options:

1. Managed futures is a pure price play with account values marked to the market at the end of each day. An accounting scandal or a

nontransparent credit default swap brewing behind a veil of corporate secrecy would not be a direct manipulative factor in commodity prices.

2. Both professional and individual investors can have daily visibility into their direct accounts. Their value is marked to the market every day, and the positions and strategies are clearly visible to knowledgeable investors.
3. The industry is tightly regulated with audited performance. Those being regulated respect the regulators and the author is unaware of any instance where those being regulated do not approach regulated issues with a strong degree of care and caution.
4. Managed futures has historically performed in both positive and negative stock market environments, so investors might not have given up performance during bull markets while benefiting through diversification in bear markets. There are significant risks, different from the risk in stock investing. Those risks should be understood and actively managed.

It's about Reducing Correlation to Stocks and the Economy

In the future the stock market will go up and down while having good days and bad. But that's not the point. The point is not to worry about it. Use methods of investing that ideally benefit from economic recovery at the right time, but are not beholden to the stock market to any debilitating degree.

Think about investing without paramount concern for the economy. This is about true asset diversification that is not solely dependent on stocks or the economy. That is the future of investing. That is high-performance managed futures.

No one can guarantee what will happen in the future and there is risk to varying degrees in all investing. However, it can be said with a degree of confidence that investors lowering their debilitating correlation to the stock market and economic conditions at large might sleep a little better at night. Diversifying with stocks and traditional assets alone doesn't work, as Nobel Prize winners have identified and practical experience dictates. The image of stocks as having a diversifying potential is starting to give way to the truth.

Bright, forward-looking professionals recognize this and have taken the time to understand a new method of investing: one designed not to be entirely dependent on the whims of economic uncertainty. It is these forward financial engineers and intelligent investors that are the reason managed futures is finding its way into modern portfolios and is among the fastest growing asset classes.

Your reading of these words represents an investment: an investment of time and interest. Hopefully you have been rewarded appropriately. But the true reward is not based just on the interpretation of that information, but based on the positive results of those actions.

On the Book's Web Site

Available to registered book readers:

- List of RIAs, BDs, FCMs and IBs that offer complete portfolio-diversification services using managed futures.
- Professional graphical statement analysis tool.
- White paper: "Managed Futures Past and Future."
- White paper: "Twelve Most Common Managed Futures Mistakes."
- Professional certification process for managed futures portfolio developers.
- Professional white paper: "Guide to Active Portfolio Management."

For more information visit www.wiley.com/go/managedfutures.

APPENDIX A

HPFM Strategy Benchmark Performance Study

In managed futures, the strategy can be significantly important—and different strategies can have different performance characteristics. Following is the Managed Futures Strategy Benchmark Performance Study as of the March 2010 reporting cycle. This study of past performance will be updated on the book's web site on a monthly basis, along with a detailed explanation of the study variables and analysis of various CTAs as measured against the benchmark study.

Average Reported Performance of CTAs with a 36-Month Track Record, as of March 2010

	All Programs	System/ Trend	Option/ Vol	Discretionary	Spread/ Arb
Returns Performance					
Compounded Annual Return (ROR)	10.64%	10.99%	12.39%	12.60%	15.59%
Avg Mo ROR	1.02%	1.04%	1.25%	1.16%	1.35%
Last 6 Mo ROR	−0.73%	−1.94%	8.18%	−0.07%	1.12%
Last 12 Mo ROR	2.57%	−0.44%	20.65%	5.93%	3.01%
Cpd ROR last 3 yrs	9.31%	10.74%	7.34%	9.04%	11.96%
Best 12 Mos	74.20%	72.08%	77.84%	76.64%	24.07%
Worst 12 Mos	−20.20%	−19.63%	−25.81%	−15.55%	−8.81%

(*Continued*)

Average Reported Performance of CTAs with a 36-Month Track Record, as of March 2010 (*Continued*)

	All Programs	**System/ Trend**	**Option/ Vol**	**Discretionary**	**Spread/ Arb**
Drawdown Performance					
Worst DD	25.95%	24.92%	34.40%	20.61%	10.85%
Av DD	9.37%	9.34%	10.23%	5.78%	5.44%
Wst DD/AV DD diff	16.58%	15.58%	24.17%	14.83%	5.41%
Avg Rec Time (mos)	4.13	4.04	3.58	3.28	3.32
Current DD	−19.11%	−17.92%	−29.01%	−13.05%	−7.09%
Worst DD first 3 yrs	−20.65%	−20.03%	−32.08%	−15.36%	−17.05%
Av DD versus Up Dev	−4.3963	−4.5366	−4.3177	−4.2522	−4.6056
Volatility/ Probability Measures					
STD	5.39	5.48	6.21	4.83	5.25
RAD	3.10	3.10	4.27	2.43	2.80
UpDev	4.49	4.63	4.42	4.31	4.66
DownDev	3.08	3.08	4.26	2.41	2.78
Up/Down Dev	1.66	1.63	1.41	2.1	1.97
Win%	59.99%	57.89%	74.25%	60.63%	63.50%
Loss%	−40.01%	−42.11%	−25.75%	−39.37%	−36.50%
AvgWinSz	4.22	4.52	3.75	3.82	3.93
AvgLossSz	3.68	3.63	5.38	2.85	3.13
Win/ Loss Size Diff	0.54	0.89	−1.63	0.97	0.8
Traditional Risk/Reward Measures					
Sharpe	0.49	0.49	0.63	0.63	0.57
Sortino	3.76	1.79	4.37	5.6	5.03
Correlation versus					
S&P Total Return	−0.02	−0.06	0.22	−0.05	−0.03
Barclay CTA Index	0.36	0.45	0.01	0.2	−0.09

Average Reported Performance of CTAs with a 36-Month Track Record, as of March 2010

	All Programs	System/ Trend	Option/ Vol	Discretionary	Spread/ Arb
Graveyard CTA	0.3	0.34	0.21	0.15	−0.12
Barclay Hedge Fund Index	0.05	0.01	0.26	0	−0.11
MSCI World Stock	0.01	0.03	0.23	−0.03	−0.07
Rogers Commodity Index	0.12	0.1	0.23	0.1	−0.08
Characteristics					
Average Minimum Account Size	$1.580 mil	$2.082 mil	$838,000	$1.539 mil	$729,000
Av Margin/ Equity Ratio	15.12%	15.56%	34.33%	12.83%	12.71%
Assets (AUM) inc prev quarter	3.3%	11.2%	4.5%	−9.8%	0.7%
%AUM increase prev quarter	1%	3%	9%	−8%	3%
AUM increase last 4 quarters	27.4%	44.7%	10.5%	20.1%	11.2%
% AUM inc first 4 quarters	9%	10%	20%	16%	41%
UpCapture versus Bcly CTA	1.35	1.57	0.97	1.04	0.65
Alpha versus Barclay CTA	0.49	0.15	0.49	0.87	1.55
Beta versus Barclay CTA	1.06	0.46	0.53	0.61	−0.41
UpCapt versus S&P	0.37	0.09	0.64	0.38	0.39
DwnCapt versus S&P	−0.19	−0.14	−0.02	−0.26	−0.27

Performance Source: Barclay MAP database.

Past performance is not indicative of future results. Average performance may not reflect individual CTA performance. These numbers can change on a regular basis and are derived from the voluntary reporting of CTAs to the database.

APPENDIX B

Twelve Questions Investors Should Ask . . . of Themselves

Now that you have completed the book, here is the next step: answering 12 basic questions that often spur valuable discussion and allow for understanding the investor's risk/reward profile to point to appropriate managed futures investments. The answers should be written down and communicated with all involved in the investment process.

1. Why is the investor considering a managed futures investment?
2. What does the investor hope to achieve with this investment? What are the investment expectations relative to risk, volatility, and return?
3. What is the investor's risk/reward profile based on the book's definition?
   a. Conservative
   b. Moderate
   c. Aggressive
4. How significant a negative drawdown or loss is the investor willing to tolerate? As a benchmark, consider the S&P 500's worst drawdown was 50.95 percent.
5. What drawdown recovery times are investors willing to accept? Consider the S&P 500 took two years to recover from its worst drawdown.
6. Score the types of risk the investor is willing to tolerate, 1 being the most tolerable risk and 4 the least tolerable risk:
   a. Highly volatile investments
   b. Significant drawdown potential
   c. Long drawdown recovery time
   d. Individual manager risk
   e. Significant exposure to Black Swan Events
   f. Other

7. What are the investor's annual return expectations? Consider the average annual S&P 500 return averages around 10 percent.
8. What percentage of risk capital in the investor's overall portfolio is being considered for a managed futures investment? If the qualified investor is aggressive, consider a 33 percent allocation of his or her overall portfolio to managed futures; moderate investors might want to follow the allocation similar to Harvard University's Lintner report and devote 20 percent to managed futures; conservative investors might consider 10 percent or just not investing in managed futures.
9. Is the investment capital required for any future need? What is the investment time horizon?
10. How important is liquidity, transparency, or potential fraud protection in an investment?
11. What does the investor's overall investment portfolio consist of? Is there specific market exposure in the existing portfolio that would be best if hedged?
12. What is the investor's level of investing experience and liquid net worth?

This questionnaire is admittedly basic, but often a good point to start a more detailed discussion. The book's web site contains an interactive question and answer process that can help guide the investor to opinions on the appropriate investment options.

APPENDIX C

Selecting a Commodity Trading Advisor

In Chapter 10 we discussed commodity trading advisor (CTA) selection, and the next two appendices add to this discussion. The discussion in Appendix C is more general in nature, while Appendix D considers a study of average performance of top CTAs based on performance measures that investors should consider.

The task of matching an investor to a risk-appropriate CTA can be a complicated job. This is because it is really about identifying and then matching the investor's investing needs with the CTA's trading personality and related performance, both positive and negative. The trick with this is twofold, requiring understanding of CTAs, their strategies, and potential volatility, and then identifying true investor needs, which are not always easily ascertained as they relate to managed futures. Recommending CTAs can be tricky—it is a very different investment model.

Each CTA can have trading characteristics; to simplify, some can be cowboys, some accountants, and some CEOs. The problem is their performance numbers sometimes don't accurately portray their true personality and risk. There are CTAs who can exhibit amazingly consistent and "conservative" performance only to have a massive blowup month. Even more common are CTAs who have much more volatile intramonth performance than their reported monthly performance numbers indicate. There are measures that help decipher the true potential risk of an investment, such as the understanding of the core strategy and margin-to-equity ratios, which are discussed in advanced chapters. But to simply consider past returns as the only basis for determining a CTA's investment worth is incomplete at best. Striving to design a high-performing CTA portfolio in a managed risk environment is much more involved that gazing at amazing past returns.

When managing high-performing but risky assets, such as managed futures, hedge funds, and stocks, the first step in determining risk-appropriate choices in which to invest is for the investor to know his or her investment objectives. In managed futures this means understanding the investor's needs and risk tolerances: A frank risk tolerance discussion should take place before investments in managed futures are advanced. Individual investors are now sitting at the grownups table at Thanksgiving dinner where frank and strategic discussions of risk management take place. This is a process that should take place in all risk investments: stocks, managed futures, and hedge funds. Once investors understand their risk tolerance and investment needs they can properly choose diversified CTA investments that meet their individual risk/reward profile. (The Appendix B questionnaire helps start this conversation.)

"Know thyself" may sound like somewhat of a cliché, but it is truer in managed futures than in other investments. This is because if the investor chooses to invest in the aggressive managed futures asset class it can result in volatile performance, to the upside as well as the downside. Unfortunately, volatility has a habit of inappropriately playing to the individual investor's emotions. This is one reason matching a CTA program to an investor's risk tolerance and personality to a degree can serve an important role, particularly for individual investors. For instance, it is not uncommon to hear investors say they are interested in single CTAs with only the highest return potential, looking to receive triple digit annual performance, which can and does occur with the most aggressive CTAs. The problem occurs when the aggressive CTA enters a drawdown larger than any in his history and the investors discover they should have chosen more moderate programs.

INVESTOR EXPERIENCE: A REQUIREMENT FOR UNDERSTANDING STRATEGIES

A factor in determining appropriate CTA selection could be the investor's level of experience and financial wherewithal. Highly experienced, qualified investors might be those best suited to invest in aggressive CTA portfolios due to their understanding and appreciation of investing risk and reward management. Many CTA strategies just are not well suited for moderate or novice investors. In fact it could be argued that managed futures is not at all the classroom for investors to cut their investing teeth—particularly with risky investments in single managers or aggressive, high-flying CTAs.

Investor knowledge is important, but even the most experienced investors may not understand all the CTA strategies in which they have invested. And this can be a problem. It is important that the investor has at least a basic understanding of a CTA's strategy, if for no other reason than confirming appropriate diversification and having a basic understanding of the risk exposure of the investment. In many cases this task falls on the broker–portfolio manager the investor chooses. Some portfolio managers provide very detailed explanations of CTA strategy and updates of position exposure, particularly with actively managed portfolios. However, many brokers simply provide the vehicle for the investors to access managed futures and leave the investors to their own devices. Before investing in a managed futures program it is important to determine how involved the investor wants to become and then match the appropriate services with the investor. This book's web site has a tool that attempts to match an investor's individual situation with appropriate CTA investments. It is not perfect, as no machine intelligence can be, but it is interesting and starts the thought process.

CHOOSING CTAs BASED ON RISK-FOCUSED CRITERIA

Investors of a certain age might remember collecting baseball cards when they were younger; poring over statistics and considering the best combination of players to create the ultimate lineup. It is interesting to consider the performance statistics different people used to build their team. Some managers might have favored players who had the best headline numbers of most home runs or best batting average. Even as early as a few years ago, baseball teams were built based on instinct and gut feel of scouts and managers. Then a change hit the sport, as gut feel gave way to sophisticated statistical analysis. Led by the Oakland As and later the Boston Red Sox, it is now commonplace to see raw statistical analysis drive decisions in baseball with a powerful degree of success.

Managed futures is similar in some respects, not only in the sophisticated computerized strategies that drive the managed futures programs, but as revealed here the methods of statistical analysis used to select CTAs.

It is interesting to note that the owner of the Red Sox, John Henry, is one of the more prominent CTAs in the history of managed futures. John Henry's success as a CTA is said to be attributed in part to his statistical prowess and skills in probability analysis and risk/reward. John Henry transferred skills learned as a CTA to the world of baseball, where his statistics-based-decision influence on the Red Sox has led them to a World Series and perhaps one of the most dramatic playoff wins ever against their Darth Vader of enemies, the New York Yankees.

In baseball, John Henry's success came in part from considering statistics at a relevant level. He wasn't so much interested in the headline performance numbers of home runs or batting average: The Red Sox understood the importance of numbers beyond the headlines. They considered the importance of on-base and slugging percentage, and other at-one-time obscure statistics that led the Red Sox to some surprising but successful baseball conclusions.

In part, John Henry's success on the ball field and in the field of managed futures might be credited, in part, to an insight, a formula really, that is helpful in the world of managed futures:

Understanding the Total Risk and Reward Equation
+ Statistical Probability Analysis
= Potential for Powerful Results

Managed futures investors can follow a similar path.

In part, choosing an appropriate CTA can resemble the decision to put a particular player in the baseball manager's lineup. Just like a manager building an appropriately correlated baseball lineup based on gut feel and headline performance statistics, in managed futures some investors might only consider the headline performance numbers of highest returns or worst drawdown. But just like little-known statistics such as on-base and slugging percentage are hidden but powerful numbers in baseball, managed futures has its interesting yet little-known risk and reward statistics that can be used with the goal to choose CTAs based on statistical probability analysis. In fact, decision making based on statistical probability is the bedrock methodology behind trend trading CTAs, the largest category of managed futures programs. So why shouldn't statistically driven analysis play a role in CTA selection?

Baseball cards have given way to sophisticated Internet applications that allow for enthusiasts to build their unique team and "play" the lineup as the season progresses. The same is true in managed futures. Investors can visit a variety of web sites and select different managers based on a variety of statistical measures and combine various CTAs into a "lineup" or portfolio and then the web site reports the team results.

In this section we are going to outline the managed futures statistical measures that enable investors to conduct appropriate analysis, and identify how different CTA statistical measures are best matched toward very specific investor goals. This book then puts forth the concept that there is no "best" risk/reward statistical measure; it is all a matter of investor goals and situation. Much like considering the statistic of on-base percentage being appropriate for the early spots in a batting order, different CTA statistics are suited to fill needs in different situations. Some statistics are appropriate for investors where significant drawdowns are the issue; other statistics are best for investors who can handle large drawdowns but prefer specific noncorrelation to other parts of their portfolio.

FOCUSING ON SHORT-TERM GAINS IS SHORT-SIGHTED: CONFUSING ONLINE CTA RESEARCH

There are a number of web sites that investors can choose to conduct CTA research, and they also have links to other major CTA database web sites. But there is a problem with some of the sites: They can be confusing at best to new investors and might even point unknowledgeable investors in the wrong direction.

On their front-facing welcome page, some CTA database web sites contain lists of potentially unscrutinized CTAs ranked by their short-term monthly headline performance—and this can be a mistake. Many investors could immediately gravitate to the short-term returns because it is the easiest to understand. For instance, if one visited a popular CTA database web site one might be greeted with the performance tease shown in Table C.1.

There is nothing necessarily dishonest about this display of information. It was taken from a CTA database reporting service considered credible. In all likelihood, this is the actual performance reported and it is a semiautomated system that displays the top monthly reported performance. The problem is that this display of incredible returns based on a short-term monthly basis can lead the investor in the wrong direction—chasing the "hot dot" investment, as we describe below. But also, this provocative display of information doesn't tell the whole story.

What investors *should* see—information that is often hidden—is shown in Table C.2.

The "Top 10 Monthly Performers" actually were also top performers in delivering some amazingly high worst drawdown numbers and low Sharpe ratios. The average worst drawdown numbers only touch the tip of the iceberg of what are some aggressive programs. (On the book's web site readers can find what is believed to be balanced and straightforward opinion and analysis of various CTA programs and strategies.)

The problem is compounded by a Sharpe ratio that requires a magnifying glass just to register. But here is what's worse: Many of the CTAs in this list of top performers might not be appropriate for investors. This is because several of the CTAs have short track records and may not have undergone a National Futures Association (NFA) audit. It is not a bad general rule to view with caution performance that has not undergone an NFA audit. Other CTAs may not even fall under the regulatory control of the NFA, with yellow and red flags that are not evident unless the investor understands where to look and find information. But here is perhaps the largest issue with the naked display of seductive monthly performance numbers: *It chases the hot dot.*

TABLE C.1 Top 10 Performers Month of October, 2009

	Current	2009 YTD
Pearl CTA—Silver Spoon Program	52.43%	−6.39%
Be Your Best CTA Capital Management—FX Program	18.20%	10.40%
Randolph Duke Trading Group, LLC—Flexible Option Strategy 1	16.37%	25.24%
P.F. Chang Finance Associates AG—Aggressive Prg	14.87%	256.69%
Jimmy Carter Road LLC—Options Overlay	12.00%	49.55%
AS IS Futures Mgt LLC—MAAP (3X–6X) Program	11.39%	65.51%
S+P Options King Investment Strategists—DPC Regular	9.86%	94.24%
Boris Becker Asset Mgt, LLC—Program 1	8.79%	41.55%
AS IS Futures Mgt LLC—MAAP (2X–4X) Program	7.90%	46.33%
DCI—Option Selling Strategy	7.45%	28.74%

TABLE C.2

	Worst Drawdown	Sharpe Ratio	Author's Limited Opinions
Pearl CTA—Silver Spoon Program	−86.39%	NA	Volatile AUM pattern in 2009 $185K to $538K, should require investigation.
Be Your Best CTA Capital Management—FX Program	−16.97%	0.10	Only four month track record, overseas potentially unregulated CTA.
Randolph Duke Trading Group, LLC—Flexible Option Strategy 1	−16.37%	0.25	Three month track record, might not have had NFA audit, only $78,000 under management.
P.F. Chang Finance Associates AG—Aggressive Prg	−6.90%	0.07	Eight month track record, might not have had NFA audit.
Jimmy Carter Road LLC—Options Overlay	−73.35%	NA	Fund structure, only 2.1 mil under management after close to 6 years in business.
AS IS Futures Mgt LLC—MAAP (3X–6X) Program	−89.67%	0.20	Credible, long track record, CPO, $49.8 million under management.
S+P Options King Investment Strategists—DPC Regular	−80.60%	−0.31	The famed options king continues after strategy returns blow up. His new strategy options look interesting, worthy of investigation.
Boris Becker Asset Mgt, LLC—Program 1	−41.07%	0.55	Yellow flag with only $400K under management after nearly 5 years in business.
AS IS Futures Mgt LLC—MAAP (2X–4X) Program	−74.76%	0.25	Good aggressive CTA. In existence since 1992, $128 million under management, $5 mil minimum account size.
DCI—Option Selling Strategy	−34.63%	0.89	Solid past performer, strong diversified strategy, portfolio foundation. Keep an eye on risk management and stop triggers.

CHASING THE HOT DOT CAN BE LIKE A DOG CHASING ITS TAIL

While these monthly performance teases are interesting, it can start the CTA selection process in the wrong direction and investors should not get distracted. Here's why:

> *Trying to chase the hot dot based on monthly performance can be a distracting exercise in futility.*

The small measure of a previous month's performance serves the purpose of focusing on the hot hand, and this narrow approach should yield to a more holistic method that considers both risk and reward performance.

The hot monthly performer is interesting, but not from the most common perspective. When viewing the list of hot monthly performers, investors tend to focus on the individual CTA and his or her related returns. But this misses the key insight: Some investors can use the hot performer as a method to identify the winds of current market behavior. The hot performers are *not* interesting from the perspective of the CTAs and their short-term performance, but more significant are the underlying strategies they use, the markets they trade, and how this can provide an indication as to the winds of the current market environment. Are we in a trending environment? Shifting volatility? These are the questions that might matter more in managed futures. When the list of CTAs is filtered to consider only what the author considers a minimum standard for qualified CTAs, the top monthly performers might see trend traders well represented as a group at one point, indicating that the markets could be trending; at another point volatility/option CTAs could take center stage, potentially indicating market volatility is moving from a high point to a low point.

In this section we travel down the path of individual CTA selection and bring it all together in the coming section on portfolio building.

CTA STRATEGY CONSIDERATIONS AND MARKET TIMING

There are different market environments that both positively and negatively impact CTA trading strategies. Markets can be in a trending environment, where the price of a commodity is moving consistently in one direction. Conversely, markets can be in what is known as a "choppy" environment, where there is no consistent price direction and the price of a commodity changes direction seemingly on a whim. There are high-volatility markets, where the price differential is very large and can quickly rise and fall to dramatic levels. Conversely, there are low-volatility markets where the price differential is small and markets seem to trade in more historical ranges or norms. There are points where fundamental supply and demand issues may change the short-term market dynamics but not impact the long-term market dynamics—and the list of possibilities can go on. *Specific managed futures strategies perform depending on the market environment*, something not often considered in manager selection.

Market theory tells us different market environments benefit particular CTA strategies, which might influence the decision regarding *when* to enter a CTA investment.

APPENDIX D

Identifying True Risk and Utilizing the Best Managed Futures Performance Measure

In Chapter 10 we touched on CTA selection and performance measures, and Appendix D offers more study. On the book's web site is a white paper that analyzes CTA performance for each strategy, recommending different performance measures depending on the strategy.

As you review the risk measures in this appendix, understand that all performance and risk measures obviously are entirely based on past results—that is why they are historical statistics—and past performance is not indicative of future results.

KEY TO SUCCESS: CONSIDER RISK FIRST, THEN RETURN

What is the "best" risk measure to use when evaluating CTA performance? Answering this question can prove difficult, much like asking an individual's preference toward a Malbec, Pinot Noir, or Cabernet. Much could depend on the individual's portfolio, risk tolerances, and performance goals.

In this appendix, the concept is put forth that there is no universal "best" performance measure because it is relative to the individual's risk tolerances and goals. And here is an insight:

> *Different performance measures work best with different CTA strategies.*

For instance, win percentage is typically very different in a short volatility strategy than a trend trading system. Volatility and drawdown can be very different in a spread trading strategy than a trend or discretionary strategy. On the book's web site readers can download a professional white paper with opinions on the most appropriate performance measures for each strategy, and importantly, each individual investor.

And here is a key in selecting the appropriate CTA investments: The CTA selection method should start by understanding the investors' risk tolerances and then customize a CTA selection process from this perspective.

Every investor has a different risk/reward profile. Cold mathematical calculation can be the trademark of the professional investor. But even different pension funds can have different individual risk/reward needs to varying degrees. Some professional investors may seek only managed futures to smooth out their portfolio volatility during times of stock market decline. For these investors, one measure to consider is obviously correlation, but under certain circumstances, a win percentage analysis during periods of correlation can prove interesting. Some pension funds may look to managed futures as a returns enhancer, willing to tolerate significant short-term drawdowns so long as the fund does not remain in the red long. These investors might want to focus on average recovery time as well as force of probability, which we list next. These are just a few of the indicators and situations under which investors should frame risk measures, always understanding they base their output on past results which do not indicate the future.

While many consider professional and individual investors worlds apart, that might not be as much the case as many think, particularly when it comes to selecting the appropriate risk/reward measures. It all involves understanding tolerances and investor goals. While it is assumed that all investors desire high returns and low risk, it is risk that can be relative to the investor. Some might be accepting of high drawdowns but with quick recovery times; others can accept volatility but not significant average drawdown.

There are several risk measures and methods to select a CTA. What follows are the author's opinions on CTA selection and risk/reward measures, which may or may not be right for all individuals and is not being represented as all inclusive on the topic.

The following is a unique analysis using common performance statistics while considering the top 20 CTAs in the following categories and then cross-referencing the performance statistics:

- Compounded annual return
- Sharpe ratio
- Worst drawdown
- Standard deviation in rate of return
- Average recovery time

TABLE D.1 Average Past Performance of the Top 20 CTAs Based on Compounded Annual Return

Top 20 Category	CpdAnR	sdROR	AvgRec	AvgDD	Worst DD	Sharpe
CpdAnR	48.2	11.32	2.24	11.46	31.6	1.42
Sharpe ratio	30.38	3.26	1.89	2.95	6.99	2.32
Worst drawdown	9.87	1.37	2.18	0.99	2.41	1.17
sdROR	4.08	0.88	2.65	1.15	3.84	0.39
Average recovery time	21.27	4.33	1.42	3.97	11.36	1.51

(For this study we focus only on what the author considers the major risk measures, but note that many potentially powerful risk measures, including average drawdown, have not been included.)

The first category in Table D.1, for example, is the compounded annual return. This top-20 category puts on display the average performance of the top 20 CTAs with the highest compounded annual return (CpdAnR) at the time of this study. Moving from left to right, readers can see the top 20 CTAs when averaged together have a compounded annual return of 48.2 percent, a high standard deviation (sdROR) of 11.32 percent, a reasonable recovery time (AvgRec) of 2.24 months, an average drawdown (AvgDD) of 11.46 percent, a worst drawdown (Worst DD) of 31.6 percent and a strong Sharpe ratio of 1.42 that one might expect when returns are generally high and deviation is moderate.

POPULAR PERFORMANCE/RISK MEASURES

Compounded Annual Return

Compounded annual return is perhaps the most common performance measure that investors consider. It is easy to understand, wrapping the investor's mind around the positive.

But are simple returns the best method to choose a CTA?

To provide potential guidance, the book conducted a limited study of the Barclay Map CTA database where the top 20 CTAs were compared in a number of performance categories. The related performance measures of the average of these groups was considered.

Those CTAs with the highest compounded annual return also had the highest standard deviation, or most volatile performance, with an 11.32 standard deviation. The highest annual return category also had the highest worst drawdown and average drawdown statistics of 31.6 percent and

11.46 percent respectively. The high relative Sharpe ratio is a respectable 1.42, but obtaining those returns came with a required tolerance of what might be significant drawdown and volatility. And this highlights a unique, perhaps timeless truth:

> *The fact that CTAs with the highest compounded annual return also have the highest negative risk measures highlights an old truism that has held the test of time for a reason: With increased reward, there is increased risk.*

In this book, all studies using compounded annual return provided by the Barclay MAP Alternative Database use the following formula:

[(Final VAMI/Initial VAMI) ^ (1/number of years)] – 1(× 100 for %)

If you don't have an even number of years, use (12/number of months) or (4/number of quarters)

Example: Initial VAMI = 1000, Final VAMI = 4000, No. of years = 2

Cpd. Ann. ROR = [(4000/1000) ^ (1/2)] – 1

Cpd. Ann. ROR = 4 ^ 1/2 – 1 = 2 – 1 = 1 or 100%

Worst Drawdown

It is not uncommon for investors to consider the worst drawdown as a headline risk statistic. And while worst drawdown is an interesting statistic, it is not the only drawdown statistic that should be considered. As an overall measure of a CTA's past success, the measure has a ways to go. The top 20 CTAs as measured by lowest worst drawdown had an average drawdown of just 2.41 percent and a low volatility measured by a standard deviation of only 1.37 (see Table D.2). Those CTAs with the lowest worst drawdown also had a comparatively low compounded annual return, at 9.87 percent.

TABLE D.2 Average Past Performance of Top 20 CTAs With the Lowest Worst Drawdown

Top 20 Category	CpdAnR	sdROR	AvgRec	AvgDD	Worst DD	Sharpe
Worst drawdown	9.87	1.37	2.18	0.99	2.41	1.17

Worst drawdown is an interesting risk measure for conservative investors to rely more heavily on than aggressive investors, as evidenced by the somewhat slight 9.87 percent compounded annual return. But as you will see shortly, it might not be right for all situations; in fact average drawdown and drawdown recovery time might warrant more consideration under certain circumstances.

Length of Track Record

Length of track record is an important basic statistic to be considered. This is not always due to any potential correlation between experience and performance, as new CTAs sometimes possess significant professional trading histories without CTA registration. It is important to focus on experience relative to the validity of a track record; it will show a CTA's performance over a variety of market conditions and allow for clarity into whether a more experienced manager can handle business and trading operations. When considering emerging CTAs, length of track record can become a consideration from the important standpoint of that CTA having undergone an NFA audit. Another interesting point to consider is that CTAs with long track records but who don't have a reasonably significant level of assets under management are sometimes cause for further investigation. Sometimes investors may find themselves asking this question: Why after a successful track record and relatively long period of time of three to five years does a CTA not have more significant assets under management?

In Table D.3, as might be expected, CTAs with a long track record also possess reasonable assets under management with an average of $278 million under management. While some may consider CTAs with a long track record most stable, in fact, as a group the top 20 oldest CTAs, who range in start date from 1975 to 1986 have a long average recovery time and a high average drawdown. While the compounded annual return of 16.76 percent could be attractive, a Sharpe ratio of 0.34 is rather stock market–like in its risk/reward profile.

TABLE D.3 Average Past Performance of Top 20 CTAs with the Longest Track Record

Top 20 Category	CpdAnR	sdROR	AvgRec	AvgDD	Worst DD	Sharpe
Longest track records	16.76	10.33	5.68	15.59	48.14	0.34

TABLE D.4 Average Past Performance of Top 20 CTAs Based on Sharpe Ratio

Top 20 Category	CpdAnR	sdROR	AvgRec	AvgDD	Worst DD	Sharpe
Sharpe ratio	30.38	3.26	1.89	2.95	6.99	2.32

Sharpe Ratio

Astute investors might also consider Sharpe ratio, perhaps the most popular of all the risk/reward statistics, which was defined in Chapter 2. As might be expected, the top 20 CTAs based on Sharpe ratio had strong performance statistics, with a 30.38 percent compounded annual return, relatively low standard deviation, a very quick average recovery time, and shallow worst and average drawdown statistics. Sharpe ratio is a popular measure for all levels of investors, but as you will see it might not be the best measure because it does not differentiate between positive and negative deviation.

The following is the formula for Sharpe ratio.

$$= \frac{\bar{r}_p - r_f}{\sigma_p}$$

where: $\bar{r}_p$ = Expected Porfolio Return
r_f = Risk-Free Rate of Return
σ_p = Portfolio Standard Deviation

Standard Deviation of Returns

The strict risk measure standard deviation of returns only measures the differential in returns/price movement of an asset from high to low. For instance, a CTA with a 20 percent loss one month and 20 percent gain the next would have a higher standard deviation than a CTA with a 5 percent monthly loss and 5 percent gain the following month. Table D.5 is very revealing. Note the pathetic returns performance of CTAs that also have the

TABLE D.5 Average Past Performance of Top 20 CTAs with the Lowest Standard Deviation

Top 20 Category	CpdAnR	sdROR	AvgRec	AvgDD	Worst DD	Sharpe
sdROR	4.08	0.88	2.65	1.15	3.84	0.39

TABLE D.6 Average Past Performance of Top 20 CTAs with Quickest Average Recovery Time

Top 20 Category	CpdAnR	sdROR	AvgRec	AvgDD	Worst DD	Sharpe
Average recovery time	21.27	4.33	1.42	3.97	11.36	1.51

lowest standard deviation, which points to the fact that volatility and standard deviation and volatility are the price one pays for returns in managed futures.

Standard deviation is said to measure the volatility of an investment, and is thus one measure of risk. Volatility has always been considered one significant measure of risk ever since Harry Markowitz used the measure in his Nobel Prize-winning modern portfolio theory. Standard deviation is a statistic used as a measure of the dispersion or variation in a distribution, equal to the square root of the arithmetic mean of the squares of the deviations from the arithmetic mean. Standard deviation is an important volatility measure, but its equal weighting for positive and negative volatility should be questioned, which becomes clear when consideration is given to the overlooked risk measures.

OVERLOOKED PERFORMANCE MEASURES

Average Drawdown Recovery Time

Average drawdown recovery, an underutilized risk measure in the author's opinion, should be considered. As you will see from the analysis of risk measures on the coming pages, this risk measure can provide one of the more interesting windows into an investment's past.

Consider the significance of recovery time, particularly as it relates to conservative and moderate risk-averse managed futures investors, which is always a relative term to managed futures risk. There are certain moderate and aggressive investors who can tolerate significant 20 percent monthly drawdowns so long as the time frame for recovery is reasonably quick. Understanding the past drawdown recovery time provides investors a peek into a very important past risk measure, with two points that are perhaps most interesting about drawdown recovery time. On the surface, quick drawdown recovery time might indicate sound trade management under certain circumstances, as evidenced by performance statistics study, but under certain circumstances it surprisingly might indicate more aggressive CTAs who can make up large losses quickly. This points to the fact that average drawdown

TABLE D.7 Top 20 CTAs Based on Lowest Standard Deviation

Top 20 Category	CpdAnR	sdROR	AvgRec	AvgDD	Worst DD	Sharpe
sdROR	4.08	0.88	2.65	1.15	3.84	0.39

recovery time is best used in conjunction with other risk statistics to provide the most complete view of risk and reward, but it can be a multifaceted risk/reward measure.

It is interesting to consider a study of the top CTAs in various performance categories. For instance, next we start by analyzing what might be hidden keys to past performance success, which doesn't indicate the future. Note in Table D.6 that the CTAs with the best average recovery times also had a relatively respectable Sharpe ratio at 1.51, a reasonable standard deviation at 4.33, a relatively moderate average drawdown and a somewhat acceptable worst drawdown of 11.36 percent. Compare this to the top 20 CTAs based on the lowest standard deviation to provide perspective, shown in Table D.7.

The top 20 CTAs based on standard deviation had a measly 0.39 Sharpe ratio and a paltry 4.08 percent compounded annual return: an investment that starts to look like a stock index. From this comes a unique insight: Identifying the "best" CTAs by considering nothing other than standard deviation in fact produced the least attractive risk/reward profile. The obvious conclusion is that in managed futures, high standard deviation and the resulting volatility is where significant past returns can be found. In other words, an academic insight that might seem unnatural for traditional stock investors:

Under the right circumstance, volatility can yield positive results.

This might go against the grain of certain popular opinion and requires understanding that we devote several fascinating chapters to explore and use in part to present an investment philosophy. Thinking about it from a different perspective might make the concept more palatable to some. In the past, investors tolerated high standard deviation as a cost to obtain higher returns, which could be considered an axiom in managed futures.

Average Drawdown

While worst drawdown tends to get the headline attention, it is really average drawdown that is more common in an investor's actual field of vision, the drawdown type most commonly experienced. From a mathematical perspective it could be considered more valid to include consideration of the most probable past result rather than the most extreme. But that is not the only insight. Average drawdown is also interesting to consider from the perspective of the spread between the average drawdown and the worst drawdown. Ideally it is most appealing to see consistent drawdown depth. A drawdown that is out of character with the performance might indicate softness in a risk-management plan, among other issues, which could be considered an overlooked, less-popular factor in CTA analysis.

Assets under Management

Assets under management (AUM) is a consideration in CTA selection from several standpoints. Significant AUM implies a degree of success in that the top CTAs may have achieved a degree of institutional acceptance and relatively long track records. As you can see in Table D.8, the 16 CTAs that have AUM over $2 billion have acceptable performance statistics, but also have an equally high average stated account minimum of $5.7 million.

AUM is interesting to consider from several perspectives, both positive and negative.

CTAs with significant AUM signify to some that the firm has a degree of gravitas and management sophistication that is attractive to institutional capital, which often requires passing significant due diligence. In order to effectively manage significant assets, CTAs with significant AUM likely have a degree of business acumen and knowledge of market liquidity dynamics. In terms of AUM, emerging CTAs might garner a degree of attention when they surpass their first $1 million under management; when they surpass the $10 million level, they might garner what could be considered a degree of acceptance, but any hard and fast rule in this area is pointless, as many other factors are at play. However, this also misses a potential opportunity:

> *One benefit of smaller-AUM CTAs is that they can be nimble in executing unique niche strategies.*

TABLE D.8 Average Performance of "Large CTAs" with Assets Under Management over $2 Billion

Top 20 Category	CpdAnR	sdROR	AvgRec	AvgDD	Worst DD	Sharpe
AUM over $2 billion	14.66	4.52	2.89	11.46	19.66	0.49

This is because, at the same time, massive AUM can create liquidity issues that might limit strategy considerations and markets in which the CTA can participate.

Certain strategies are most nimble at lower AUM levels, and increased AUM can actually make the strategy more cumbersome. Market liquidity relative to a particular strategy can be an issue in some niche markets, but not most of the primary markets. While many futures and options markets are highly liquid, there are certain strategies that might require execution in less liquid markets, which means that AUM might be limited. For instance, CPO A-1 is a single-advisor commodity pool that trades sophisticated niche spread strategies in the interest rate complex. The highly successful fund had to close to new investors when they reached certain AUM because the initial strategy traded could not accommodate additional assets without denigrating performance. Rather than have all investors suffer performance denigration, the fund chose to remain exclusive and true to its initial investors. (Later the fund slightly revised the strategy and successfully launched a second fund featuring the new strategy and the additional benefit of diversification.)

Another measure is to consider the pattern of asset growth: Is it ascending or descending and at what rate? This can provide clues into the health of the business operation and potential survivorship issues.

Sortino Ratio

One of the better but often overlooked risk/reward measures in managed futures is the Sortino ratio because it starts to differentiate between good and bad volatility. Like the Sharpe ratio, the Sortino ratio considers expected return along with the risk-free rate of return. The difference is the Sortino ratio recognizes positive and negative returns through its weighting of negative deviation of asset returns. This weighting of negative returns in a formula is a solid development, because it is interesting when a risk/reward measure differentiates between positive and negative returns to a degree.

$$\text{Sortino Ratio} = \frac{\langle R \rangle - R_f}{\sigma_d}$$

where: $\langle R \rangle$ = Expected Return

R_f = Risk-Free Rate of Return

σ_d = Standard Deviation of Negative Asset Returns

TABLE D.9 Average Past Performance of Top 20 CTAs based on Best Sortino Ratio

Top 20 Category	CpdAnR	sdROR	AvgRec	AvgDD	Worst DD	Sharpe
Sortino	27.58	2.94	1.9	2.1	5.36	2.2

As you can see in Table D.9, the top 20 CTAs based on best Sortino ratio also have significant compounded annual return and very low standard deviation and drawdown statistics.

OTHER PERFORMANCE MEASURES

Upside/Downside Deviation

Perhaps another major overlooked performance measure is the Upside/Downside ratio. Upside deviation can be an interesting performance measure based on knowledge of the various CTA strategies and their trading patterns. Managed futures with strong upside deviation can indicate normalized positive performance from this practical standpoint: It can be common for strong managed futures programs to let profits "run" and this can create high upside deviation, particularly in high-performing managed futures. However, high downside deviation could be a significant problem. Downside deviation can indicate inconsistent past risk management, spiky negative past performance. This is a significant issue. As all professional investors understand, no measure is perfect. More common is a shade of gray rather than stark black and white, and much can be analyzed to varying degrees. This obviously depends on the strategy. Professional investors may recognize that short volatility strategies, for instance, can be slightly exempt from this upside deviation to a degree. Having said that, short volatility options traders who don't use risk management—the nightmare of this strategy—could exhibit significant downside deviation while more stable upside deviation, assuming that their selling strategy is remaining consistent in terms of the standard deviation, or distance they sell options from the market. In technical terms, the options delta they sell remains consistent. Further, certain "gamma scalping" option strategies could experience similar upside/downside deviation characteristics. These option strategies seek to benefit from the rate of change in the option time decay, or theta. Readers of this book don't need to understand these rather technical and finite strategies; the point is to illustrate that different strategies can have different upside/downside deviation ratios.

Here are the formulas for both upside and downside deviation:

Downside Deviation (Formula Used in Barclay MAP) Take all of the those returns in the target period that are less than zero, square each of these returns, take the sum of all these squares, divide the entirety by N (the number of returns in the complete period, whether the returns are up or down), then take the square root of the whole thing.

In symbols:

Suppose R = { R1, R2, . . . , RN }, the set of N sequential returns for a program or fund over some period of time.

From this we can get:

r = { r1, r2, . . . , rk | ri ∈ R and ri < 0, i = 1, 2, . . . , k ≤ N }; that is, the subset of all returns less than zero, of which there will be at most N, and which may be empty (i.e., no returns less than zero).

The formula for downside deviation, D, can then be written

D = [(S1k ri2] / N)1/2, for all ri ∈ r (i.e., for all returns less than zero in the target range), and:

D = 0, when r is empty (i.e., there are no returns less than zero).

Note: We are comparing each return with zero, but some other constant could be used, say, Z:

D = [(S1n (ri – Z)2] / N)1/2, for all ri ∈ R where ri < Z for each i = 1, 2, . . . , n.

In Barclay MAP, Z = 0.

Upside Deviation The formula is virtually identical to the downside deviation formula used above, except the returns greater than zero would be used; that is, the returns $r_j \in R$ such that $r_j > 0$ for each j = 1, 2, . . . , q.

Returns Distribution

Perhaps one of the more significant performance measures in managed futures is returns distribution. Critical degrees of success can be found among CTAs with somewhat even returns distribution. Returns distribution does have statistical tendencies depending on managed futures strategy, which provides interesting insight during the CTA selection process when returns distribution is benchmarked against an industry standard.

Sterling Ratio

Sterling ratio considers worst drawdown in its formula, which is interesting. Investors who tolerate volatility as long as the average drawdown is not significant might do well to consider this risk measure.

$$\text{Sterling Ratio} = \frac{\text{Compounded Annual Return}}{\text{Average Maximum Drawdown} - 10\%}$$

It is the author's opinion that recovery time can be a more significant risk measure than is standard deviation. In fact, a risk/reward measure that utilizes drawdown recovery time might be perhaps most interesting to those investors most sensitive to experiencing extended negative performance.

Calmar Ratio

Calmar ratio is another effective risk/reward measure that looks at worst drawdown. It could be argued that average drawdown and drawdown recovery time are more valid drawdown risk measures. This could highlight a weakness in this risk measure. While worst drawdown is important, average recovery time and average drawdown might be better suited for investors who desire to understand what might be the typical drawdown performance, not the extreme performance. This emphasizes the fact that worst drawdown can highlight aberrations of the investment's past experience.

$$\text{Calmar Ratio} = \left(\frac{\text{Compounded Annual Return}}{\substack{\text{Maximum Drawdown} \\ \text{(using the absolute value)}}} \right)$$

RISK MEASURES SHOULD CONSIDER PROBABILITY OF SUCCESS AND SIZE OF WIN

There is not a major risk/reward measure that considers probability of success. While Sortino might be the closest in that it weights negative asset returns, which is one reason this risk/reward measure might have a solid tale to tell, this is still not a pure probability risk/reward measure. And this should be a consideration.

Following are measures that consider probability and force of success.

Win/Loss Percentage

This tells investors the likelihood for experiencing past success during any given time period. The ratio is often used on a monthly basis, thus a positive win/loss ratio would indicate the investor would meet success during a large percentage of months.

It could be argued that probability of success is most effectively measured in a risk/reward ratio for individual investors based on the percentage of time the investment was a winner, along with the force, or magnitude, of that win.

It is the author's opinion that in managed futures those CTAs that generate quick, massive, but relatively rare positive returns are more difficult for the investor to "catch" and require a more disciplined, patient investor. This is why understanding the nature of the investor's needs can provide a valuable look at setting up the appropriate CTA structure.

Using win/loss percentage in combination with average drawdown and drawdown recovery time, the investor can receive a picture of the past risk, time to recover from pain, and percentage of time that the investor experienced success.

Size of Win/Size of Loss

Size of win versus the size of loss can matter in managed futures as it points to strong trade and risk management. This can tell you if both positive and negative returns have occurred in bunches and can provide insight into the probability and force of past success. There are CTAs that can do really nothing for most of the year and then suddenly experience powerful performance surges with the bursting speed of a game-changing kickoff return specialist. The problem is that many investors don't have the patience to watch paint dry or endure drawdowns while waiting for what can be a powerful sprint that could end in a relative nanosecond.

Force of Probability (Past Magnitude and Past Likelihood)

There really isn't a standard measure that considers both the probability of past success or failure and the force, or magnitude, of that resulting past success or failure. For this reason, we created the force of probability index. The measure considers win percentage and loss percentage, as well as the size of the win and the size of the loss. To measure this we use the following formula:

$$(\%\ \text{Win} \times \text{Avg win})/(\%\ \text{Loss} \times \text{Avg loss}) = \text{Past Probability and Force}$$

Generally the higher the number the better, meaning that the CTA had a significant number of past winning months and those winning months were of significant size. Note that this formula offers interesting insight but the measure is relative to the strategy. For instance, option premium collection strategies should have a large percentage of wins but those wins might not necessarily come with significant gains. Conversely, on the downside the options premium collection strategy might have a small percentage of losses but those losses could be significant. A discretionary position trader could have a much lower win percentage but a higher returns magnitude.

It is also important to note, that each managed futures strategy have indicators that might be considered best suited for their individual strategy. On the book's web site we offer a more extensive white paper on the best managed futures performance measures based on trading strategy, where all these indicators are further explored on the web site and applied to specific CTA analysis.

APPENDIX E

Regulated versus Unregulated Entities

In Chapter 5 we discussed industry regulation, but we didn't touch on activities that might not technically fall under such regulation, such as highly dubious sales pitches and get rich quick schemes.

"Learn how to trade and double your money every year just like Jim Smith did. He turned $50,000 into $1 million in just four years working from home just 30 minutes per day!"

Investment professionals in regulated futures industries cringe at such outrageous claims. Never mind that most individual investors turned "traders" end up losing their capital, but the cherry-picking of results and appeal to investor naked greed with what could be described as a statistically unlikely scenario is what gives the entire industry a bad name—and this activity is generally in the crosshairs of industry regulators like the NFA and Commodity Futures Trading Commission (CFTC). However, entities that do not fall under the regulation of these entities have much looser communications and marketing standards than do those regulated entities.

The worldwide interbank foreign exchange market (FOREX) is perhaps the most widely used example of an unregulated marketplace. Firms that offer investments originating from these are often not directly regulated by the NFA and CFTC, and their claims are sometimes over the top relative to profit potential and the occasional use of high-pressure sales tactics. Although this lack of regulation is likely to change, it is important to note that entities not regulated by the NFA and CFTC have much less restrictive confines in which to work. It is recommended that investors interested in Foreign Exchange (FOREX intra-bank currency markets) place investments through NFA registered firms, which can be identified on the NFA web site at www.nfa.futures.org.

Another example of unregulated entities includes certain industry educators. While many educators are legitimate, some educators make claims regarding "hypothetical" past performance that are outside the realm of statistical norms, and could be cherry-picking only the best results and ignoring the poor performance of certain accounts. While technically not fraud in a court of law, sometimes due to the couching of language this type of marketing communication would not pass the strict guidelines of the NFA or CFTC. Investors considering any commodity investment should ask two simple questions: "Are these results audited by the National Futures Association? Can you prove it?" (The book's web site contains a link that allows investors to check the background of all NFA members. If a search does not yield a result, the individual may not be an NFA member and likely is not regulated by this organization, which should always be a caution sign for investors.)

WHEN UNREGULATED ENTITIES ENSNARE REGULATED FIRMS

Unregulated entities are not *directly* within the reach of the NFA and CFTC, but that does not mean that they are outside their sphere of influence.

When a regulated entity engages in business with an unregulated entity, and that unregulated entity makes deceptive claims or otherwise violates NFA guidelines, it is the regulated entity that can become responsible. This is kind of like sitting next to a troublemaker in grade school and being included in the bad kid's punishment. While this might not seem fair, the answer might be not associating with the bad kids in the first place. Consider an example.

Assume an unregulated entity or person is operating a futures trading system to trade client accounts. The person or entity is not a registered CTA and does not have an audited past performance, yet he advertises only selected past performance, cherry-picking the top performing accounts but neglecting to balance the discussion with mention of poor performance. The unregulated entity or person uses pressure sales tactics and violates several NFA rules. While this individual is not registered, accounts must be held at a registered futures commission merchant (FCM). The FCM might even pay the unregulated trading system for sales leads of potential customers. In either case, the FCM or any regulated entity that participated in the marketing could be held responsible by the NFA and CFTC for the unregulated entity's activities, even if the regulated entity did not directly participate in any action. This guilt by association may seem onerous, but it can have the impact of eliminating fraudulent loopholes. There are other such regulations that ensnare the unsuspecting. For instance, if a regulated individual first enters the industry and unknowingly works for an FCM or introducing broker (IB) that has had serious NFA infractions, this individual could become what is known as a tainted broker just due to his association with a disciplined firm. There are a variety of situations where firms and individuals in this industry have had NFA or CFTC issues that to an outsider might seem odd. But when the investor is put first in an aggressive regulatory environment this can be the fallout. The book's web site contains links to specific locations where investors can conduct research on past violations of various CTAs, commodity pool operators (CPOs), and brokerage firms. Readers are always encouraged to visit the NFA web site at www.nfa.futures.org or the CFTC web site at www.cftc.gov to learn more about the industry's strong regulation.

APPENDIX **F**

Markowitz and Lintner: A "Modern" Investment Method Half a Century Old

Throughout the book we discuss the work of Markowitz and Lintner. This appendix provides more of an anecdotal background of their work, with details on the book's web site.

What was he thinking?

On the chilly, wind-swept shores of Lake Michigan in the 1940s, a young University of Chicago graduate student, Harry Markowitz, was looking for a topic for his doctorial thesis and decided to study the stock market. A man of Markowitz's superior academic ilk would be presumed to consider more serious, higher-level topics of the day; anything but the disgusting stock market.

At the time the stock market was considered dirty, questionable subject matter, as aptly described in Ben Warwick's book *Searching for Alpha* (John Wiley & Sons, 2000):

> *In the late 1940s (the stock market) was an unusual subject for serious academic study. The memories of the Great Depression, along with the well-publicized scandals of such market luminaries as Richard Whitney (the Chairman of the New York Stock Exchange who was caught in a stock fraud scheme with his brother) and J. P. Morgan (recently vilified by a congressional subcommittee on banking and finance) generally soured the public's view on the stock market as an investment medium. . . . In addition, the proliferation of so-called bucket shops—brokerage houses of ill repute that charged outlandish commissions and manipulated stock prices—only served to further separate the stock market from the average investor.*

Today it might be difficult to comprehend the societal backdrop of the 1940s. The stock market was not a viable mainstream investment, much like managed futures is viewed today. Stocks were viewed as a Wild West road show of sorts with the popular contempt reserved for snake oil salespeople. Contrast this with today's hero-worship relationship between investors and equities. The stock market is *the* investment source, the unquestioned singular temple of investing, the state-mandated religion forced down investors' throats by societal norms that place it on such a high plateau the words *stocks* and *investing* are considered synonymous. And while the following is not an insight, perhaps it should be: Stocks might not deserve to be the center of the investing universe. But the notion might be a little radical at this point in time, perhaps like true asset diversification and risk/reward management were when modern portfolio theory (MPT) was first released.

Regardless of the opinion of the day, Markowitz was his own man; a man of vision with the confidence and fortitude to push forward against the headwinds of resistance. This fortitude would later be tested when none other than University of Chicago legend Milton Friedman delivered a public browbeating to Markowitz, claiming that his MPT was "not economics." But Markowitz, confident in his quest for true diversification and the efficient frontier future of investing, was undaunted, and in 1990 the Nobel Prize committee ultimately rewarded his out-of-the-box thinking and validated his investment methodology with the world's highest intellectual honor.

INVESTORS SHOULD ONLY TAKE RISKS FOR WHICH THEY ARE PROPERLY COMPENSATED

Today, with the benefit of hindsight, it seems so logical almost to the point of obvious. Markowitz believed that investors should only take risks for which they are compensated. That sounds simple, but in the last decade have stock investors, most with negative or very small returns, taken risks for which they were properly compensated?

Markowitz believed investors should be different from riverboat gamblers who were willing to risk their entire net worth on one investment. Rather, investors should act like intelligent, rational decision makers who prefer to spread their risk among various investment opportunities.

But in the 1940s, just before Markowitz created his work, it was a stock picker's environment where risk management through diversification was generally shunned. Investing thought was exemplified by "home run hitter" Gerald Loeb, author of *The Battle for Investment Survival* (John Wiley & Sons, 1996) and a top producing broker of the day, who believed that wealth was accumulated through concentration of investment, not diversification.

In other words, Loeb liked to put all his eggs in one basket, chasing returns and the hot stock. Even today the concentration concept is used as an aggressive method to build wealth in stocks: a high-risk, high-return approach.

HOW IT WORKS: MANAGING RISK THROUGH INTELLIGENT DIVERSIFICATION

At a basic level Markowitz's MPT is a graphical method to evaluate the risk and reward of an investment portfolio.

Figure F.1 shows a simplified version of Markowitz's representation of an investment's risk and reward plotted on a graph. (Note that alterations to Markowitz's graphical display have been used to further simplify the concept, but on the book's web site readers will find the explanation in more technical detail.)

At its most basic level, MPT plots various investments on a graph to visually illustrate risk versus reward. The method can be used to measure risk and reward of individual stocks or a diversified portfolio with different asset classes such as managed futures.

To understand this at a basic level, look in the upper left. The first graph illustrates where those high-performing investments are plotted: in the upper left of the graph. The worst performing investments are plotted in the lower right. Investments are considered high risk when they are plotted nearest the right side of the graph, low risk closest to the left side of the graph.

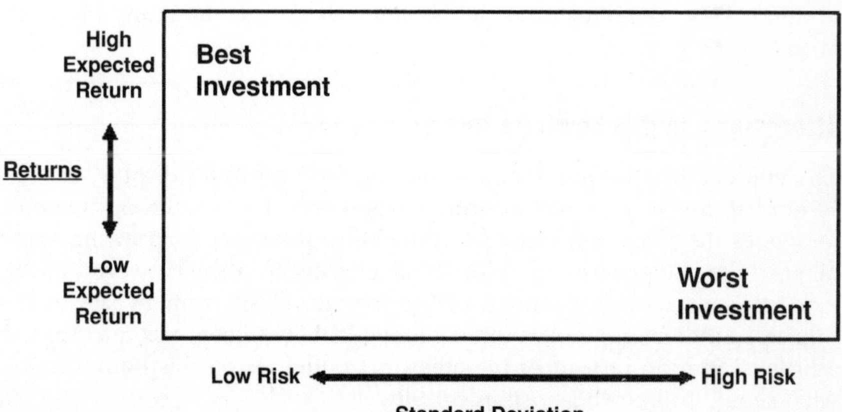

FIGURE F.1 Investment Risk versus Reward, a Basic Graphic

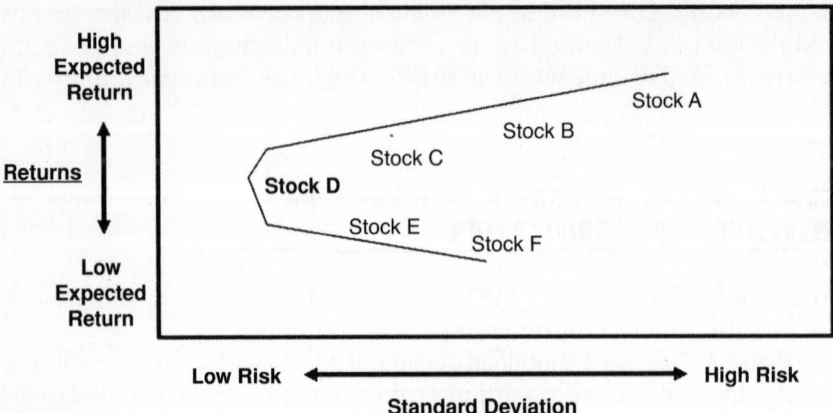

FIGURE F.2 Modern Portfolio Theory Graphic
Based on Harry Markowitz, "Portfolio Selection: Efficient Diversification of Investments," *Journal of Finance* (March 1952/1991).

Investments considered high return are plotted near the top of the graph, low return near the bottom of the graph.

THE BOTTOM LINE UTILITY OF MPT

An MPT graph (see Figure F.2) then combines both the risk and the returns to give the investor one picture of the investment. Markowitz used a curved line to map the efficient frontier, the point at which risk and reward was optimal. This is explained on the book's web site for the more advanced investor.

Alterations to Markowitz's Graph

The efficient frontier graphic, a swooping loop portfolio display, can be somewhat awkward from several perspectives. The portfolio "swoop" known as the efficient frontier has valuable applications for viewing overall portfolio components and plotting an efficient frontier. However, under many circumstances it is more useful to view the graph from an easy quadrant setup that makes understanding individual investment risk and reward a little clearer. So instead of the efficient frontier curve, this book utilizes what should be known as *risk quadrants*.

Note the four risk/return quadrants in Figure F.3, with automotive reference to add interest. The central concept of plotting an investment's

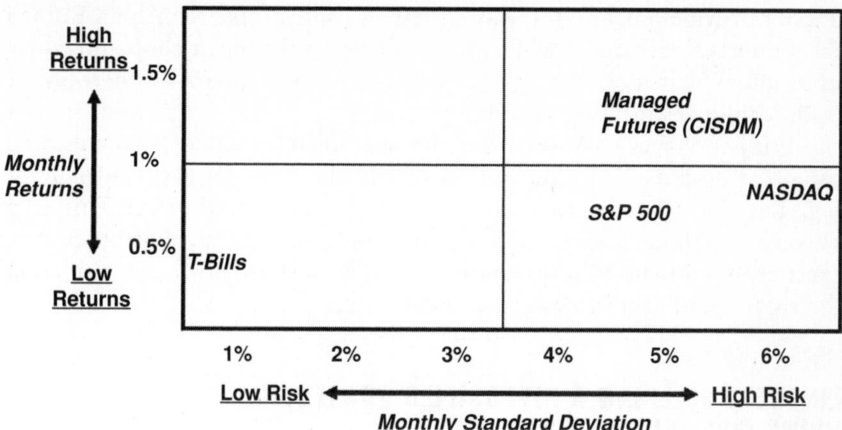

FIGURE F.3 Author's Simplification of Modern Portfolio Graphic

risk/reward on a graph remains similar. The upper left is the dream quadrant, the rare but desirable section of the graph where the highest returns are met with the lowest risk. So as to be memorable we could liken this quadrant to solid luxury cars, such as the brands Lexus and BMW, which are known for their high performance without an overly expensive price tag, their easy maintenance, and positive resale value. While the size and scope of the graphic can be relative to the variety of investments, few investments reside in the dream quadrant, which can change relative to the standard deviation and the expected returns of the investments plotted.

The next quadrant, in the upper right, is the high-risk/high-return quadrant. The author likens this section to a Lamborghini, an exciting, high-performing sports car but somewhat flashy, that can generate risky and volatile performance and potentially require costly repairs if the car is not maintained properly. An analogy to managed futures could not be more fitting, and interestingly this is where the asset class resides in many relative studies in this book.

The lower left quadrant, just under Lexus and BMW, is the low-risk/low-return quadrant. This is the safe and solid area of the investing risk spectrum, where many of the low-returning but low-risk government-backed interest rate products reside. Like a Honda Civic, it can be very useful and practical but generally boring without much in the way of risk or reward.

In the lower right quadrant, we find the high-risk/low-return quadrant. This lower right corner is the worst of all options. Sort of like an expensive car that is difficult and costly to maintain, the high-risk/low-return category isn't a good value. It can be fun—sometimes risk can be exciting—but it doesn't provide much in the way of reward, sort of like the Alpha Romeo the author's father drove while he was single: in the repair shop and costly more often than not. But as you will see, this quadrant is where many traditional investments tend to fall.

With apologies to Markowitz, this simplified version of a complicated topic was described with the author's particular twist for easy understanding. But don't let the easy and entertaining context deceive: This is a powerful method to measure risk and reward and put investments in perspective. In particular the quadrant method is most useful when considering the risk/reward profiles of various asset classes.

LINTNER: BUILDING A DIVERSIFIED PORTFOLIO USING MANAGED FUTURES

Lintner was fascinated by the work of Harry Markowitz. He unequivocally believed, "Diversification can substantially reduce the risks involved in portfolio returns," as he stated in a landmark paper delivered to a conference of financial analysts in 1983.

In the early 1980s, Lintner began his quest for advancing Markowitz's work by considering a variety of investment ideas and landed on what is arguably the asset class most noncorrelated to the stock market: managed futures.

Lintner started his study by considering a typically conservative portfolio, 60 percent in stocks and 40 percent in bonds, and then added managed futures at every possible level. His conclusion is probably one of the most quoted academic insights in the managed futures industry: "... Judicious investments in leveraged managed futures accounts show substantially less risk at every possible level of expected return than portfolios of stocks (or stocks and bonds) alone."

Lintner concluded that the addition of managed futures to a traditional portfolio of stocks and bonds improved portfolio performance, enhancing returns. The surprising component is that Lintner concluded that adding managed futures, a volatile and risky investment with stocks, another volatile and risky investment, actually had the impact of reducing portfolio risk.

Managed futures have an accurate reputation as being a risky investment. While significant risks exist in all investing such as stocks, managed futures, and hedge funds, in part this managed futures risky reputation is built on a rough and tumble industry where unknowing investors could wake up one morning taking delivery of thousands of bushels of corn on their front lawn (a phenomenon few, if any, have witnessed). The reputation is further soiled because certain types of direct futures investments carry with them the baggage of a theoretically undefined loss potential. Despite this, the core message from the Harvard Lintner report was received: Managed futures could reduce an investor's portfolio risk. But again, in the face of popular Wall Street opinion, Lintner's conclusions, reprinted in the book *Managed Futures* by Carl Peters, (Probus Publishing Co., 1992) stand today:

> *Indeed the improvements from holding efficiently selected portfolios of managed futures are so large... that the return/risk tradeoffs provided by augmented portfolios... clearly dominate the tradeoffs available from portfolios of stocks alone. Moreover, they do so by very considerable margins.*

Dr. Lintner's conclusions had significant reverberations that are still being felt today, but unfortunately the good doctor never saw the impact his study created in a then budding cottage investment industry. He had been rumored to be in line to receive the Nobel Prize in economics with Markowitz and Sharpe, but he suddenly died in a car crash months after delivering his landmark conclusions, dashing his eligibility for the Nobel Prize, which is awarded only to living recipients.

Is Lintner's Message Really about Managed Futures?

Lintner understood that Markowitz had built a framework for analyzing risky assets, which at the time were primarily stock investments. While he thought Markowitz's work was groundbreaking, and in fact collaborated with Markowitz on several occasions, Lintner thought the theory was being narrowly implemented. He noted that in the 1970s many major institutions had broadened their diversification to include minor fractions of their portfolios in risky real estate and even very risky nontraditional holdings such as venture capital and oil well exploration.

Using Lintner's Report as a Basis to Create a Truly Diversified Portfolio

Many studies and ideas have sprung from Lintner's original work. Perhaps the most interesting and relevant is the most recent study from the Chicago Mercantile Exchange (CME) titled *Portfolio Diversification Opportunities*. The study confirmed Lintner's conclusions with powerful resolve.

The CME first considered a conservative portfolio of 50 percent stocks, as measured by a globally "diversified" basket of stocks through the MSCI

World index, and 50 percent bonds, as measured by the J.P. Morgan Government Bond Global index. Then the study added just 20 percent managed futures, reducing the stock and bond holdings to 40 percent each. To determine the managed futures investment the CME used the CASAM CISDM CTA Equal Weighted index. The study then considered a 100 percent allocation to managed futures, which, like a 100 percent allocation to the stock market, is not recommended to any investor—even those without concern for risk.

The results in Figure F.4 confirm the wisdom of creating a portfolio with true asset class diversification. The portfolio of 50 percent bonds and 50 percent stocks delivered low returns, as might be expected due to the 50 percent allocation to bonds, which makes the portfolio conservative. And here is where it gets a little surprising: This "conservative" portfolio is in fact near the high risk quadrant, based on standard deviation. What's more, the study methodology may even be masking the true volatility of the stock

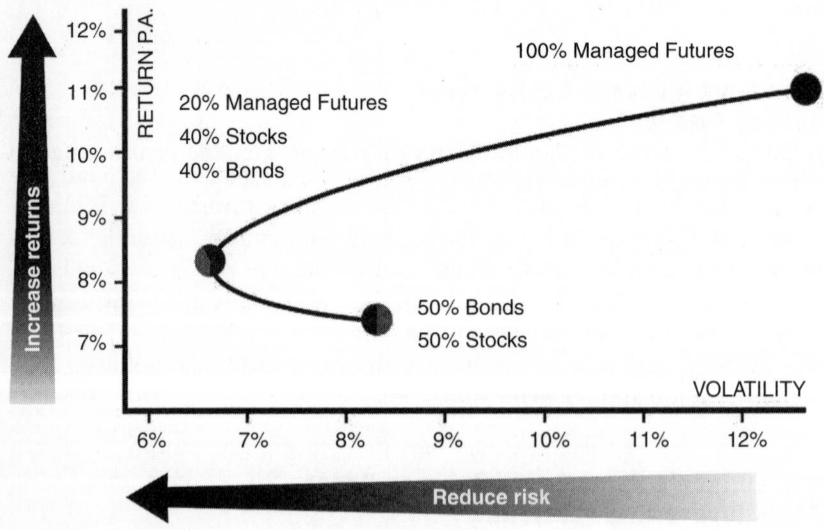

*1) *Managed futures: CASAM CISDM CTA Equal Weighted;*
2) *Stocks: MSCI World;*
3) *Bonds: JP Morgan Government Bond Global;*

FIGURE F.4 Portfolio Study With and Without Managed Futures
Graphic courtesy of CME Group.
Source: Bloomberg.

and bond portfolio. While the term of the study was in excess of 20 years, which provides a statistically diverse period of time, the study unfortunately ended in February of 2008—before the massive stock meltdown began in September of that year, thus reducing the true volatility of the stock market. If the true, up-to-date past performance of the stock market were included one could only imagine where the conservative stock and bond portfolio would fall on the chart.

Next, the study added just 20 percent alternative asset allocation of managed futures. This noncorrelated allocation moved the portfolio closer to the sweet spot, up and to the left, increasing the returns while reducing its risk measure of standard deviation. The standalone managed futures investment offered significantly higher returns but also more risk, as expected.

It is important to note that the author is in no way indicating that managed futures or any alternative asset class is an investment that does not carry risk: to the contrary. These investments involve risk all investors should understand. The message the author is conveying is the interpretation of Lintner's work that uncorrelated diversification can perhaps generate a more attractive risk/return payoff. Investors are properly compensated for the risks they take, regardless of the asset class.

Unlike Lintner's report, where a limited dataset was available and performance auditing might not have been as robust, the CME study was conducted during modern times. This is an important consideration.

In modern times, NFA performance auditing can provide a degree of confidence that the NFA-audited returns are in fact the returns that investors generally experience. Further, as the industry has grown, new and more dynamic programs have entered the marketplace, upgrading the professionalism of an industry once filled with Wild West cowboys. While there is still room for the industry to improve, researchers should consider the benefit of modern times.

Faults with Lintner's Report

Lintner's major concept of true diversification with asset classes noncorrelated with the stock market should continue to remain unquestioned, despite the fact that most financial advisors have not integrated his method. The brilliance of the conclusions is not being questioned. However, some examination of the methodology Lintner used to form his conclusions warrants additional consideration.

Lintner's study of managed futures programs included a very limited dataset and was done at a time when performance reporting, auditing, and market regulation were not as robust as is the case today. Any study with limited datasets can lead to statistically unreliable results. In this case,

Lintner used 15 publicly available managed futures and 15 funds. In part this could be due to the limited availability of funds to study at the time, as the managed futures industry was just beginning to blossom. So due to no fault of his own, Lintner had a limited amount of data to work with. This is why additional studies warrant consideration.

It is important that these post-Lintner reports are considered because three primary changes have impacted Lintner's conclusions. First, managed futures has grown from a cottage industry sideshow in 1983 with under $5 billion in assets to a significant industry force in 2009 with over $200 billion in assets under management. Second, the number of programs has risen from a handful of options in 1983 to over 1,000 registered managed futures programs in 2009. Third, and perhaps most important, strict industry regulation and required regulator auditing of performance now rides roughshod over an industry once rife with lightly regulated transgressions. Another risk factor not addressed in the Lintner report, which the author has never seen published, is individual manager risk and risk of margin and leverage: issues we address in detail on the book's web site and in an active management program.

Notes

CHAPTER 1 Understand It

1. The institutional interest in the product is defined by The Chicago Board of Trade publication *Managed Futures: Portfolio Diversification Opportunities* (2006); noted on p. 1 is the significance of institutional interest in managed futures, noting the asset class's significant growth may be due to institutional interest in the product resulting from the need for asset diversification. Investopedia also defines institutional interest at http://investopedia.com/terms/m/managedfuturesaccount.asp and defines the asset class as an account like a mutual fund. The terms *Wall Street establishment* and *Wall Street institution* are euphemisms for these professional investors. A limited focus group study of financial advisors indicated that less than 7 percent understood managed futures. While this may be a limited study, it confirms the author's general experience. The asset class may be deliberately obscured from investors, based on the author's conversations resulting from this focus group study as well as additional conversations outside the realm of scientific study.
2. *Managed Futures: Portfolio Diversification Opportunities,* Chicago Mercantile Exchange (September 2008); p. 8 of the publication quotes return statistics from the CASAM CISDM CTA Equal Weighted index, U.S. stocks with the S&P 500 Total Return index, and the MSCI Index for world stocks. The S&P 500 Total Return index includes dividend payments in its calculations. In this book we use both the total return index and the basic price index for calculation to provide balance, as well as using both the CASAM CISDM indexes and the Barclay indexes for alternative investments to provide balance. The CME publication is available for download at www.cme.com. Past performance is not indicative of future results. The study showed that from 1980 to February of 2008 the asset class managed futures, as measured by the CASAM CISDM, generated a $513,467 return while the U.S. stock market, as measured by the S&P 500 Total Return index, generated a $287,890 total return. The largest drawdown for the CASAM CISDM CTA Equal Weighted index was 9.3 percent and was recovered in two months, from 01/92 to 04/92. By contrast, the S&P 500 Total Return index had a 44.7 percent drawdown that took two years to recover; the NASDAQ composite had a 74 percent drop, losing close to three-fourths of its value. This publication is available for download at www.cme.com. It is the author's opinion that a 9.3 percent drawdown and two-month recovery time is dramatically more attractive than a 44.7 percent drawdown that took two years

to recover. Note that in this chapter and book we use different broad indexes as performance measures. Indexes, particularly in managed futures, may not reflect the performance an investor would experience in an individual managed futures program. We make this clear throughout the book. Also throughout this book and in this chapter different index measures will be used. We substitute different managed futures index performance from both the CASAM CISDM indexes and the Barclay indexes. Further, while the S&P 500 stock price index is available on the CASAM CISDM web site, which was used for this research, the S&P 500 Total Return index was used on the CME study, yielding different results. Past performance is not indicative of future results; investors may have difficulty replicating the performance of a managed futures index. As is detailed throughout this book, to mimic the exact return performance of any index is difficult due to the fact that no such investment product is currently offered and it may be impractical for investors to invest in an equal weighting of all CTAs contained in the index due to many of the high minimums of investment. Note the S&P price index used on the CASAM web site does not include dividends and has lower returns than does the S&P 500 Total Return index, which could be considered common knowledge. The methodology the index uses to calculate returns is as follows:

CASAM CISDM CTA/CPO Index Rules—Equal Weighted Indexes

Only funds that have reported monthly returns and assets at the time the indexes are calculated are included.

Only funds with more than USD 500,000 in assets and one year of reporting history are included in the indexes.

The indexes are calculated as simple arithmetic averages for that group. For example, if there are 30 CTAs classified as Physicals that meet the criteria above, the return would be a simple arithmetic average of the returns of those 30 CTAs.

Once calculated, index performance numbers are never revised.

The institutional interest in the product is defined by The Chicago Board of Trade publication *Managed Futures: Portfolio Diversification Opportunities* (2006); noted on p. 1 is the significance of institutional interest in managed futures, noting the asset class's significant growth may be due to institutional interest in the product resulting from the need for asset diversification. Investopedia also defines institutional interest at http://investopedia.com/terms/m/managedfuturesaccount.asp and defines the asset class as an account like a mutual fund. The terms *Wall Street establishment* and *Wall Street institution* are euphemisms for these professional investors. Regarding the low drawdown numbers, this is cited in a publication of the Chicago Mercantile Exchange, *Managed Futures: Portfolio Diversification Opportunities* (September 2008). The statistics appear on pp. 6–7 of the document.

3. This statement regarding correlation represents the author's opinion and is based on the structural nature of the various managed futures strategies and their potential to perform regardless of the positive price movement of the

markets in which they invest and the stock market, which is the conclusion of other published work on the topic. Further, as is outlined in Chapter 9 on correlation, past returns correlation indicates that managed futures is significantly uncorrelated to other high performing asset classes in a variety of economic periods of time. Past performance is not indicative of future results, and the studies in this book are not represented as all encompassing. The author's opinion that managed futures is the most uncorrelated asset class is based on the following: Chapter 9 on correlation includes a correlation matrix showing how the managed futures index correlates to other major asset classes, and it is in fact the most uncorrelated to any major asset class. But more to the point, the core strategies available to managed futures managers, unique to the futures markets, are behind the author's assertion. In this chapter the strategies are outlined that are often based on unique contract structures only available in futures and option derivative markets. To provide examples of a few CTA strategies that are not necessarily correlated to the up or down price movement of any market, a CTA could buy the July contract and sell the November contract of the same product. This strategy is not necessarily dependent on the up or down price movement of the underlying product, but the price differential between the July and November contract, which could be influenced by different factors that would influence the up and down price movement of a market. Another example is an option premium collection CTA who sells options on both sides of the market. This option strategy can be profitable regardless of market direction to varying degrees depending on the volatility of the market and how far the market moves out of a trading range, not necessarily the direction in which the market moves. This time-based contract structure is unique to derivative futures and options and thus drives the lack of correlation, in the author's opinion.

4. www.investopedia.com/terms/m/managedfuturesaccount.asp, "What Does Managed Futures Account Mean? An account that is like a mutual fund, except that positions in government securities, futures contracts, and options on futures contracts are used to manage the portfolio." Note that the comparison here is only relative to the concept that investment decisions made by a mutual fund are done through an individual investment manager who is skilled in the markets in which he or she invests. There are obvious significant differences between a stock mutual fund and managed futures, including the markets traded, the risk factors, leverage, margin, and other variables.
5. Ben Warwick, *Searching for Alpha* (New York: John Wiley & Sons, 2000). Nobel Prize Winner William Sharpe concluded that all stocks are subject to systematic risk, or overall market risk, and thus true diversification among stocks cannot take place without diversification from this systematic risk.
6. The sentiment was echoed by the NFA in its January 22, 2010 *NFA Investor Newsletter*. It seems odd that government regulators are out front on the right side of an issue, taking the lead in advocating true asset diversification, something Wall Street is slow to embrace. www.finra.org/Investors/ProtectYourself/InvestorAlerts/MoneyManagement/P120716. Another good article on managing risk: www.finra.org/Investors/SmartInvesting/AdvancedInvesting/ManagingInvestmentRisk/index.htm.

7. On p. 46 of the book *Commodities for Every Portfolio* (Hoboken, NJ: John Wiley & Sons, 2007), author Balarie cites a 2004 study published by K. Geert Rouwenhorst of Yale School of Management and Gary Gorton of the University of Pennsylvania titled "Facts and Fantasies About Commodities." Note studies exist which run counter to this and the author is not making a definitive judgement in this regards.
8. *Managed Futures: Portfolio Diversification Opportunities*, Chicago Mercantile Exchange (September 2008); p. 8 of the publication quotes return statistics from the CASAM CISDM CTA Equal Weighted index, U.S. stocks with the S&P 500 Total Return index and the MSCI index for world stocks. The S&P 500 Total Return index includes dividend payments in its calculations. CASAM CISDM Equal Weighted CTA index and S&P 500 price index, which is used on the CASAM web site as a benchmark. This web site was the source for these statistics and readers can view the current statistics at: www.casamhedge.com/IndexDetail.aspx?ID=7130&G=3. Study conducted 1/2010 and screen shots for all research, when applicable, are available on the book's web site. The monthly standard deviation for the equal weighted CTA index is 4.70 and monthly returns; the S&P 500 had a monthly standard deviation of 4.51 and average monthly returns of 0.85 percent. This information is available at: www.casamhedge.com/IndexDetail.aspx?ID=7130&G=3#. Source for NASDAQ and T-bill data: Barclay Alternative Asset Database. Note that the lower-performing S&P price index, not the total return index, is used on the CASAM CISDM web site. The CASAM CISDM equal weighted CTA index is the highest performing index, one of several alternative investment indexes operated in part by the Center for International Securities and Derivatives Markets (CISDM) at the University of Massachusetts, Amherst. The index has become a standard of sorts for the reporting of performance for the managed futures industry, as it was featured in the industry benchmark report published by the Chicago Mercantile Exchange, *Managed Futures: Portfolio Diversification Opportunities* and provides the managed futures return data published by *Barron's* magazine. Past performance is not indicative of future results. There is substantial risk of loss in investing.
9. Harry Markowitz, "Portfolio Selection," *Journal of Finance* (March, 1952).
10. Ben Warwick, *Searching for Alpha* (New York: John Wiley & Sons, 2000). Nobel Prize Winner William Sharpe concluded that all stocks are subject to systematic risk, or overall market risk, and thus true diversification among stocks cannot take place without diversification from this systematic risk.
11. Brinson study, "Determinants of Portfolio Performance," *Financial Analysis Journal* (May–June, 1991); William Sharpe, "Asset Allocation: Management Style and Performance Measurement," *Journal of Portfolio Management* (Winter 1992); Zvi Bodie, Alex Kane, and Alan Marcus, *Essentials of Investments*, 4th ed. (New York: McGraw-Hill, 2001).
12. Study available at www.iijournals.com/doi/abs/10.3905/jai.1998.407848; www.lindzon.com/docs/dealing.pdf, *The Journal of Alternative Investments*, Summer 1998, Vol. 1, No. 1: 56–65.

13. Study available at www.iijournals.com/doi/abs/10.3905/jwm.2004.412354, *The Journal of Wealth Management*, Summer 2004, Vol. 7, No. 1: 44–47.
14. Study available at www.iijournals.com/doi/abs/10.3905/jai.1998.407842, *The Journal of Alternative Investments,* Summer 1998, Vol. 1, No. 1: 56–65.
15. Study available at www.iijournals.com/doi/abs/10.3905/jai.2002.319032, *The Journal of Alternative Investments*, Spring 2002, Vol. 4, No. 4: 57–61.
16. *A Former Institutional Investor's Perspective on Managed Futures,* seminar delivered at the Chicago Mercantile Exchange on February 26, 2008, by Tom O'Donnell with Liz Flores, Associate Director, Interest Rate Products, CME. Paraphrasing takes place in this report but the author believes the representation to be accurate. The presentation is available at https://admin.na5.acrobat.com/_a777821181/p89835260/ or available for download at www.cme.com.
17. Barclay MAP alternative investment software. For this study, the database was filtered for all funds with a 36-month track record and the average performance was noted. Then the study lifted the fund restriction, adding direct accounts. The fund-only performance was compared to the performance of both fund and direct accounts. An analysis of only direct CTA accounts would have yielded even higher performance numbers for the direct CTA account versus the fund. The word "whisper" is used earlier in this paragraph because the author has no direct experience regarding brokers dealers requesting a fee for a managed futures fund to be listed on their platform, but has been part of several discussions with credible fund managers and other related industry participants regarding the issue. Not all broker dealers may require a fee from a managed futures fund to be listed on their platform.
18. Barclay Alternative Asset MAP database. Study looking at the rate of return of all CTAs in the database that reported as options strategies (44) or systematic strategies (388) with a minimum 36-month track record. 2009 year to date (YTD) performance ended in November, but does not diminish the point being made.
19. BarclayHedge. Yearly performance of Barclay CTA index available at www.barclayhedge.com/research/indices/cta/sub/cta.html.
20. The numbers of trend-following strategies can vary from index to index. See note 18 for an approximation of the number of trend-following CTAs reporting to the Barclay index.
21. The conversation with Papagiannis took place during the winter of 2010 and occurred on phone and via e-mail.

CHAPTER 2 Define It

1. *Managed Futures: Portfolio Diversification Opportunities,* Chicago Mercantile Exchange (September 2008); p. 8 of the publication quotes return statistics from the CASAM CISDM CTA Equal Weighted index, U.S. stocks with the S&P 500 Total Return index and the MSCI index for world stocks. The S&P 500 Total Return index includes dividend payments in its calculations. In this book we use both the total return index and the basic price index for calculation to provide balance, as well as using both the CASAM CISDM indexes and the Barclay

indexes for alternative investments to provide balance. The CME publication is available for download at www.cme.com. Past performance is not indicative of future results. The study showed that from 1980 to February of 2008 the asset class managed futures, as measured by the CASAM CISDM, generated a $513,467 return while the U.S. stock market, as measured by the S&P 500 Total Return index, generated a $287,890 total return. The largest drawdown for the CASAM CISDM CTA Equal Weighted index was 9.3 percent and was recovered in two months, from 01/92 to 04/92. By contrast, the S&P 500 Total Return index had a 44.7 percent drawdown that took two years to recover; the NASDAQ composite had a 74 percent drop, losing close to three-fourths of its value. This publication is available for download at www.cme.com. It is the author's opinion that a 9.3 percent drawdown and two-month recovery time is dramatically more attractive than a 44.7 percent drawdown that took two years to recover and a 74 percent drawdown. Note that in this chapter and book we use different broad indexes as performance measures. Indexes, particularly in managed futures, may not reflect the performance an investor would experience in an individual managed futures program. We make this clear throughout the book. Also throughout this book and in this chapter different index measures will be used. We substitute different managed futures index performance from both the CASAM CISDM indexes and the Barclay indexes. Further, while the S&P 500 stock price index is available on the CASAM CISDM web site, which was used for this research, the S&P 500 Total Return index was used on the CME study, yielding different results. Past performance is not indicative of future results; investors may have difficulty replicating the performance of a managed futures index.

2. Source: CME Group, Managed Futures Diversification Opportunities. Current assets under management information is available at: http://www.barclayhedge.com/research/indices/cta/mum/CTA_Fund_Industry.html.
3. Barclay Alternative Asset MAP database. Study conducted 9/09. In the Barclay database a search was conducted of all CTAs with a 36-month tenure that exhibited returns performance from 7 to 15 percent; 15 to 30 percent and 30 to 60 percent at that moment in time. Screen shots showing the software study methodology and results are available on the book's web site. *Note:* The Barclay Alternative Asset Database includes both commodity pools as well as CTAs. Past performance is never indicative of future results. As is outlined in Chapter 11, the use of margin and leverage can create unique risks that can cause investors to lose more than they invest when investing in direct managed futures accounts. Studies that rely on past performance to determine asset class categorization could be subject to hindsight bias.
4. Ibid.
5. Ibid.

CHAPTER 3 Work With It

1. Barclay Alternative Asset MAP Database. These returns are hypothetical due to the fact that the CTAs have not traded together in a regulated environment and

the portfolio developer had the benefit of hindsight when developing the portfolio. See the hypothetical risk disclaimer in note 7 for Chapter 3. These portfolios are for illustrative purposes and, particularly with the aggressive portfolios, might not pass the author's due diligence, including uneven returns distribution and significant exposure to individual manager risk.

2. Barclay Alternative Asset MAP Database. The top CTA with a $200,000 investment minimum was determined based on the highest compounded annual return for all CTAs with a 36-month track record reporting managing client assets to the database at the time of the study and is used for illustrative purposes only. It should be noted that no due diligence was conducted on the individual CTA reporting the top performance in the $200,000 category, a move that could highlight the need to look past simple returns headlines.
3. Investing in a CTA on a drawdown is a sophisticated method for qualified investors and is a risky, highly speculative investment strategy and as outlined in the book there is no guarantee at which point an investor could exit a program or that a margin call will stop losses. This is not recommended for all CTAs and only risk capital should be used. The concept was addressed in the book *Managed Trading: Myths and Truths* by Jack D. Schwager (New York: John Wiley & Sons, 1996) and was also studied in the *Attain Managed Futures Newsletter* dated April 26, 2010 in the article "Should You Buy, Hold, or Fold a Drawdown in Managed Futures?" Both studies are well researched, in the author's opinion. On the book's web site we also offer a professional download of the white paper study on the topic.
4. Barclay MAP Database. Performance measure benchmarks were established for this book using the following methodology for the example given herein for the trend/systematic strategy: All managed futures programs voluntarily reporting to the Barclay database trading categorization as systematic were searched, and the performance of each was averaged through the Barclay software. These benchmarks are available on the book's web site for registered users.
5. Short volatility strategies have various methods of risk management when the market turns against them, which include liquidating the position at a loss, rolling the spread over to the following month, rolling the spread down or up to move the options out of the money, inverting an iron condor or butterfly, or offsetting the short options position with a futures contract. There are no guarantees any risk management technique will operate as designed.
6. *Notionally Funded Accounts Disclosure*: You should request your CTA to advise you of the amount of cash or other assets (actual funds) which should be deposited to the advisor's trading program for your account to be considered fully funded. This is the amount upon which the CTA will determine the number of contracts traded in your account and should be an amount sufficient to make it unlikely that any further cash deposits would be required from you over the course of your participation in one of the CTA's programs. You are reminded that the account size you have agreed to in writing (the nominal or notional account size) is not the maximum possible loss that your account may experience. You should consult the account statements received from your futures commission merchant in order to determine the actual activity in your account, including profits, losses,

and current cash equity balance. To the extent that the equity in your account is at any time less than the nominal account size you should be aware of the following:

(1) Although your gains and losses, fees and commissions measured in dollars will be the same, they will be greater when expressed as a percentage of account equity.
(2) You may receive more frequent and larger margin calls.
(3) The conversion chart below may be used to convert actual rates of return (RORs) to the corresponding RORs for particular funding levels.

Rate of Return	100% funded	75% funded	50% funded	25% funded
−20%	−20%	−30%	−40%	−80%
−10%	−10%	−15%	−20%	−40%
−5%	−5%	−7.5%	−10%	−20%
0%	0%	0%	0%	0%
5%	5%	7.5%	10%	20%

Additions or withdrawals will materially affect RORs of notionally funded accounts. This is because the advisor will continue to trade the account at the agreed trading level without taking into consideration additions or withdrawals, and thus any additions or withdrawals of actual funds will not result in a corresponding proportional increase or decrease in the nominal funding of an account. For example, assume that a client opens an account with an actual funding level of $100,000, and instructs the advisor to trade the account at a nominal level of $200,000. If the client withdraws $50,000 of actual funds from the account, the advisor will continue to trade the account at a nominal level of $200,000. Before the withdrawal, the account would be traded at a 50 percent funding level, but after the withdrawal the account would be traded at a 25 percent funding level. If the trading program were to experience a −5 percent rate of return, then if that performance occurred before the withdrawal the actual performance would be a −10 percent return but if that performance occurred after the withdrawal the actual performance would be −20 percent. Please note that the increased leverage resulting from notional funding may lead to more frequent and larger margin calls in the event of a drawdown in an account.

7. *Hypothetical Risk Disclosure*: This composite performance record listed is hypothetical and these trading advisors have not traded together in the manner shown in the composite. Hypothetical performance results have many inherent limitations, some of which are described below. No representation is being made that any multiadvisor managed account or pool will or is likely to achieve a composite performance record similar to that shown. In fact, there are frequently sharp differences between a hypothetical composite performance record and the actual record subsequently achieved. One of the limitations of a hypothetical composite performance record is that decisions relating to the selection of trading advisors and the allocation of assets among those trading advisors were made with the

benefit of hindsight based on the historical rates of return of the selected trading advisors. Therefore, composite performance records invariably show positive rates of return. Another inherent limitation on these results is that the allocation decisions reflected in the performance records were not made under actual market conditions and, therefore, cannot completely account for the impact of financial risk in actual trading. Furthermore, the composite performance record may be distorted because the allocation of assets changes from time to time and these adjustments are not reflected in the composite.

CFTC Risk Disclosure: The risk of trading commodity futures, options, and foreign exchange (forex) is substantial. The high degree of leverage associated with commodity futures, options, and forex can work against you as well as for you. This high degree of leverage can have the effect of substantially magnifying potential losses as well as gains. You should carefully consider whether commodity futures, options, and forex are suitable for you in light of your financial condition. If you are unsure you should seek professional advice. Past performance does not guarantee future success. In some cases managed accounts are charged substantial commissions and advisory fees. Those accounts subject to these charges may need to make substantial trading profits just to avoid depletion of their assets. Each CTA is required by the Commodity Futures Trading Commission (CFTC) to issue to prospective clients a risk disclosure document outlining these fees, conflicts of interest, and other associated risks. Hard copies of these risk disclosure documents are readily available by clicking on each CTA's "request disclosure document" button. The full risk of commodity futures, options, and forex trading cannot be addressed in this risk disclosure statement. No consideration to invest should be made without thoroughly reading the disclosure document of each of the CTAs in which you may have an interest. Requesting a disclosure document places you under no obligation and each document is provided at no cost. The CFTC has not passed on the merits of participating in any of the following programs nor on the adequacy or accuracy of the disclosure documents. Other disclosure statements are required to be provided to you before an account may be opened for you. Past performance is not necessarily indicative of future results. Prospective clients should not base their decision to invest in these trading programs solely on the past performance presented. Additionally, in making an investment decision, prospective clients must also rely on their own examination of the person or entity making the trading decisions and the terms of the advisory agreement, including the merits and risks involved.

CHAPTER 4 Realize It

1. Source: CME Group: Managed Futures, Portfolio Diversification Opportunities. Barclay Alternative Asset MAP Database; as of this writing, historical assets under management information can be downloaded without charge. www.barclayhedge.com/research/indices/cta/mum/CTA_Fund_Industry.html.
2. Source for mutual fund comment: www.investopedia.com/terms/m/managedfuturesaccount.asp "What Does Managed Futures Account Mean? An account

that is like a mutual fund, except that positions in government securities, futures contracts, and options on futures contracts are used to manage the portfolio. Note that the comparison here is only relative to the concept that investment decisions made by a mutual fund are done through an individual investment manager who is skilled in the markets in which they invest. There are obvious significant differences between a stock mutual fund and managed futures, including the markets traded, the risk factors, leverage, margin, and other variables."

3. Barclay Alternative Asset MAP Database; see Appendix A for details.
4. Ibid.
5. Ibid.

CHAPTER 5 Don't Be a Victim

1. CFTC Regulations require FCMs to maintain separate accounts, funds, and assets to satisfy all of its current obligations to customers trading futures, and options on futures on foreign commodity exchanges. FCMs may not commingle set-aside funds with their own or their proprietary or noncustomer funds or accounts. www.cftc.gov; www.ccftc.gov/files/tm/tmclearingcorpphase1part190.pdf; www.nfa.futures.org; www.nfa.futures.org/news/newsComment.asp?ArticleID=334.
2. Penalties can be severe for not adhering to account segregation rules: www.futuresmag.com/News/2009/9/Pages/CFTC-sanctions-JP-Morgan-.aspx.
3. Based on interviews and e-mails that took place between the author and Patricia Cushing, Director of Compliance at the National Futures Association, and Larry Dyekman, Director of Communications and Education for the National Futures Association, over the summer of 2009.
4. Ibid.
5. Ibid.
6. NFA President Roth testifies before Congress: http://banking.senate.gov/public/_files/roth.pdf. The "wild west road show" comments are those of the author.
7. See note 3.

CHAPTER 6 Recognize It

1. The 2007 Berkshire Hathaway Annual Meeting Top 20 Questions. The full quote was: "The measurement of volatility: it's nice, it's mathematical, and wrong. Volatility is not risk. Those who have written about risk don't know how to measure risk. Past volatility does not measure risk. When farm prices crashed, [farm price] volatility went up, but a farm priced at $600 per acre that was formerly $2,000 per acre isn't riskier because it's more volatile. [Measures like] beta let people who teach finance use the math they've learned. That's nonsense. Risk comes from not knowing what you're doing. Dexter Shoes was a terrible mistake—I was wrong about the business, but not because shoe prices were volatile. If you understand the business you own, you're not taking risk.

Volatility is useful for people who want a career in teaching. I cannot recall a case where we lost a lot of money due to volatility. The whole concept of volatility as a measure of risk has developed in my lifetime and isn't any use to us." www.jvbruni.com/Berkshire%202007annualmeeting.pdf.

2. Barclay Alternative Asset MAP Database. Study identified the CTAs with the highest standard deviation, worst drawdown and longest average recovery time, isolated the 20 highest "worst" CTAs in each category, then averaged the results.
3. Barclay Alternative Asset MAP Database, study conducted January 2010. Study identified the CTAs with the highest worst drawdown, isolated the 20 highest, and then averaged the results. After this a standard returns-based correlation analysis was conducted and identified the eight most uncorrelated CTAs. These CTAs were placed in a portfolio using equal weighting for all CTAs to illustrate a mathematical concept.
4. Barclay Alternative Asset MAP Database Study identified the CTAs with the highest standard deviation, isolated the 20 highest, and then averaged the results. After this a standard returns-based correlation analysis was conducted and identified the eight most noncorrelated CTAs. These CTAs were placed in a portfolio using equal weighting for all CTAs to illustrate a mathematical concept.

CHAPTER 7 Use It

1. This study is a simple mathematical study and the study and the RAD formula are available in Excel spreadsheet format on the book's web site. This study is not indicative of performance of any asset or investment but rather a mathematical illustration.
2. Barclay Alternative Asset MAP Database. To accomplish this, a rules-based filtering process was utilized based on the author's opinions on "credibility." First, the entire database of CTAs was culled. Second, a search eliminated CTAs who possessed a track record less than six years, reported under $20 million under management, compounded annual return of less than 15 percent, and positive up/down deviation ratio of less than 1.5.
3. Barclay Alternative Asset MAP Database. To accomplish this, a rules-based filtering process was utilized. First, the entire database of CTAs was culled. Second, a search eliminated CTAs who possessed a track record less than six years, reported under $20 million under management, compounded annual return greater than 15 percent, and positive up/down deviation ratio greater than 1.5. Note that the establishment of the control group is not as significant as the fact that the risk measures change and how it impacts that control group.
4. Barclay Alternative Asset MAP Database. To accomplish this, the total results from the study control of 41 CTAs were downloaded into an Excel spreadsheet along with key risk statistics. The study then organized this group of 41 by a variety of risk measures, including average drawdown.
5. Barclay Alternative Asset MAP Database. To accomplish this, the total results from the study control of 41 CTAs were downloaded into an Excel spreadsheet along with key risk statistics.

6. Barclay Alternative Asset MAP Database. To accomplish this, the total results from the study control of 41 CTAs were downloaded into an Excel spreadsheet along with key risk statistics.
7. Barclay Alternative Asset MAP Database. To accomplish this, the total results from the study control of 41 CTAs were downloaded into an Excel spreadsheet along with key risk statistics.
8. Barclay Alternative Asset MAP Database. To accomplish this, a rules-based filtering process was utilized. First, the entire database of CTAs was culled. The study then organized this group of 41 by a variety of risk measures, including CTAs in this group with compounded annual returns in excess of 30 percent. The study then organized this group of 188 CTAs by a variety of risk measures, in this case based on the top 10 drawdowns. This Excel spreadsheet is available on the book's web site with screen shots of software used in the study.
9. Barclay Alternative Asset MAP Database. The study then organized this group of 188 CTAs by a variety of risk measures, in this case based on the top 10 drawdowns.

CHAPTER 8 Protect it: Principal-Protected, Conservative, and Risky Investments

1. These numbers are chosen to illustrate a concept and are not representative of any investment. There exist a variety of methods to calculate interest, all dependent on the product. For the purpose of illustration, the value of the investment the two components are broken down into separate calculations. The Protection VAMI starts with the initial amount, which is multiplied by the interest rate each month. This interest rate amount is added to the yearly value. This new yearly value is then multiplied by the interest rate to obtain the next year's VAMI. The Excel spreadsheet is available on the book's web site. With principal protection there is no absolute guarantee principal is protected. The principal protection concept works best when interest rates are high and the source of protection can generate an appropriate return. The interest rates and returns used in this chapter are for mathematical illustration and are not based on any specific investment. In fact, the interest rates quoted on a compounded basis are significantly higher than interest rates as of this writing, but the point is to illustrate the protection concept under ideal circumstances.
2. This point bears repeating as it is mentioned in the text. When the protection amount is used as margin, it is not "protected" because a margin call could reduce the protection amount to an undefined level. This point is outlined in the CME publication, "Why Managed Futures?" CMEGroup, 2008, John W. Labuszewski, Research and Product Development, available for download on the book's web site.
3. Ibid.
4. Ibid.

CHAPTER 9 Use All of It

1. This statement is based on the author's opinion that the futures and options derivative contract structure enables spread trades across various time frames and markets and using different futures and options strategies that can easily go long, short, or even neutral to the underlying market movements to a degree. More to the point, the core strategies available to managed futures managers, unique to the futures markets, are behind the author's assertion. In this chapter, the strategies are outlined that are often based on unique contract structures available only in futures and option derivative markets. To provide examples of a few commodity trading advisor (CTA) strategies that are not necessarily correlated to the up or down price movement of any market, a CTA could buy the July contract and sell the November contract of the same product. This strategy is not necessarily dependent on the up or down price movement of the underlying product, but the price differential between the July and November contract, which could be influenced by different factors that would influence the up and down price movement of a market. Another example is an option premium collection CTA who sells options on both sides of the market. This option strategy can be profitable regardless of market direction to varying degrees depending on the volatility of the market and how far the market moves out of a trading range, not necessarily the direction in which the market moves. This contract structure is unique to futures and options and thus drives the lack of correlation, in the author's opinion.
2. *Managed Futures: Portfolio Diversification Opportunities,* Chicago Mercantile Exchange (September 2008).
3. An interesting story, some might consider it an urban legend, about the movie "Trading Places" and Richard Dennis is located on the book's web site. Richard Dennis is a turtle trader who some credit as popularizing trend trading. See Michael Covel, *The Complete Turtle Trader: The Legend, the Lessons and the Results* (New York: HarperBusiness, October 2007). The source of information on this CTA was the Barclay MAP database.
4. This is entirely a hypothetical example and is not based on any actual CTA trades or strategy but an illustration based on the author's conceptual knowledge of various CTA strategies. The shorter the track record, the less applicable the correlation analysis.
5. Barclay Alternative MAP Database, using all-period correlation and started from the point of the shortest index track record, October 2006, until September 2009. Updated results are on the book's web site along with screen shots of the study methodology. The shorter the track record, the less applicable the correlation analysis.

CHAPTER 10 Build It

1. *Hypothetical Risk Disclosure*: This composite performance record listed is hypothetical and these trading advisors have not traded together in the manner shown

in the composite. Hypothetical performance results have many inherent limitations, some of which are described below. No representation is being made that any multiadvisor-managed account or pool will or is likely to achieve a composite performance record similar to that shown. In fact, there are frequently sharp differences between a hypothetical composite performance record and the actual record subsequently achieved. One of the limitations of a hypothetical composite performance record is that decisions relating to the selection of trading advisors and the allocation of assets among those trading advisors were made with the benefit of hindsight based on the historical rates of return of the selected trading advisors. Therefore, composite performance records invariably show positive rates of return. Another inherent limitation of these results is that the allocation decisions reflected in the performance records were not made under actualmarket conditions and, therefore, cannot completely account for the impact of financial risk in actual trading. Furthermore, the composite performance record may be distorted because the allocation of assets changes from time to time and these adjustments are not reflected in the composite.

2. Investing in a CTA on a drawdown is a sophisticated method for qualified investors and is a risky, highly speculative investment strategy and as outlined in the book there is no guarantee at which point an investor could exit a program or that a margin call will stop losses. This is not recommended for all CTAs and only risk capital should be used. The concept was addressed in the book *Managed Trading: Myths and Truths* by Jack. D. Schwager (New York: John Wiley & Sons, 1996) and was also studied in the *Attain Managed Futures Newsletter* dated April 26, 2010 in the article "Should You Buy, Hold, or Fold a Drawdown in Managed Futures?" Both studies are well researched, in the author's opinion. On the book's web site we also offer a professional download of the white paper study on the topic.

CHAPTER 11 Understand It

1. Study conducted with BarclayHedge over the summer of 2009. BarclayHedge sent one e-mail to all those reporting to the managed futures index. This yielded responses from 75 CTAs who answered several questions, including the question: How many times has your CTA strategy received a margin call where fully funded customers were required to deposit additional funds? There were six total questions asked, each of which confirmed the basic findings. The reporting of this information was entirely voluntary and participation was a smaller percentage of the overall universe of CTAs. This information and the accuracy of the information provided was not confirmed by the book, the author or BarclayHedge. This study is limited in scope and should not be construed as a definitive study on the matter, but rather it highlights a study topic that should receive more academic attention. There is significant risk of loss when investing in managed futures and no attempt is being made to diminish the potential for a CTA to experience a margin call. Complete screen shots from the study are available on the book's web site. This study should not be used or construed in any manner that would

diminish the risk potential in managed futures. Past performance is not indicative of future results.

2. "Why Managed Futures?" CMEGroup, 2008, John W. Labuszewski, Research and Product Development. On p. 11, first column, the official expresses the opinion that a managed futures investment falling to zero might be considered an "unlikely probability." The entire sentence is as follows: "If, for example, the managed futures investment declines to zero (an unlikely probability), the underfunded guarantee portion will advance to a level which falls short of 100 percent of par." Past performance is not indicative of future results. There is significant risk of loss in managed futures and margin calls can and do happen regardless of past behavior.

About the Author

Mark H. Melin has written/edited three books, including the industry-standard textbook *The Chicago Board of Trade's Handbook of Futures and Options* (McGraw-Hill, 2006). Melin has worked extensively in the futures and options industry as a consultant for organizations such as the Chicago Board of Trade and OneChicago, the single stock futures exchange, as well as several futures commission merchants (FCMs) and broker-dealers (BDs). He is currently a division director at one of the largest non-clearing FCMs, where he works with financial professionals and qualified investors to integrate managed futures into investment portfolios.

Melin's interests include educating investors and financial professionals on an amazing asset class that can no longer be ignored... as well as surfing, skiing, ice boating, hockey, and mountain biking, all of which are almost as invigorating as managed futures. For more information visit www.wiley.com/go/managedfutures.

Index